THE
STUDY
OF
SOCIAL
STRUCTURE

M. G. SMITH

RESEARCH INSTITUTE FOR THE STUDY OF MAN
NEW YORK

First Edition 1998

Library of Congress Catalog Number: 98-066501

ISBN 0-9633741-5-X Paperback
ISBN 0-9633741-6-8 Hardcover

Published by Research Institute for the Study of Man
162 East 78th Street
New York, NY 10021
212-535-8448

This publication was made possible in part by financial
assistance from the Ruth Landes Memorial Fund.

Printed in the United States of America

We take the liberty
of dedicating this book
to that "one-woman army"

Mary Smith

M.G. Smith's wife, friend,
and extraordinary partner
for nearly half a century

PREFACE *by Lambros Comitas*

Although M.G. Smith wrote many books, I believe that none contained an introduction penned by anyone but himself. Given the posthumous nature of *The Study of Social Structure*, however, a few notes that place both the book and the author in context may be appropriate.

* * *

Soon after his retirement from Yale University, M.G. Smith (Mike or MG to friends and colleagues) delivered a series of lectures at Teachers College, Columbia University to the students and faculty of the anthropology programs. He believed it offered him an opportunity to crystallize his thinking about social structure, a subject he had dealt with throughout his career and one he considered to be at the core, albeit the oft neglected core of social anthropology. The lectures were given in his extraordinarily precise yet low-keyed style over a two week period in 1987 to an increasingly appreciative audience. They were converted into book form several years later, although it is remarkable that he could have summoned the time and energy. *The Study of Social Structure* was completed by Mike Smith while "in retirement," during a time when he was directing a major research project on education and society in the Creole Caribbean, carrying out field research in Grenada at the age of nearly seventy, and while encumbered by a host of other writing obligations. The final draft of the book was completed at home in Glastonbury, England in 1992 just months prior to his untimely death the following year.

Testamentary in quality, this book unfolds key elements of the epistemology of one the leading social anthropologists in the post World War II period while reopening the subject of social structure to systematic inquiry. Throughout his career, Smith was steadfast in the belief that the study of social structure, despite recent disinterest, was central to the anthropological enterprise, and he was even more resolute that the subject itself be critically reexamined. In both regards, he called for the development of new conceptual frameworks "free of unverifiable postulates" to facilitate the study of social structural phenomena. He wrote that traditional Western ideas of societies as normatively and functionally integrated systems of action had to be supplemented, "perhaps" even replaced, by concepts that suspend such assumptions so as to permit the investigation of social units and relations "directly as concrete empirical structures." His plural society and corporation work provide examples of viable alternatives to what he called "the familiar system model." *The Study of Social Structure*, which rests on Smith's compelling logic, deals with those perspectives and approaches that objectify and thereby unravel social structures and their component parts.

Born in Jamaica in 1921, M.G. Smith was always a brilliant student. As a schoolboy at Jamaica College, his schoolmates claimed him as their "intellectual hero" who, in 1939 at age seventeen, achieved the highest marks of all Higher Schools Certificate candidates in the entire British Empire. More than a student scholar, he later emerged as a published poet of very considerable promise. In fact, the Nobel Laureate Derek Walcott once ranked Smith as "one of the two important writers of recent Jamaican poetry." Douglas Hall in a recent biography entitled *A Man Divided; Michael Garfield Smith - Jamaican Poet and Anthropologist, 1921-1993* deals with this significant aspect of his life. But it was his scholarly feats that earned him the prestigious Jamaica Scholarship for study abroad which led not to Bombay as he had wished but rather to McGill University in 1941, and then, soon afterwards, to war-time service with the Canadian Army in the European theater. Demobilized in London in 1945, he turned from literature to law which he studied for a year before the fateful switch to anthropology. As his wife Mary reported, Mike found the law "an ass" and not, as he had hoped, about justice. He took to anthropology quickly and anthropology to him. Soon he became a prize student in Daryll Forde's department at University College London, completed his undergraduate work in short order, and after very successful field research in Northern Nigeria, was awarded the Ph.D. in 1951.

Smith's professional career in anthropology, straddling three continents and the Caribbean, was truly distinguished. His first appointment, which made possible a return home after eleven years, was to the Institute of Social and Economic Research in Jamaica. When the ISER was melded into what is now the University of the West Indies, Smith was also anointed a Senior Lecturer in Sociology. During a hectic period of eight years, he embarked on an ambitious program of Caribbean research, carried out a year's field work in Nigeria, published prolifically on both the West Indies and Africa, and firmly established his reputation as a first-rate anthropologist. In what I would consider the "golden age" of ISER, it would be not be unfair to say that Mike Smith was the most productive and arguably the most creative member of an illustrious research complement of anthropologists, sociologists, and economists. In 1961, he left Jamaica to become Professor of Anthropology at the University of California at Los Angeles. Lasting eight years, this first stay in the United States provided the impetus for four books and some thirty articles. Mike, Mary and their three boys returned to Great Britain in 1969. It was a move made for personal rather than academic reasons without any prior proffers of employment. As I remember, he was not only pleased but surprised when offered the chair of his old department at the University College London. Yet, when in 1972 while at UCL, his old schoolmate and Prime Minister of Jamaica, Michael Manley, requested his services as Special Adviser, he accepted this added appointment as well, not only because of close friendship with the Manley family but also out of a continuing attachment to and love for his native land. This punishing, policy-related assignment lasted until 1977 and was carried out during one of the darkest and most violent periods of modern Jamaican history. Smith returned to the United States in 1978 as the Franklin M. Crosby Professor of the Human Environment at Yale University, a post he held until his retirement in 1986. His last academic affiliation was with the Research Institute for the Study of Man.

Smith was both superlative theorist and extraordinary field worker. His personal field research in Africa and the West Indies, always impeccably planned and thoroughly executed, stretched over half a century. In 1949-50, 1958-59, 1972, and 1977-78, he studied the Hausa, Kagoro, and Kadara in Northern Nigeria. In 1952-53, he worked in Grenada and its dependency Carriacou on social stratification, religion, kinship, and community. In 1955, 1960, 1964, and 1974-75 he carried out a variety of field projects, some with an applied bent, in Jamaica. And, finally in 1990, when he was nearly seventy years old, he returned to Grenada to study the course of education since independence. These forays into the field were always productive and led to twenty-four monographs as well as an exceptionally large number of significant articles on important anthropological themes. His books on Africa include: *The Economy of Hausa Communities of Zaria; Government in Zazzau, 1800-*

1950; Pluralism in Africa (with Leo Kuper); *The Affairs of Daura;* and *Government in Kano, 1350-1959.* On West Indian themes, they include: *A Framework for Caribbean Studies; A Report on Labour Supply in Rural Jamaica; A Sociological Manual for Extension Workers in the Caribbean* (with G.J. Kruijer); *The Ras Tafari Movement in Kingston, Jamaica* (with R. Augier and R.M. Nettleford); *West Indian Family Structure; Kinship and Community in Carriacou; Dark Puritan; The Plural Society in the British West Indies; Stratification in Grenada; Culture, Race and Class in the Commonwealth Caribbean; Poverty in Jamaica* and *Pluralism, Politics and Ideology in the Creole Caribbean.* At least two books, *Corporations and Society* and the present volume, *The Study of Social Structure,* transcend regional emphases and deal directly with theoretical and methodological issues. Another ten manuscripts of substance and quality await publication.

Among the many awards presented to M.G. Smith were the Wellcome Medal for Anthropological Research, the Curle Bequest Essay Prize, the Amaury Book Prize from the Royal Anthropological Institute, the Musgrave Gold Medal from the Institute of Jamaica and honorary degrees from McGill University and the University of the West Indies. In 1972 Jamaica fittingly bestowed upon its native son its very highest honor, the Order of Merit.

*　　　*　　　*

It is evident that Smith was concerned about how best to present this book to the reader - what style to use, graphics to include, elements to incorporate - in order to make the "exposition easier to follow". He believed that he had resolved these issues as well as possible, that some textual repetition was necessary, and that the charts and diagrams, while perhaps cumbersome, were integral to the text. Knowing how he felt about these matters, the editing that preceded this posthumous publication was kept to an absolute minimum. The very few typographical errors and textual anachronisms were corrected; several charts and diagrams were redrafted to facilitate clarity and printing; and citations of references within the text were standardized. Since complete references had not been submitted, a reference section was generated based on citations in the text. As a consequence, several references could not be fully verified. In all other respects, the manuscript as submitted by the author was reproduced without change.

The Research Institute for the Study of Man, with which M.G. Smith was affiliated as Senior Research Fellow, is privileged to have played a part in bringing forth *The Study of Social Structure*. We are particularly indebted to a member of our staff, Mr. Lewis Burgess, who expedited the various phases in the preparation of this book for printing. While carrying out his own doctoral research in Korea, he may well have been the first anthropologist who, relying on his notes from Smith's 1987 lecture series, made effective field use of the ideas now embodied in this book.

FOREWORD

In October/November 1987 I was invited by Professor Lambros Comitas to give a brief course of lectures on the study of social structure to students and faculty of anthropology at Teachers College, Columbia University, New York. When delivered the lectures were recorded to facilitate their revision, and diagrams were distributed to students and faculty. But when these were played back for revision, I quickly recognized that they had to be rewritten and expanded extensively to realise the intentions that prompted the course, namely, to communicate fully and clearly what I had to say at the conceptual level about the study of social structure. As opportunity allowed in the years that have passed, I therefore reworked and expanded the text of the course and modified the original diagrams as necessary. Now, even though the argument remains in parts undeveloped, I think it is sufficiently clear and complete to be presented to a wider public.

My primary aims in these lectures were, firstly, to replace the conventional causal and functional approaches to social theory by an analytic structural framework free of those illusions; secondly, to present a comprehensive, discriminating and realistic conception of social structure and its components, and a set of operationally effective procedures for their study, applicable to any situations and processes in human society; finally, to refine and develop these rather static descriptive models of social structure, I outlined a set of concepts and procedures for their dynamic analysis designed to lay bare the interrelations of structural units and conditions with one another, and with their environments, and so to facilitate the analysis and prediction of structural change. In pursuing these aims I have tried to formulate my concepts and criteria as clearly as possible, in order to exclude ambiguities and facilitate the verification of any hypotheses or conclusions based on them. I have also avoided those assumptions about the nature and bases of societies we have inherited from social philosophers and from the founding fathers of modern social science. These theoretical reservations are ample reason to redouble the search for adequate value-neutral conceptions and procedures that may be used in the comparative study and intensive analysis of specific social situations, conditions and processes, including societies and change.

However, as my thinking has been influenced by the concepts and theories of those who made or shaped social science, it may be regarded partly as a reaction to their teaching. I have therefore briefly reviewed their work and some of the principal themes and ideas we have inherited before presenting my own. As those objectives have guided the selection of writings and writers cited in the following pages, although broadly 'historical', they are neither a sketch nor a substitute for the history of social thought, although they may provide some sort of an introduction to it.

To focus the argument on social units and collectivities, I have not given the attention they deserve to culture and to social processes, though I think they are adequately indicated. To a lesser degree, the same criticism applies to my treatment of collectivities, which is much less intensive than social units. However, to ensure comprehensiveness, as when the lectures were given, I have relied on charts to summarize analyses that are not presented here for reasons of space and focus.

Struck by the scope and seriousness of the topic and by its relevance for humanity today, as well as for anthropology, Dr Philip Burnham and Professor Jean LaFontaine have together suggested many improvements to the text to ensure that it reaches a wide readership with the impact it deserves. Some of these are quite beyond me. However, the study of social structure as an objective phenomenon has declined sharply following the rise of structuralist anthropology. This duly spawned Neo-Marxism, transactionalism, hermeneutics and its successors, the deconstructionist and post-modernist fashions, all of which have diverted efforts from the comparative study of social structure towards various highly subjective 'cultural' projects. Yet without a model of social structure, empirically grounded in an appropriate value-free methodology and globally comprehensive data to guide its faltering steps on the dark road ahead, mankind moves blindly and anthropology has failed in its principal aim. Hence, without pausing to comment on these schools of thought or their feminist, racist and other political alternatives, I hope that the case presented here for the study of social structure as an objective scientific pursuit is sufficiently strong to halt the trend and to encourage many others to tackle the task with renewed energy and confidence.

In her thorough and very helpful review of the manuscript, Professor Jean LaFontaine of the London School of Economics has sought to dissuade me from relying on charts as substitutes for an orderly exposition of my arguments, urging their difficulties of publication and use when reading. However, while welcoming most of her suggestions, at the risk of losing some readers, I have retained the format used in the lectures with its repetitions, examples, illustrations, occasional digressions and summaries, and have also included the charts, in the hope that those who are interested will find the exposition easier to follow when graphically presented. As Professor LaFontaine and Dr Philip Burnham both recommended, to simplify the exposition I have shortened some sentences, but still feel that the text is indigestible without the charts, ethnographic and historic illustrations, and the odd repetition. I appreciate warmly other questions, comments and suggestions from Dr Philip Burnham of University College London, who also reviewed the text, and from Professor Lambros Comitas of Teachers College, Columbia University, New York, without whose encouragement and support the project would never have been undertaken or completed. Finally, as always, I am very grateful to my one-woman army, Mary Smith, for her fortitude and skill with the word processor and otherwise.

M.G.S.,
Glastonbury, England, 1992

CONTENTS

LIST OF FIGURES

DIAGRAMS IN TEXT

CHARTS

I S S U E S
IN THE
LEGACY

1. BEGINNINGS AND ASSUMPTIONS

Systematic social and cultural studies are rather recent academic developments and have only taken root as continuous scholarly pursuits worthy of establishment at universities in western Europe during the past two centuries. Until then the peculiar and distinctive nature of social phenomena had rarely been recognised, and the problematic character of society and social processes had either escaped attention or been discussed in religious and moral terms in all civilisations. The three earliest efforts to establish a secular analytic study of society known to me all fell flat, like so many premature false starts. Only the first, in ancient Athens, began the process of taking institutional shape, and that was misdirected from its very beginning by Plato's search for normatively acceptable answers to the many pressing problems of Greek society in his day. A second heroic effort, made some 1600 years later by the great Muslim historian, Ibn Khaldûn of Tunis, simply had no successors in his own tradition or any other. Neither, immediately, did the third, Giambattista Vico's attempt to build a Scienza Nuova, which long remained unknown outside Italy, being published in Italian rather than Latin, at that time still the language of scholarship. The continuous study of society and culture in universities is thus a rather late development of Western thought, and developed during the decades that followed Vico's work, under different influence and on different lines.

Most of the social philosophers to whom we owe the ideas that underlie and guide secular modern society, together with our theories about it, both analytic and programmatic, from Suarez and Althusius, Grotius, Hobbes and Locke to Rousseau and Marx, tacitly assumed that all the societies for which they theorised were uniformly homogeneous in their culture, language and ethnic composition. They did so even though the countries in which they lived and for which they wrote, namely, France, England, Spain, Holland and Germany, were highly heterogeneous in culture, speech and ethnic composition and sharply divided by religion. Nonetheless by assuming that all societies were ethnically and culturally homogeneous, and that no society was otherwise possible, they freely formulated fundamental principles of natural law and natural rights on the bases of those fictional contracts from which they derived human society. Historically, as Hume remarked, few if any human societies ever began thus, and many if not most are and have long been heterogeneous in ethnic composition, language and culture. In France the Franks were dominant, having overrun the Gauls, Bretons, Catalans and other indigenous peoples. In England, though the English derived from the association of Angles, Saxons, Jutes, Danes, Normans and others in conflict with Welsh, Scots and Irish as well as the French, the rulers began to proclaim their nation's common ethnic identity by the mid fifteenth century. Somewhat later, at English insistence, the British were invented as a hypothetical amalgam of English, Welsh, and Scots, following the union of the kingdom in 1707, despite the central role that Locke's ideas of natural law and social contract had played in framing the modern British state and their tacit exclusion of ethnic and cultural diversity. Even without their Jewish populations, in broad outline the social history and composition of Dutch, Spanish and German societies at that time were not radically dissimilar from those of England and France. By inference from prevailing postulates of ethnic and cultural homogeneity as the essential basis of human society, even such oligarchic and polyethnic states as 18th century Britain were held to demonstrate high levels of normative consensus, institutional integration, stability and order. For theorists to recognise and account for social disorder therefore becomes a tortuous problem. Yet without going to Hobbes' extreme and postulating a war of each against all, we should not see disorder as a problem, but as inseparable from order, much as social continuity and social change are inseparable aspects of social process and develop together.

However, when Europeans first created colonies overseas, whether by conquering other peoples and settling their territories, as in the New World empires of Spain and Portugal, or by importing new populations from Africa as slaves after eliminating the aborigines, as in the Caribbean, the assumptions of ethnic and cultural homogeneity from which social philosophers of the sixteenth to eighteenth centuries derived their theories of natural law, social contract and human rights, being clearly irrelevant, were either ignored entirely, or restricted exclusively to citizens of the imperial state. It is therefore especially ironic that, having assumed ethnic, cultural and linguistic homogeneity as the indispensable basis of human society, in their colonies West Europeans created plural societies peopled by diverse races, speaking different languages, worshipping different gods, practising different economies and ecologies, and sharply divided by conflicting interests and needs as rulers and ruled, exploiters and exploited, slaveowners and slaves, Christian and heathen, whites and non-whites, etc. Nonetheless, whatever the philosophers said, each of those European colonies became a distinct new society, despite its non-contractual foundations and the ethnic and cultural differences of its people.

The 14th century Muslim historian, Ibn Khaldûn, who hailed from a different tradition, had a different view of society and a different scholarly commitment. By his theory of society he sought to account for history purely by social processes. As the son of a Berber woman and Arab father, in his own person Ibn Khaldûn illustrated one characteristic outcome of military conquest; and as a student of human society and history he could neither ignore the predominance of conquest states, their mixed and varied ethnic, cultural and social composition, nor the parallels in their development and decline. Thus, given the Arab conquest of Berbers in his native Tunis, Ibn Khaldûn could neither entertain philosophic illusions of ethnic and cultural homogeneity as a *sine qua non* of human society, nor their sociological implications of normative consensus, institutional homogeneity and integration, functional coherence, order and stability. Instead he perceived the acute collective divisions, conflicts and struggles within societies as motive forces that underlay the development and decline of their political regimes, economies, populations, artistic and intellectual culture and religious life, until they either fell apart through internal strife and decay, or were overrun by invaders when they had lost the *asabiya* or solidarity they needed for order, vigor and cohesion. In his *Muqaddimah*, the prolegomena to his history of the world, Ibn Khaldûn therefore presented a theory of human society based on the regularities of social organisation and development he had found in the available historical and ethnographic record. Unfortunately Ibn Khaldûn wrote in Arabic and had no successors. Earlier, as we have seen, in ancient Athens, and later at Naples when Giambattista Vico published his *Scienza Nuova* in 1725, there were other heroic attempts to initiate a rational comparative study of society, but like Ibn Khaldûn's, these proved to be premature and failed to reach a wide, responsive audience.

To study social structure we must begin by resolutely excluding any presumptions about the levels of consensus, integration or stability that society requires or involves, leaving those and similar conditions to be determined at the end of our enquiry by its results. All questions of that kind should surely be set aside until the empirical data have been analysed. Many scholars, however, including Karl Marx, Herbert Spencer and Emile Durkheim, seem to preface their studies by assuming those conclusions in advance, especially as regards the nature or bases of social order, causality and motivation. In doing so they only reflect the traditions they have inherited and personal factors. Thus, although a rabbi's son, the French scholar, Durkheim, nonetheless assumed the ethnic and cultural homogeneity of French society, even during the trial and disgrace of Alfred Dreyfus, on which he wrote passionately and at length. Perhaps he did so, having uncritically adopted in childhood and from his teachers, Fustel de Coulanges and Comte, those assumptions about society that permeated the philosophies of natural law and social contract on which traditional Western social theory rests. By contrast Marx, having rejected his Jewish identity and the traditional consensualist view of human society, thereafter denounced ethnicity, nationality and religion as regressive modes of false consciousness that blinded workers to the reality of their status and interests as exploited proletarians.

The final attempt to initiate a continuous study of society was made in France by another historian, Baron de Montesquieu, in a book that expressed his reaction as an empiricist to the speculative theories of natural law and social contract that had dominated European social philosophy and jurisprudence for centuries from the collapse of feudalism in northwest Europe to the rise of commercial capitalism, the establishment of independent Protestant polities, and the early development of modern science. Philosophic theories based on arbitrary and opposing speculations about the pristine nature of man and human relations and rights in presocietal or prepolitical conditions, of which for obvious reasons there is no record, were increasingly seen to be inconsistent with incoming ethnographic reports of the customs and cultures of peoples in the Americas and other regions of the hitherto unknown world, and with historical accounts of societies in Europe, Asia and Africa from the earliest times. It was therefore opportune to present an alternative view.

In *The Spirit of the Laws* Montesquieu was probably guided by the physicists' concepts of closed and coherent systems. Isaac Newton's model of the solar system seems to underlie Montesquieu's idea of society as a kind of system whose true laws, like Newton's laws of motion, state the "necessary relations" between social things. For Montesquieu, as necessary relations between social things, such laws differed in their nature and bases, and followed paths quite different from the rules of natural law theorized by philosophers as necessary bases for the appropriate organisation of secular modern society. They also differed from the codes of positive law devised by jurisprudes to regulate relations in states. These issues and ideas underlay the American Revolution and constitution of the late eighteenth century and the French Revolution that followed a few years later. Montesquieu's contribution to the development of secular constitutions for such governments consisted in his understanding of republican virtues and their preconditions, and his emphasis on the need for a clear division of powers between the legislature, executive and judiciary in modern states, whether monarchic or republican, as the essential basis of civil liberty. No less fundamental was his emphasis on the diffuse functional interconnections of the diverse conditions and aspects of activity and process in each society that shape and reflect its distinct ethos and direction, providing the spirit that animates its laws and institutions, and rendering coherent and intelligible practices which by themselves appear disfunctional and bizarre.

In the *Spirit of the Laws* Montesquieu casually indicated, by the wide range of conditions he discussed, the intrinsically systemic nature of society and its institutions, and so incidentally laid the basis for their systematic study. His attempt was largely successful because it immediately caught the imagination of a group of outstanding Scottish thinkers that included Adam Ferguson, Adam Smith, John Millar, Lord Kames, all influenced in different ways and degrees by Montesquieu and his friend, the philosopher David Hume. By their writings those scholars established a Scottish school of social and cultural anthropology that sought to follow up, discuss, develop and supplement Montesquieu's theses and comparative work.

In that study, having indicated the great diversity in beliefs and institutions as well as laws among societies, Montesquieu sought to explain or account for such differences by invoking geographical factors of habitat, climate and soil jointly as decisive determinants. That seemed necessary since the endogenous development of such societal differences were not easily harmonised with his general assumption that each society was a functionally integrated self-regulating system of interdependent parts. The geographical factors Montesquieu invoked as ultimate determinants of differences in the contents and structures of societies and their cultures now seem quite simplistic. As a geographical determinist he tried to attribute the bulk of those differences to what we would now call conditions of cultural ecology, a concept as yet unnamed. Montesquieu's geographical theses accordingly attracted considerable criticism even from his greatest admirers, such as Ferguson among the Scots. Nonetheless as a general theory of society, its laws and institutions, that hypothesis of geographical determinism, and the alternatives it provoked, stimulated the cumulative research and continuous discussion that laid the foundations of modern social science.

Having unleashed the Terror, the French Revolution provoked an incisive critique from such conservatives as J. de Bonald and Joseph de Maistre, champions of the old regime, and from others including Edmund

Burke, who had been perhaps the most eloquent champion of the American Revolution. In response to that critique and to continuing controversy about the revolution and its development, Comte Henri de Saint Simon tried to identify the factors that were decisive in the breakdown of the ancient social order in France, and the unprecedented dramatic developments that followed it. Clearly, Montesquieu's geographical determinants were irrelevant to that enquiry, which was probably the single most productive issue in the development of social science, since it continued throughout the 19th century, and continues today, to engage the attention of social scientists of all kinds as well as philosophers and historians. Independently, and through his influence on Auguste Comte and Karl Marx, Saint Simon played an especially formative role in promoting the study of societies as systems in process, being particularly concerned with social integration and change, which he saw as the result of continuous interactions and adjustments between a society's technology and economy, its material basis, and its ideological superstructure of beliefs, values, norms, philosophy, art, science and law.

Auguste Comte, who served as Saint Simon's secretary for several years, elaborated and systematised his master's ideas with very different emphases, since he regarded ideology as the decisive determinant of social order, a position quite distinct from that of Saint Simon, and the reverse of that of Marx. Following the breakdown of the *ancien regime* in France and the collapse of Montesquieu's general theory, thinkers concerned to understand the nature and bases of the social order sought to identify the causal factors that underlay and governed social systems in such phenomena as environment, demography, the material and economic basis of society, or its prevailing sets of beliefs and ideas. According to Comte, collective beliefs and ideas determined the nature of social order. If harmonic and coherent, as in Western Europe in the Middle Ages, they would establish an integrated institutional system, sustain and perpetuate it. Alternately, when contested and in conflict, as in Western societies during the 17th and 18th centuries, they would lack the authority required to secure acceptance, thereby throwing society into chaos and conflict, a conclusion that closely echoed Joseph de Maistre's important critique of the French Revolution.

For Karl Marx, the material underpinnings of society, and especially the ways in which men are constrained to work together collectively to earn their living, provide the best guide we have to understand society and its development, being their determinants. In Marx's view, the mode of production, that is, the way in which the production of material commodities is organised, has decisive influence on the structure and content of social formations and determines their character. Hence we should expect to find different kinds of social formation accompanying different modes of production.

Whereas Montesquieu implicitly regarded societies as systems, and tried to ascribe their differences to such extrinsic factors as differences of habitat, climate and soil, Marx's concept of social formations clearly combined the idea of societies as systems with that of systems having structures. For Marx, the social formation is still a system in the sense that relations between its components determine its development, *in toto* and in detail. In his scheme, the sub-stratum, or material organisation of the means and relations of production, and all that is involved in the mode of production, ultimately determine the content, structure and development of the rest of the social order. However, as a system, the social formation is simultaneously structured, since it has a material substratum with its own components and internal articulations, together with social and ideological superstructures which Marx frequently assimilated to one another. Thus while structured, as Marx conceived it, the social formation has clear systemic properties.

Though our ideas of societies as systems probably derive from the work of Montesquieu and may have Newtonian models as their ultimate bases, the concept has since been variously developed by such writers as Spencer, Durkheim, Malinowski, Radcliffe-Brown, Talcott Parsons and others in different directions for different purposes.

I have serious reservations about the validity of the presumption that societies are systems or may be considered as if they are. Such use of the system concept, which has perhaps been most elaborately applied to society in the work of Talcott Parsons, seems to me to beg so many important questions concerning the systemic and other, non-systemic properties, qualities and aspects of society that I do not regard society as in any sense a real, empirical system, a meaningful system in the scientific sense of that term. Even though as students of society we may all agree that it is useful to look carefully at society as if it were a genuine system, because in doing so we raise a great many relevant questions about the interrelations and contributions of its components that we might otherwise not ask, I cannot accept as Levi-Strauss and others do the view of society as a set of structured models which are so systemic that if any parts of any one of them are modified, that automatically generates modifications in the remainder. Such a postulate seems to me to fly blindly in the face of too many important and diverse historical facts and ecological processes that clearly controvert it. Large libraries of historical records amply demonstrate the non-systemic character of human societies, whether considered separately, or together as a world system after the fashion of Wallerstein and his colleagues. Hence, though it may be necessary and methodologically useful that as researchers and analysts we should operate as if a society is a system for purposes of research design, data collection, formulation of hypotheses, and analysis, we should never forget that that is very strictly an 'as if' situation, a heuristic, methodological procedure which should be pursued only as long as it is serviceable for the delivery of insights, for the questions it raises and the results it yields. To analyse societies as empirical units, we must also recognise how deeply they differ from our familiar but highly theoretical concepts of them as social systems.

As for Marx, despite the high opinion of his work, I find his sociology confused. For Marx the basic concept is production, and from that he develops a cluster of concepts, of which the three that permeate his writings, namely, mode of production, means of production and relations of production, are pivotal to his theory. Together these constitute the material basis of society, the substratum which he says determines the remainder, including its political institutions and law, ideology and religion. However, as the relations of production which distinguish proprietors and workers and regulate their shares of the common product clearly presuppose property law and the political institutions that establish, enforce and regulate relations between labor and capital, it seems rather that those central elements of the substratum are "determined" by the law and polity than the opposite, as Marx claims.

For Marx the classes of human society are defined by their relationships to the means and mode of production. He believed classes to be universal in human societies at any level of development from the Pygmies and Hadza to the USA and the USSR. Hence as classes are distinguished by their relations to the means and mode of production, the key question becomes what does Marx mean by production? How does he define the term? On that we should consult the opening chapters of volume one of *Capital*. There Marx clearly defines production as the production of commodities, of material things. By that definition, universities and schools are engaged in essentially unproductive activities. Likewise on that view administration is unproductive, and so too are any activities that do not produce a commodity, that is, something material that we can handle and consume, or exchange or sell, and which another person in turn can consume, pass on, or sell. All else is not production. Thus such activities as medicine, law, nursing, finance, sport, education, research, transport, communications, religion, art, music, and social work, all service activities in fact, are unproductive, including notably all the various domestic services that women provide everywhere and in all ages for their menfolk and families. Since for Marx classes are distinguished by their relations to the means and mode of production, all not engaged in productive activity are excluded from his classes. In the *Grundrisse* Marx reiterates the view of production just cited. In consequence Marx's array of social classes includes only a fraction of the gainfully employed population in capitalist society. They certainly are not recognisable in primitive societies, despite the recent elaborate efforts of several devoted French scholars to find them. Such an inappropriate basic idea of production inevitably generates other inadequacies in such derivative concepts as the means, mode and relations of production, value, class, class struggle, and class conflict, and in the general theory of which they are part.

Thus far we have had two important original conceptions of social structure; or perhaps more accurately, two antecedents of the modern idea of social structure. Both regard society as a functional system, whose diverse parts and processes are intimately and continuously connected by the functional relations and laws that Montesquieu sought, the substance, structure and capacities of the system as a whole being in his theory exogenously determined by geographical conditions. While sharing the assumption that society is a system, other theorists invoke differing causal determinants to account for differences between social systems and developments within them. Those, like Marx, who regarded the mode of production as the sole or ultimate determinant of the structure and content of the whole society, posited an endogenous variable as the decisive cause of differences between and developments within such social formations. For others, like Auguste Comte and Friedrich Hegel, collective ideas were the true determinants. Yet others, including Saint Simon and Max Weber, identified the relations and interactions of their material and ideological levels as the principal source of their development and diversity. As a consequence of continuing controversies on these and cognate topics between idealists, materialists and others, the search for a general causal theory came to dominate the emerging social science, with the result that we now have several competing theories that claim to account for societal differences and internal changes besides those mentioned here.

The most thoughtful, sustained attempt to evaluate, refine and develop Marx's ideas was made by his compatriot, Max Weber, at the turn of this century. Since Marx held that men's beliefs and ideas were determined by the material conditions of their existence, and especially by their mode of work, he focussed attention on those objective conditions, and treated ideas and values as secondary. Weber, on the other hand, following his early study of the nature and development of Protestantism, and the social changes associated with it, held that men's beliefs and values influence their perceptions and interpretations of situations, and often exercise decisive influence on their actions. Accordingly in his view, to understand human society, we should give priority to its subjectively meaningful aspects and try to interpret social action in those terms. By *verstehen* or understanding, which Weber adopts as the central aim of sociology, he seeks to identify the values, beliefs and meanings that motivate individual action and enable people to conceive their society as a field for meaningful action.

In his essays on Protestantism and his monographs on religion in China and in India, and especially in his book on ancient Judaism, Weber documents and establishes these theses. In his most general work, *Economy and Society*, he is almost wholly concerned with structural and processual typologies, beginning with the classification of cultures and value systems as traditional, charismatically proclaimed, or rational and pragmatic. In that work, which I find most important, Weber distinguishes and analyses social processes and structures by their salient conditions and features, using as cutting tools his conceptions of ideal types. He does so often without invoking individual ideas, values or motivations as their explanations, perhaps because individual beliefs are essential elements of the ideal types that inform his structures. Instead he discusses different kinds of social units, groups, conflicts, roles, and structures of traditional or charismatic leadership, their staffs and followers, entrepreneurs of differing kinds and such religious virtuosi as shamans, mystics, seers, hermits, priests, prophets and exemplary teachers, all individuals acting in roles that are either structurally defined or self-created. This analytic section of Max Weber's work I find exceptionally illuminating, having found little elsewhere to compare with it as social theory, except the *Muqaddimah* of Ibn Khaldûn. Unlike Talcott Parsons and many others I do not find that Weber's individual psychology or phenomenological interests are central to the development or use of this comprehensive analytic scheme and typology. Although I appreciate that such *verstehen* was the author's ultimate aim, and that perhaps to him such typological studies as his *General Economic History* and *Economy and Society* were merely the stepping stones toward it, I am personally content to stand by those stepping stones, if such they are.

Clearly unless an actor understands his role and has appropriate motivation, he is unlikely to perform it adequately. However, although most people in society differ in their knowledge and conceptions of their roles, few come to grief in their performance or bring the social process to a halt, since our interactions routinely involve continuous processes of mutual correction and steering to balance or cancel such deficiencies. Roles do not exist in social voids, as we shall see. Most are continuously subject to social sanctions of differing kind, source and intensity to ensure appropriate performance routinely. Even in the most unstructured roles, such as those between lovers or friends, we find that routine interaction involves continuous processes of mutual steering, normally unmeditated and often unconscious to the actors. It seems to me, therefore, quite reasonable to take the important influence of ideas and values in human action for granted, provided we recognise that individuals may and do differ widely in their values, priorities, knowledge and motivations.

Supplemented by such concepts of status and role that emerged after his death, my debt to Weber's work is great. However, Weber had several agenda that conflicted with his own prescriptions for objectivity and value neutrality in social science. He was as fervent a German nationalist as Durkheim was a French one, and as keenly concerned as Durkheim to promote the interests of his nation state. Coming to sociology, like Ibn

Khaldûn, with deep historical interests and knowledge, he understood that any society is a historical structure continuously in process of change and development, due both to its internal dynamics and to its need to adapt to external exigencies of differing kinds. Like Ibn Khaldûn and Karl Marx, he seems to have been mainly concerned to formulate a general framework and method by which we could study such change, unravel its intricate and varied strands and sequences, and understand the diverse sources, conditions and kinds of development that so often proceed simultaneously, though at different rates, in reshaping societies. Undoubtedly in those longitudinal and comparative studies of social structures and processes, Weber had other commitments and interests, such as his long subliminal argument with Marx about the nature and future of capitalist society, and his deep abiding commitment as a German to the interests of his nation and state. However, if we identify those commitments that even against his will introduced various biases into his work, and if we make the necessary effort to apprehend and criticise his teaching despite its immense scholarship, we shall have an excellent basis for our study of human society.

2. FUNCTIONALISM

Modern ideas of social structure and social function can ultimately be traced, along with the essentials of structural-functionalist theory, back to the important work of Herbert Spencer, a Victorian engineer turned philosopher of evolution, who wrote extensively on the structure and evolution of societies in the latter half of the nineteenth century. As an engineer, Spencer was familiar with machines as structures designed to perform such functions as locomotion, by harnessing sufficient pressure from steam to drive boats, engines, and other machinery. Not surprisingly, therefore, in the social groups and organisations of the diverse peoples studied in his monographs on descriptive sociology, Spencer identified the progressively increasing complexity of more advanced societies and economies by the greater variety of their structural arrangements, as well as the greater number of structural levels exhibited by societies of greater differentiation and development. For example, societies of foragers dependent on hunting and gathering typically lived in kin groups or bands that lacked any superstructure to coordinate and regulate their relations, thus creating polycellular societies with one level of organisation. By contrast, lineage-based societies of hoe-farmers tend to have two or even three structural levels which correspond in scale, composition and functions with significant levels of their segmentary organisation. More advanced societies show a greater number of structural levels between the local group or its subdivisions, and such central regulative agencies as the paramount chief and his council or the monarch and his court, which administer the collectivity and its affairs.

In studying biological organisms Spencer had noted striking parallels with the structures and functions he found in human societies, having identified the distinctive structures of organisms as their organs, whose functions were such vital processes as breathing, ingestion, movement, elimination, defence and reproduction. Being concerned to exploit the parallels between social and biological phenomena in a general theory of evolution applicable to both, Spencer classified the characteristic social structures and processes in human societies by their function on broadly similar lines, and grouped them in systems of three kinds, which he claimed to be universal in all societies. These were firstly, the *sustaining* system, which provided such basic necessities as food, shelter, water, required to sustain their populations; second, the *reproductive* system of institutions such as marriage, family and kinship through which each society reproduced itself by replacing its members in an orderly way; and thirdly, the *regulative* system which maintained the social order, and in which law, government or politics and religion were central.

By such analogies Spencer came to regard societies as merely the largest and most complex organisms whose institutional sub-systems were essentially similar in their vital functions and needs to the more advanced organisms studied by biologists. He thus sought to demonstrate the similar nature of social and biological structure, function and process, despite the obvious differences between the anatomy and physiology of animals and the chiefships, temples, clans, bands and other organs of human societies. Convinced by the facility with which he could find parallels in society to biological phenomena, Spencer adapted various theses of evolutionary biology which he regarded as proven to construct a general theory of societies and their development. Among these, besides his principal idea of the three hierarchically related subsystems of human societies, namely, the regulative, reproductive and sustaining, he held that structurally distinct parts of society emerged in response to its functional needs, and therefore depended for their maintenance and development on the efficient performance of the functions through which they contribute to the unit's viability. Thus for Spencer, functionless structures were a contradiction in terms, since structures that had no function would either disappear and decay, or persist like such atrophied organs as the human appendix. In effect, then, Spencer held that any durable structure that played a significant part in an organism or society owed its existence as well as its composition and form to the functions that it performed for the vitality of the unit of which it was part.

A leading theorist of social Darwinism and an arch liberal, Spencer set the individual and his interests at the centre of his social theory, and ranked societies on his evolutionary scale, as more or less developed, more or less advanced, according to the nature and number of individual rights and liberties they provided, though not their extent. Having identified social organization as the essential and distinctive condition of human society, Spencer defined it as the voluntary or coerced co-operation of individuals in society for individual or collective ends. In the more primitive and archaic societies, including ancient civilisations and such imperial systems as Egypt and Rome, Spencer found great reliance on the coercion of individual cooperation to carry out essential collective activities routinely. He contrasted that with the presumptively spontaneous pursuit of individual interests through which bourgeois capitalist societies such as Victorian England and other Western countries, organized the cooperative work they needed to sustain and perpetuate themselves and regulate their affairs. For Spencer, the free pursuit of individual interests provided the ideal end and primary force that created and perpetuated human society. Overlooking the inequalities and coercion of society in industrial Britain, he valued highly those societies that encouraged the spontaneous pursuit of individual interest and regarded the collective coercion of individuals as primitive and low. Such a combination of individualistic sociology and evolutionary biology produced Spencer's philosophy of Social Darwinism which provoked the prolonged and hostile criticism of Emile Durkheim, who had taken from Comte as a central tenet the primacy of collective interests as the source of human society.

Current sociology and social anthropology owe many guiding ideas about the nature of society and how to study it to Emile Durkheim. Nonetheless, like his teacher, Fustel de Coulanges, and like Auguste Comte, though keenly concerned with society as a complex organisation, Durkheim was primarily a student of the influence of culture as the collective ideas of a population on the organization of social life. Like Comte, he tended to regard culture as the principal determinant of the form and content of social process, sometimes virtually assimilating the collective consciousness and society. Whereas at the end of his study of *Suicide* Durkheim claimed that the sum total of the different kinds of relations in a society together determined the full range of attitudes and ideas in its collective conscience, in most of his work he seems rather to hold that social structures and relations are governed either by specific collective representations and norms, or by the collective consciousness as a whole. Thus while social relations and organization were important to Durkheim, and he made important contributions to the study of segmentary lineages, clans and other corporate structures in simple and industrial societies, I regard his work, like that of Edward Tylor, another disciple of Comte, as an expression of cultural idealism in its stress on the explanation of social customs and institutions by the ideas, beliefs, and values that constitute the basis for collective understandings, and motivate men to act together, as well as in their own interests.

For Durkheim social "facts" or phenomena fell into two great classes, those like institutions and their elements that prescribe behavior and constrain individuals to conform, being sanctioned and coercive, and others, to which he gave less attention and thought of as 'social currents'. The category of social facts designated 'social currents' by Durkheim includes what we now call mass behavior and collective behavior, which are discussed below. However, though most modes of mass and collective behavior are non-institutional or at best weakly institutionalized, as, for example, audience behavior of different kinds, others such as crime, sabotage, or terrorism are implicitly or explicitly anti-institutional in their rejection of the prevailing institutional order or attacks on it. It seems then that implicitly though not explicitly, Durkheim divided the universe of social facts into two great classes, namely, institutional phenomena and all else, whether non-institutional or anti-institutional. In that way he broadened the concept of society beyond Herbert Spencer's view of it as an essentially utilitarian set of institutional arrangements, and redefined institutions to stress their external moral and coercive qualities instead of the utilitarian nature and functions stressed by Spencer.

Durkheim's leading Anglophone successor, A.R.Radcliffe-Brown, spent a lifetime trying to develop analytic conceptions of social structure, based partly on Durkheim's work, but mainly on his diverse ethnographic experience in Polynesia, Australia, South Africa, North America and other parts of the world. It is fascinating to trace the gradual evolution of Radcliffe-Brown's ideas on social structure at different points in his career. Having taken his bachelor's degree in anthropology at Cambridge under A.R.Haddon and W.H.R.Rivers, Radcliffe-Brown reacted with aversion to their teaching, and warmly welcomed Durkheim's work when he came across it. After leaving the Andaman Islands, in a series of surveys Radcliffe-Brown studied the kinship systems of several Australian tribes, and so gradually developed his own idea of social organization as a distinct system of relations between individuals, groups and social categories based on kinship and marriage. Unlike Rivers (1924), Radcliffe-Brown's idea of social organization in 1930, when he summarized the results of studies of the kinship systems of several Aboriginal societies in a masterly paper, was virtually synonymous with the dimension of kinship, marriage and family in society, while stressing its systemic character as reflected in the elaborate terminology that identifies and classifies the relationships, statuses, and roles involved. Thereafter it was nearly ten years before he moved forward to broader conceptions of social structure, following some years at the University of Chicago during which Ralph Linton, then at the University of Wisconsin, published an influential work that introduced the concepts of status and role on which so much sociology and socio-cultural anthropology still rest. As formulated by Linton, the ideas of status and role nicely fitted Radcliffe-Brown's idea of social organization as the network of relations between persons holding kinship statuses that prescribed the reciprocal roles that regulated their interaction. By the end of his long academic career in 1955 Radcliffe-Brown regarded societies as functional systems in process, and conceived social structure primarily in terms of individual interactions in relations and roles, with a secondary emphasis on corporate groups based on kinship and locality in simple societies. Those ideas informed his presidential address to the Royal Anthropological Institute in 1940 on social structure, and expressed his tendency to treat individuals regarded as persons, as key units of the social order and its analysis, an approach that probably derives from his lifelong study of kinship in simple societies, which focussed on the individual's kinship roles and relations as the foundation of his or her *persona* or social personality.

To Bronislaw Malinowski, Radcliffe-Brown's rival for the leadership of British anthropology, who viewed Durkheim's work differently, the basic structure of a society consists largely in the interrelations of its institutions and their components. Together, such institutional articulations and processes constitute the society as an ongoing functional system which meets the biological needs of all or most of its members, and assures its own perpetuity by the ordinary processes of kinship-regulated social reproduction. For Malinowski, then, societies, or cultures as he conceived them, are empirically as well as ideally systemic, since all their components and processes are functionally necessary, integrated, and biologically essential for their members. Accordingly in his scheme, when totally free from external interference and pressures, societies are coherent and self-perpetuating systems of human life and activity, incapable of endogenously self-generated social and cultural change. In consequence, Malinowski's model of societies as systems, although structured differently from the social systems of Radcliffe-Brown, has much the same static quality as a result of its closure and self-perpetuating properties. However, whereas for Radcliffe-Brown the basic unit of social action and analysis is the individual, whose social *persona* is a combination of individually specific roles and relations, and the social structure is a network of such interpersonal and group relations, according to Malinowski, institutions are the basic units of social organisation and activity, and therefore the appropriate units for social analysis.

Though Malinowski has been criticized for assuming that institutions are always identified with specific social groups, and although he certainly devoted much attention to those forms of institutional action, he also regarded as institutional such social phenomena as language, rank and customary law in societies without tribunals or courts, to which we might add money, certain forms of exchange, house building and house style, dancing and art, even though these all lack discrete social groups. In various parts of the world, people who speak a common language, such as English, German or Arabic, may or may not be organized in distinct groups, and are sometimes mutually opposed. Thus, though often identified with discrete social groups, language is not always so. To operate efficiently and routinely, while many institutions such as the family require groups, and so conceptually lend themselves to definition as either institution or group, others, such as the division of labor by sex, the means of exchange, and various market systems, like language, do not. Unlike Durkheim, who recognized the prevalence of non-institutional 'currents' or processes in all societies, and who also saw that certain institutional processes, including the division of labor, could be 'anomic' or disfunctional, Malinowski's functionalist scheme seems to exclude both possibilities. Like Durkheim, however, he clearly conceived institutions as cultural and normative forms of organized action, legitimated by ideological charters as inherently right and effective. Moreover, in his schematic model of institutions which distinguishes their rules and norms, social organization, tasks, resources and tools, time and place issuing in the resultant activity and its effects or functions, Malinowski implicitly redefined them as integrated clusters of requisites and entailments. This insight he later generalized to cultures as closed self-regulating systems whose integration and perpetuation presupposed the adequate implementation of their 'integrative imperatives' by appropriate institutional action.

Like Malinowski, Radcliffe-Brown regarded societies as functionally coherent systems committed to perpetuate themselves by the kinship-regulated processes of social reproduction to which he devoted attention. However, whereas for Malinowski such systems initially developed to meet the biological needs of their individual members, for Radcliffe-Brown, as for Spencer, even though individuals were the basic social units, their needs *qua* individuals were a matter of indifference to the student of society, since that pursued the functional consistency necessary to ensure its integration and satisfaction of its system needs. There are thus radical differences in the ethnographic and analytic implications of these superficially similar models of societies as static systems.

Based on a biological analogy, Spencer's guiding idea in the study of society was that of organism. Besides self-sustenance through essentially ecological and economic processes, society had to coordinate its organic activities and perpetuate itself by reproduction. Spencer accordingly identified the three institutional subsystems in societies that performed those functions, as sustaining, regulatory and reproductive. For Emile Durkheim on the other hand, while displaying organic features, societies were united by the beliefs, values and ideas their members shared. They could therefore be regarded as moral-symbolic systems, as Evans-Pritchard, basing himself on Durkheim, later declared, in attacking Radcliffe-Brown's Spencerian view of them as natural systems, distinct from the cultural systems of Durkheim, Malinowski and others. Nonetheless both Malinowski and Radcliffe-Brown regarded society as a functional system with strong tendencies towards equilibrium, whereas Spencer, although an engineer, stressed its inherent dynamic properties and evolutionary tendencies. For Talcott Parsons and his colleagues, societies are highly differentiated structural-functional systems with complex hierarchies of analytic subsystems such as goal-formulation, adaptation, integration and the cultural latency system which exercises regulatory control. However appealing analytically, since those subsystems are artificial constructs based on functional criteria of the observer's choice, they do not prove that any human society is a genuine empirical system, despite Parsons' (1952) book with that title. Indeed, despite their equilibrial tendencies and functional aspects, their moral-symbolic features and imperfect closures, viewed systemically, societies have such vitalistic qualities that some students conceive and analyse them with the aid of general systems theory (Bertalanffy 1973). Despite the obvious inadequacies of the institutional subsystems in Spencer's organic analogy, analytic models of such subsystems as the economic or the political system within societies share the same basic weaknesses as the system model of society as a whole, namely, its imperfect closure and articulation as an empirical entity. Moreover, despite their careful definition and construction, in practice the analytic subsystems of Parsonian theory also display a heterogeneous composition, since it is impossible to segregate any coherent subsystem of human activities, relations and interests from all others on strictly functional criteria, as perhaps is most easily recognised in the materialist political economy of Marx and Engels.

Perhaps for these reasons among others, while explicitly rejecting functionalism, Claude Levi-Strauss claimed, *contra* Radcliffe-Brown, that in speaking of social structures we are simply dealing with models of our own construction, and not with empirical realities, but with models designed to approximate and summarize them. To clarify what he meant by a model, Levi-Strauss listed several attributes and properties which clearly indicated its highly systemic character. Thus, being persuaded that neither societies nor their structures, however defined, are truly systemic, I cannot accept Levi-Strauss' models as empirically adequate, despite their interest and appeal. I shall not dwell therefore on other difficulties in Levi-Strauss' concept of social structure. Briefly, he distinguishes three orders of social structure, namely, dynamics, statics and morphology, each of which requires appropriate models. While the classifications are analytically interesting, I doubt if they are either appropriate or operationally useful. For example, to abstract or construct the model of a static social structure, we must assume that the empirical society experiences no change, and thus that it constitutes a totally static system. Thus abstracted, social statics and dynamics are merely complementary aspects of the same social process that proceed together. Thus, while we may abstract for a moment whatever we wish from a given social situation and process to develop a static model of it, since the reality modelled is an imperfectly dynamic and changing complex, even while we observe or participate in it, that static model is pure fiction, like its dynamic complementary alternative. Faced with such alternatives, I prefer to conceive social structure and study it as an empirical reality, rather than as a set of imaginary constructs that distort the reality by accentuating and abstracting one of its aspects to the exclusion of others, such as statics to the exclusion of dynamics, dynamics to the exclusion of statics, or morphology to the exclusion of both. Instead I assume that social structure exists as an empirical reality in the interactions and relationships of human populations; and although I am not sure that we can always document and map it accurately or fully, I think the attempt to do so eminently worthwhile and feasible. In making that attempt the problems that beset us have to do with the validity, variety and ubiquity of social processes since, even as we seek to abstract regularities from them, given that process is dynamic, often repetitive and always underway, those processes may be changing their contents, directions, rates and other properties in ways we cannot know. To be accurate, the structural model we may derive from such observations should reproduce those changes, even though we are unaware of them or misunderstand their nature.

While as a stand-still point in time the idea of an ethnographic present provides a convenient convention for modelling social structures as perfectly static over the period of our ethnographic observations, we all know that it is a dangerous fallacy, and quite misleading. Hence if our theories rest on the models people build with such presumptions of society and their structures, those theories, like the maps we make to assist us when working in society to pursue our immediate and remoter goals and interests, however interesting, can only mislead. Though in practice necessary, and created and used in different ways by almost everyone in society, such maps or models should not be advocated as appropriate and accurate representations of that society for serious study. It is true that without such mental maps of their societies and situations, however inadequate, citizens may be socially lost, and may waste their efforts in incoherent actions as they pursue their chosen goals. Yet if we assume that the continuous motion and change our maps should display are the empirical reality, and that in theory we can record it accurately and in sufficient detail, we will surely recognize that, however dynamic, our models of that structure are bound to be imperfect, and should therefore make our best efforts to reduce those errors.

In 1951 Raymond Firth proposed a middle way between these diverse approaches by conceptualizing social structure as the ideal models people have of the forms of their societies, or the proper ways of doing things, in contrast to the social organization, which he defined as the way in which they have actually dealt with various exigencies by activities in which they cooperated and related to one another, disputed, ordered their lives, pursued their various goals, and so on. By this formula, Firth equated social structure with Radcliffe-Brown's concept of structural form as the perduring ideal pattern instead of the empirical reality that Radcliffe-Brown had claimed for social structure as a network of relations. Like Malinowski, Firth was keenly concerned to locate actors as goal-seeking individuals at the centre of his model of society which he regarded processually as a dynamic, self-modifying complex of activities, relations and interests in which individual and group stratagems, opportunistic tactics and short-term tactical manoeuvres are the essential and ubiquitous means by which actors pursue their goals and, in the process, either modify or uphold the traditional forms of action and relationships.

While at Yale Malinowski extended and developed an essay on culture (1944) he had written for the 1934 *Encyclopedia of Social Sciences* that distinguished the basic needs of individuals as actors in society as their organic needs, from their secondary or derived needs, and finally the integrative needs of the cultural system. As the extended version of that essay was published posthumously, Malinowski probably had little chance to revise the text. Nonetheless, despite the critique launched by structuralists in Britain and elsewhere at the time, the hierarchy of needs and other salient ideas in that essay were picked up later by Talcott Parsons in his contribution to a book on Malinowski's work edited by Raymond Firth, Malinowski's student and successor in Britain. Parsons' article on Malinowski's theory of needs interpreted the integrative imperatives of Malinowski's theory of needs as the functional requisites of societies as orderly social systems. Ultimately those functional requisites ended up as Parsons' famous system, when he finally identified four functional requisites or imperatives. The needs of actors as individuals having organic biological needs and drives, and the needs of collectivities as social systems composed of individuals, together provided the basis for Parsons' final list of functional requisites.

In 1950, nine functional prerequisites identified as preconditions for social systems were listed by David Aberle, Kingsley Davis and others who had studied with Parsons at Harvard. Their list included provisions for adequate relationship to the environment and for sexual recruitment, thus identifying two distinct requisites for sustainable ecological relations and for social reproduction. Role differentiation and assignment were a second set of requisites. Communication, which Levi-Strauss (1953) placed first, came third; shared cognitive orientations, fourth; a shared articulated set of goals, fifth; normative regulation of means, sixth; regulation of affective expression, seventh; adequate socialisation, eighth; and effective control of disruptive forms of behaviour, i.e., social control, ninth. These were seen as functionally necessary conditions for the emergence and continued existence of societies as systems of human action. It all seems very dated when you read it at this remove. In the following year Marion Levy added a tenth requisite, but in later years Parsons reduced the list to the four basic requisites, namely, goal attainment, adaptation, integration and latency (A-G-I-L), on which he built his last elaborate model of society as a system. Specification of what is a functional requisite or prerequisite seems to change from one moment in time, and from one author to another, partly due to the nature of those concepts.

In a seminal work influenced by Talcott Parsons, Marion Levy Jr. (1952) tried to clarify the terminology and conceptual apparatus of structural-functional theory, beginning with the distinction between functions or *eufunctions*, that is, effects that contribute positively towards the operation or persistence of the societal or some specific structure, and *disfunctions*, those which do not, and which might indeed have severe negative effects. This directed attention to a critical point that Durkheim, Radcliffe-Brown, Malinowski and others had largely overlooked, namely, that not all effects of institutional or other activity made positive contributions to the persistence of a social order or cultural system, even when those activities were unavoidable aspects of routine social processes. In the same work, Levy tried to distinguish the *functional prerequisites* and *requisites* of social phenomena such as clearly defined structures, processes or conditions, from one another and from their *structural requisites* and *prerequisites*. By a *requisite* he meant any thing or condition without which the particular phenomenon or event could not exist, and by a *prerequisite* any phenomena or condition without which the particular event or structure could not occur or come into being. *Functional prerequisites* are therefore functional preconditions for the existence or operation of a particular social structure or process, while *structural prerequisites* are the structural preconditions for its emergence and operation. In like fashion *functional* and *structural requisites* denote specific conditions and structures which are necessary for the existence or operation of a phenomenon. The attempt to define and distinguish structural and functional requisites and prerequisites was clearly overdue, and should permit a closer analysis of the necessary conditions and preconditions of particular processes and structures in any society, thereby reducing severely the scope for loose 'explanations' of events as functions of some antecedent or consentaneous process. However, despite the clarity of Levy's presentation, it is not always clear from his account how to distinguish prerequisites and requisites, whether structural or functional.

Of even greater importance for the development of analytic conceptions of social structure was Marion Levy's (1952) distinction between analytic and concrete structures. According to Levy, *concrete structures* are simply membership units while *analytic structures* are functionally defined abstractions from ongoing activities within a society, which include all aspects of activity and organizations that fit the defining criteria. To illustrate: an economic system is an abstract analytic structure of a specific kind that differs in its scope and components according to the set of criteria used to distinguish economic from other kinds of activity or pursuits. In like fashion, according to their definitions of what is specifically political, political scientists may construct analytic models of the political system by abstracting from the ordinary social processes of everyday life those aspects of social relations and activities that conform to their chosen criteria of political action. In similar fashion we might distinguish as analytic structures or systems within society the religious aspects and processes of social life, the reproductive, educational, recreational, or ecological. Within any analytic structure such as the economic, we may also distinguish subsystems or structures that deal exclusively with saving, production, consumption and distribution or exchange, according to the criteria selected for identification of those activities and processes.

In this way Marion Levy directed attention to the differences and relations of the two basic kinds of structure with which we have to deal in social analysis. Analytic structures, such as the political, economic, kinship, educational and religious, are more or less orderly sequences of processes, activities and relationships through which those various kinds of transactions proceed as routine aspects of society. At different points in time they may engage different sets of actors grouped or aligned in particular ways according to the nature of their activities which, being generally recurrent, normally have relatively fixed sequences that yield processual structures for analysis. Such a structure, being dependent for its identification and boundaries on the highly specific but variable criteria used to isolate it, will vary when analysts use different criteria to constitute or define it; but as an analytic artefact it will also differ more fundamentally from the concrete structures or membership units with which as ethnographers we have directly to deal. Units of the latter kind are not open to creation or modification at the will of analytic observers, being constituted independently of the observer's inclinations by the routine operation of ordinary social relations and processes among the population under study. Consequently, as extant structures, such membership units can only be understood in their objective contexts and particulars, whereas, as conceptual systems, analytic structures are created freely by different students using various criteria for various instrumental purposes.

Of special interest is the fact that the analytic structures Levy distinguished and discussed at length in his important work of 1952 are functionally defined activities and relations abstracted from the structural and processual contexts in which they occur by specific functional criteria that serve to separate out those subsystems from one another analytically in order to facilitate further study of their structure, content, composition and interrelations. It follows that, however analysts may distinguish them, if they discharge different functions, the differing aspects of activities in which groups and other social units routinely engage, are parts of different analytic structures or systems. Concrete structures such as social groups and other kinds of membership unit are therefore typically multifunctional. Even though, as in Malinowski's institutional models of families, lineages and clans, they may serve some specific set of primary functions, they commonly also discharge various other functions which may seem subsidiary to their main purpose or manifest function, but which may in practice prove cumulatively as significant as their primary function. For example, while families are commonly constituted and identified by their reproductive functions, which include the primary socialization of children, they also subserve legal, economic, religious, residential and status placement functions that are essential for the orderly processes of social life. On such grounds it seems unlikely that concrete structures in society could ever be as functionless as Spencer feared by extrapolating from such functionless features of biological organisms as the human appendix. Indeed, since as effects, functions cannot produce themselves, as analytically distinct aspects of social processes and activities, they presuppose individuals and membership units, as the responsible agents, and must derive from the routine operation of the concrete structures to which the members of societies belong. On these grounds alone it seems unlikely, *contra* Talcott Parsons, Edward Shils and their colleagues, that any institutional social unit or form of social relation could ever be as functionally specific as their pattern-variable theory requires to provide an adequate contrast with the functionally diffuse alternative; and indeed such multifunctionality seems implicit in the repetitive fourfold functional aspects of social structures and processes,

A-G-I-L, according to Talcott Parsons' analytic model of societies as structural functional systems.

3. OF FUNCTION AND CAUSE

The inherently multifunctional properties of membership units have important implications for sociology and the study of social structure. For if all or most of the concrete structures in human societies are multifunctional, they will unavoidably display numerous instances of functional equivalence, substitutability and complementarity, as well as disfunctions, mutual discord, and functional compensation in contexts of functional attrition or loss, due to changes in other spheres of activity. In consequence, analytic structures, however clearly defined and established, must always engage some aspects of most of the institutional concrete structures in each society, as implied by the mature Parsonian model of societies as functionally differentiated structural systems. Such pervasive functional diffuseness of the membership units or concrete structures in any society obliges the student first to develop appropriate criteria and valid procedures by which to identify, determine and rank in relative primacy the differing functions performed by those structures. Then he should establish for each social structure the relative primacy of its diverse functions for the maintenance or change of that unit and others to which it relates, for the structure of a specific analytic system, or the structure of the inclusive society as the ensemble of all these diverse "systems". Clearly such a complex of interdependent functional sub-systems whose modes and degrees of substitutability and equivalence will vary as aspects of the diverse activities and operations of the concrete structures that produce them at different levels of society, present many formidable problems, as we can see in the works of Talcott Parsons. However, since the total set of functions performed by its ensemble of concrete structures together ensure the society's operation, they must clearly be sufficient to meet its existential needs, though how adequately or appropriately remains unknown.

Malinowski, who defined function as the satisfaction of basic organic needs for the individual and derived systemic needs for the collectivity, was particularly prone to identify particular kinds of social arrangement or process with one or two primary functions. In his scheme the primary functions were generally both the chief purposes of those involved and the manifest results of the activity. Thus, in his view the purpose and function of marriage was to provide sexual satisfaction, which it apparently does, at least for men, while the aims and functions of war are self-preservation and defence, even though European wars were more often initiated as aggression in expectation of substantial reward. Such direct, explicit relationships between the effect of an activity and the intentions of the actors illustrate its *manifest* function, as Robert Merton (1949) showed; but not all manifest functions of activities are consciously intended by the leading participants. Moreover, although most frequently the basic distinction between the manifest and *latent* functions of a given social event or process is that between its *intended* and *unintended* effects, not all the latent functions or unexpected results of activities are unintended by all who participate in them. Perhaps two equally important and necessary distinctions should be made between the direct and indirect effects of an action or process, and between its immediately recognisable effects and other consequences which, being remoter in time and space, are not only unexpected and problematic, but less easily recognised by those responsible.

Whereas for Malinowski the primary function of a social activity is its relation to the need satisfaction of those responsible, for Durkheim and Radcliffe-Brown that was properly its relation to the needs of the society as a self-sustaining and self-perpetuating system of collective beliefs and norms. Neither set of criteria enables us to identify certain kinds of activity as disfunctional, counter-productive or inappropriate for the units concerned, whether those be individual actors seen as biological organisms *à la* Malinowski, or normative social systems following Durkheim and Radcliffe-Brown.

That leads me to wonder whether it is useful, by Parsonian or other means, to seek to identify the specific functional contributions of each structure to the total process so as to assess their relevant significance, and demonstrate their interrelations. It seems self-evident that unless the essential conditions for the continued existence and operation of a society or any of its components during the short and middle term are routinely met by the operation of those processes within it that generate the functions it requires for regulation, socialization, subsistence, resource allocation, etc., neither the society nor its components could continue to exist in its current form and state. However, since they do, the totality of requisite functions must be fulfilled and discharged routinely by the ordinary operations of its concrete structures and their characteristic processes of activity. That being so, since it would appear that each of these institutional structures and processes routinely conveys a plurality of the functions the society requires to exist, I wonder what is the point or value of pursuing the functional analysis of societal structures and processes, as has hitherto been done. Being convinced of the multifunctional properties of most concrete structures, together with the functional equivalence and substitutability of their operations for most societal requisites, I shall therefore not devote much time in the following discussion to the functional aspects of social structure, especially as I am not sure exactly how to identify, isolate, demonstrate or measure the "functions" of routine social processes and structures, and find the concept of function vague and ambiguous.

To illustrate these objections, let us consider Durkheim's functional interpretation of crime. For Durkheim, the principal function of crime is to stimulate the members of a society to express their commitments to uphold the societal norms, whatever they may be, by reference to which the action is identified as a criminal offence. By function here, Durkheim clearly means an effect unintended by the actor, in this case the offender. While such affirmative public response may be typical in simple societies, that is hardly true in modern impersonal or despotic ones, such as the Nazi state or Stalinist Russia, or even in liberal democracies. Yet even if it were, there are other functions of crime, and a great diversity of crimes - against the person, property, the peace, community, society or state, against the deities and other sacred emblems of a society, and so on. While true that in many instances, especially those to which the criminal law traditionally applies in most societies, the administration of justice and punishment of criminal offences obliquely reassert in a symbolic way the society's commitment to enforce the norms that classify certain actions as crimes, that is not so in all cases, notably in cases of white-collar crime, since there is often dispute whether certain acts are misdemeanours or crimes and whether they should or should not be punished thus. Moreover, many crimes are committed with impunity, being either unreported, undiscovered, or failing to be convicted in court. Many others are routinely committed by the police and other agents of the state. Other crimes in modern legal systems may entail civil liabilities to the injured party as compensation rather than punishment. As the literature on criminology demonstrates, and as the multifunctional nature of social processes entails, crimes have other functions than that to which Durkheim directed attention. The same point holds for other activities, such as feud, ritual, magic, witchcraft accusations, gift exchange, war, marriage, play or games and education, which have typically been identified with one or two primary "functions" or unintended effects, to the exclusion of others.

For functionalists the problem is to distinguish on value-free grounds the positive or functional from the negative effects of specific activities, processes or kinds of social relation, objectively and comprehensively, whether we use as reference points individuals, the society as an institutional order, or the groups and units involved and affected by their effects. Crime may be positively "functional" for the criminal but disfunctional for society when the criminal escapes detection and punishment. If we follow Durkheim, crime is only "functional" for the society when punished; though even then, surely not irrespective of its other effects. However in such situations and contexts as families, bureaucracies, slavery, stock exchanges or revolution, various crimes may become the norm rather than the exception. If we take a broader but more realistic view of crime than Durkheim did, as something in which societies, states and their rulers engage as well as individuals, we have to acknowledge that states and their leaders are rarely punished either by their people, their enemies or others for crimes that they commit. Indeed, states and their leaders often justify such criminality in normative terms as upholding the social order and historic ideals of the societies they govern. Horrendous examples of such political crimes abound in 20th-century Europe, Latin America, the USSR, Asia and Africa. These include the purges, terror and man-made famines in the Ukraine by which Joseph Stalin eliminated several millions of Soviet citizens; the vicious and genocidal conflicts in Yugoslavia during and after World War II as well as more recently between opposed religious and ethnic groups; events in Cambodia under Pol Pot, in Sri Lanka, Ulster, Lebanon, Uganda; and so on. In such cases, those responsible for the crime often try to justify its enormity in highflown normative terms, while methodically suppressing true reports, broadcasting falsehoods, and eliminating any challenge or critique of their claims, and all who may make them. There are also many situations in which, like genocide and ethnocide, such activities as the enslavement and sale, murder or 'disappearance' of persons, kidnapping by commandoes or press-gangs, and the distribution and promotion of such drugs as opium, heroin, cannabis and cocaine, are undertaken or encouraged by states, their representatives or agents without regard to criminality. We cannot therefore accept Durkheim's insistence that the contribution of crime to the perpetuation of a prevailing normative order is always the appropriate or sufficient criterion, or that the functions of those processes or events are positive and necessary. Rather, given their diversity, in many specific contexts we may regard their contributions toward the maintenance, development, or change of the prevailing social order as a more appropriate measure of their functional value.

There are moreover analytically important differences between functional statements about specific events and situations, such as a particular war or conflict, a particular tax or set of taxes, or the succession or appointment of a particular individual to some significant office, on the one hand, and others that refer to such categories of events as taxation, war, marriage, or similar recurrent processes, on the other. Whereas, whatever their weaknesses, functional statements about such recurrent processes or institutional categories as language or trade can only be general, those made about specific events, processes or situations should be no less specific. While functional statements about general categories of social process or relations normally rest on numerous observations by one or more observers, that is not always true of functional statements about unique specific events and processes, which are particular and non-recurrent, even though they may illustrate broader categories, such as taxation, succession, appointment, marriage and the like.

To the degree that an event or relation is distinct and relatively unique, extrapolations about its origins or functional effects, based on analyses of other instances of the category to which it belongs, are obviously inappropriate in the wider context, even for those immediately engaged. As effects of their particularity, the functions of specific and relatively unique developments or relationships cannot be validly deduced from the general categories to which they belong. For instance, though most individuals marry at some point in adult life, the implications or consequences of marriage differ in some manner and degree for every individual that undertakes it. Clearly also individual experiences in monogamous societies committed to lifelong marriage differ from those

31

characteristic of monogamous societies with easy divorce, or from the experience of marriage in polygynous societies on the one hand, and polyandrous societies on the other. Though most functional statements normally refer to recurrent processes of social life, or to such general categories of event as suicide, taxation, law, administration, crime or feud, even those statements are ultimately no less problematic in their exhaustiveness and accuracy than comparable statements about their functions or effects for those engaged in them and for others in their social environment. Despite greater opportunities for detailed systematic observation presented by recurrent processes, other than simple inference or unsupported assertion that such-and-such and no more is the function of those events or processes, I cannot say on what basis such statements are made, since I know of no acceptable methodology or procedure, including Durkheim's rules, for their derivation, demonstration, measurement or exhaustive enumeration.

To illustrate some of the problems that functional analysis must resolve, I cite an example I owe to George C. Homans. In the 14th century A.D., Edward III, king of England, sought by frequent invasions to subdue Scotland, but found his revenues insufficient. To equip his feudal levies with the necessary supplies, to arm his cavalry and other troops, and to bribe his Scottish agents and allies, Edward needed more than his revenues provided, even after plundering the Jews of London and soliciting loans elsewhere. To avoid alienating his barons by further demands, he called his council and asked them to advise how best he might raise the sums required for further campaigns. After some discussion the council advised him to levy new taxes on exports of raw wool.

At that time East Anglia and Yorkshire produced much of the raw wool the weavers of Flanders used to produce their staple cloth. Every year after sheep were shorn in East Anglia the Flemish merchants crossed the Channel, bought the wool and took it back to Flanders where it was then dyed and woven, before they returned to England with large bales of woollen cloth which they sold at a profit. His council persuaded Edward that this trade was inequitable, and that it could be lucratively reduced by imposing new taxes on exports of raw wool, which he did. The new tax duly brought the extra revenues Edward wanted for his wars against the Scots, which being their purpose, was their manifest function, though not the only one. What were the other, unintended effects or latent functions of Edward's tax policy? Where and how shall we look to find them, and how may we conclusively establish their functional links?

In this case, besides providing the revenues Edward needed to continue and conclude his Scottish wars, the wool tax had latent functions which took far longer to reveal their significance. As the records show, Edward's wool tax and its subsequent increases soon reduced English exports of raw wool to Flanders, and concentrated the production of woollen cloth in East Anglia, Yorkshire, and other parts of England where sheep farming thrived. In such regions, the early stages of carding, dyeing and weaving wool laid the basis for a thriving textile industry, which gradually expanded until it supplied most of the woollen cloth the country needed. On that firm base, guilds of craftsmen and merchants engaged in the industry continued to expand production, selling their surplus cloth abroad in Flanders and elsewhere. The production process was organised initially in the domestic and putting-out systems through craftsmen working with traditional looms and instruments of production, but was later concentrated in the workshops of guildmasters and senior craftsmen and in the first small factories.

During the 18th century, as supplies of raw cotton increased, and the demand for cotton cloth rose sharply, traditional arrangements for textile production proved increasingly incapable of producing sufficient cotton and woollen textiles to satisfy the growing demand at home and abroad. The series of technological and economic innovations by which entrepreneurs sought to overcome this impasse and to resolve successive bottlenecks in the processes of textile production as they arose, by inventing new machines and economic arrangements such as joint stock companies, and by organizing factory production with machines and full time wage workers, together formed what we call the Industrial Revolution (Goody 1982). By those means the machine production of textiles in factories advanced rapidly through successive technological solutions which removed short term bottlenecks in the manufacture of cotton and woollen textiles for sale at home and abroad. It seems therefore that the most important function of Edward III's wool tax, a latent one, was to lay the basis for those developments of textile production that ultimately promoted the rise of the bourgeoisie, mercantile capitalism and the Industrial Revolution in England some four centuries later. Please note that on this account, in this case the interval between the wool tax and the full expression of those latent functions was nearly four hundred years.

In like fashion, despite an interval of almost 2,500 years between the events, we may identify modern advances in nuclear fission and fusion as among the most important latent functions or unintended effects of those concepts of the atomic constitution of matter first proposed in ancient Greece by Leucippus and Democritus, to Plato's horror. If to avoid such tenuous and extensive linkages of the initial events and their effects across cultures, civilisations and indefinite periods of time, we restrict the range of functional analyses, on what grounds and by what measures shall we do so, and how can we then assert their validity, adequacy or completeness? On the other hand, if we extend the arena under study over such indefinite ranges of space, time and culture in which to trace those linkages that identify latent functions of social phenomena, how shall we ever know that we have indeed exhaustively identified all the many diverse and unintended effects of any process or event, or even of those that are most important for the societies that they affect? To determine functional primacy, by what verifiable, objective criteria can we estimate the relative importance of functions that manifest at uneven intervals of time and space?

These alternative kinds of *reductio ad absurdum* illustrate some problems of ever being sure that any functional analysis is as exhaustive and conclusive as it claims to be, since it can only be so by foretelling future developments, not only in the society or culture where those links began, but in all through which their other effects multiplied and ramified. However, that is only one of several difficulties I find with functional analysis. Among others, since most social processes are multifunctional, to attribute any function to a specific event, structure or process, presumes an accurate causal analysis of all others. To regard one set of functions above others as the sole or principal function of a process or event is to privilege it, and to restrict or discourage intensive study of others, thus frustrating analysis and encouraging distortion, often for ideological reasons, especially since we can neither convincingly demonstrate all the functions we identify as latent effects, nor their relations to the processes or events we identify as their cause.

A functional analysis which claims to specify and enumerate the effects of particular social processes, relations or events on their societal milieu, on those directly engaged, and on other social units is thus highly questionable and problematic. No less so, in my view, are causal accounts or "explanations" of those events and processes, despite the frequency with which they are made in sociology and anthropology. To anyone familiar with Aristotle's fourfold typology of causal factors, the problems confronting such explanation should be no surprise, even if we do not accept Aristotle's concept of causation. As John Stuart Mill demonstrated, the factors we may validly identify as causal in situations or processes of any kind can only be those residuals the evidence suggests are decisive in generating specific effects. Such a conclusion we may hope to achieve by repeated experiments in laboratory situations, but rarely, if ever, in sociological, historical or anthropological studies, least of all when we have to deal with such unique sequences as specific industrial disputes, making political decisions, passing particular laws, and so on.

J. S. Mill wrote about causality before statisticians had developed satisfactory methods of calculating the precise measures of association between two or more sets of factors such, for instance, as the appearance of sunspots and economic recessions, or meteorological conditions and changes in birth-rates. Nowadays, given appropriate information, such calculations readily yield correlation ratios whose significance may be analysed statistically. Nonetheless, given the built-in tendency of human thought to pursue the chimera of certainty offered by monocausal 'explanations' of social processes and events, even such probabilistic measures of association as correlation coefficients are rapidly converted into spurious statements of causation. From force of habit many writers conceive those correlations as essentially "causal" relations, when they are quite clearly not so, but estimate the probabilities of association for two or more phenomena. Given the influence of linguistic structures on our forms and habits of thought, perhaps people who speak Indo-European, Semitic and most other languages find it particularly difficult to accept probabilistic relations and measures as 'explanations' or partial explanations of human events, and seek instead the deductive certainties offered by linear causal models of the familiar Cartesian geometric kind illustrated by French structuralism and neo-Marxism. Empirically however, inductive analyses based on the careful collation and comparison of sufficient instances of similar events may provide better guides to the understanding of social relations and processes than the illusory logico-deductive 'method', or global theories constructed upon it.

Given the plural "causation" of social phenomena, in any event the proximate cause or decisive residual factor presupposes many other conditions and factors which are together necessary to constitute the situation or sequence in which the factors identified as decisive and causal had their effect. However, by themselves those factors could not have generated the effects ascribed to them, if the entire sequence and situation in which they operated did not exist exactly as it did. Hence even if we can identify the likely causal factors of particular social events, to demonstrate their efficacy and significance, we have to list, weigh and unravel the relations of the innumerable, unspecified conditions, antecedents and structures such causation presupposes. Without such background factors the entire sequence could not have happened, and together they are more complex and often more important for the result than the agents we say are causal.

Moreover, as historians repeatedly state, it is common to find that effects of virtually identical content and form, such as economic slumps, the enslavement of a people, or abolitions of slavery, have "causes" of differing kinds, thus directing attention to various inadequacies and uncertainties of causal analysis as social explanation. For if effects of the same kind may have diverse "causes", it is equally true that the same "causal" factors may give rise to quite diverse effects, thus leaving the utility of causal explanations of social affairs in question; and of functional analyses, even more so.

Given such variability in the "causal" links between empirical events, certain writers have sought to escape contingency in the "causal" explanation of social affairs by postulating various factors as their sole universal determinant, following the examples of Montesquieu, Comte and Marx, who invoked geography, ideology and economy respectively as pervasive ultimate causes. In that way, some writers have tried to avoid trivializing their "explanations" of social phenomena as effects of infinitely various "causes", while claiming that, though easily mistaken for proximate "causes", the immediate antecedents of those effects are not the decisive factors that produced them. It is, for example, obvious that the final cigarette or pipe of tobacco taken by an individual before he or she is diagnosed as having lung cancer cannot be its genuine "cause". This applies equally to causal explanations of other developments such as social and biological evolution that emerge slowly by continuous recurrent processes over long periods of time. According to Marx's famous formula, the dominant mode of production in an economy ultimately determines the structure and content of the social formation built upon it (Marx & Engels 1948). However convenient as an article of faith, that universal determinant, like its rivals, such as the ideas that men hold, or the geographical situation in which they live, is so general and remote from the particular developments, situations and structures identified as their effects that, given their asserted universal efficacy, they may plausibly be held to determine developments of radically opposite kinds and content in similar contexts, thus illustrating once more the vacuous nature of such global "explanations", and the contingent linkages of "cause" and effect such theories seek to eliminate.

In another sense also the application of universal determinist theories to the explanation of social phenomena and development involves contingency, since with each step in the hypothetical "causal" chain from the phenomenon to be "explained" through its immediate antecedents to its postulated ultimate "cause", the asserted "causal" relation becomes more contingent, problematic and hypothetical. The greater the number of links in the "causal" chain, the weaker the connection, and the greater likewise the probability of error and inadequacy in its structure and validity. For if, as Spencer remarked, every "cause" may have a multitude of effects, each of which in turn acts as a "causal" agent to produce its own effects, so too each effect, like a newborn baby, has an increasing number of causal antecedents, the remoter the linkage to its antecedents in any generation. For "causal" analysis, this means that the number and variety of factors or conditions that operate as causal antecedents of any discrete effect multiplies with each successive step backwards in the chain of imputed causation up to the hypothetically final point of the ultimate "causal" agent or agents, whatever their nature is said to be by Montesquieu, Hegel, Marx, Comte, Gobineau or some other.

For these and other reasons, the most unreliable and unsatisfactory "causal" analyses or explanations of social events are those that claim to identify specific events or conditions as effects of some general conditions or factors that are held ultimately to determine all varieties of social process and development. To illustrate the problem, if the industrial revolution of the eighteenth century in Britain is treated as a functional effect of the taxation policy of Edward III in the fourteenth century, then by the same token the ultimate "cause" of the industrial revolution was that ruler's taxation policy. Yet, even if that historical chain of relations could be securely established, derivation of the industrial revolution directly from Edward's taxation policy is unacceptable, since the former assumes so many other factors, conditions, developments and institutions that, however important taxation policy may have been in initiating the sequence of which industrialization was a result, that policy could not possibly have produced the industrial revolution as its independent effect. On such grounds, having rejected functional explanations and analyses as unreliable and indemonstrable, I find "causal" explanations and analyses of social affairs no more reliable or valid, though especially prone to misdirect and mislead enquiries towards erroneous and unsatisfactory conclusions. Accordingly in studying social structure I shall avoid both "functional" analyses and "causal" explanations, even though, as indicated already, when the data permit, I shall try to formulate predictive statements about future developments which may then be subject to empirical test.

4. REQUISITES

Having thus rejected functional and causal analyses of social structures and processes as illusory and indemonstrable, questions arise how and to what end then do we study society? What kind of understanding do we hope to find by so doing, and how shall we proceed with the task? In the following chapters I shall try to present an operational framework of analytic concepts designed to apply to societies of any developmental level, and to the social situations, processes and subdivisions of which societies are composed. I shall also try to describe a method or procedure for the application of that conceptual scheme to social aggregates of any scale or complexity, to any single instant or any time span, in order to determine whether and how their routine processes or other conditions perceptibly perpetuate or modify their structures and substance or content. I shall also suggest how we may learn how individuals come to occupy their different places in society, and how those positions affect their participation and interactions.

To use the conceptual scheme I have in mind, we should first undertake an intensive study of all the various kinds of social entities, units and relations that together constitute the structure of a society; and in so doing we shall also study the relations of that society with its material and social environments. The analytic scheme that requires such information fortunately facilitates its collection by clearly identifying the different kinds of data needed to provide adequate descriptive accounts of all the various kinds of social unit, process and relationship to which it refers. However, as this text is not about fieldwork, it does not deal directly with data collection. For those units, situations or processes for which we have the necessary detailed information, the conceptual scheme should also allow us to formulate falsifiable predictions about the reactions of specific social units, including categories, to changes of differing kind and degree in other units or certain specified conditions. However, to develop an adequate account and understanding of any social situation or structure, it is essential that we should examine it as thoroughly and objectively as possible, without any presumptions about its 'nature', history, or such properties as its functional coherence, internal stability, normative consensus, systemic qualities, institutional integration, or ethnic, cultural or structural homogeneity. If such conditions objectively prevail within the society or unit we study, the data collected from and about it should demonstrate this. On no account should we assume that they do in advance, as Durkheim, Radcliffe-Brown, Malinowski and Parsons have done.

To that end I shall first seek the logically necessary conditions and preconditions for the existence and operation of specific social phenomena such as events, relations, units or processes, and then try to identify their logically unavoidable entailments or immediate implications. Instead of their hypothetical functional or misleading causal relations, I shall therefore be seeking relations of logical necessity in the construction, articulation and operation of social units and relations. As far as possible I shall try to order such conditions by their relations of logical priority as prerequisite, requisite or entailment, in order to identify and derive links between antecedent, simultaneous and subsequent states or events of a given structure or process, some of which, if logically necessary, should be invariant in all recurrent instances of that kind, a possibility that invites empirical tests by comparative study.

To apply this kind of analysis to social phenomena, by observation and experience, by first-hand enquiry and other research where necessary and possible, we must first learn all we can about the object of study, whether that is a social unit, a process, or situation, so that we may list all its essential attributes, components or conditions, and if a sequence or process, reconstruct it correctly by relating all its elements exactly in space and time. Having listed those particulars, we next have to isolate the essential principles or conditions which are sufficient and necessary to identify its nature, basis and form, so that we can reconstitute it as an abstract model for further study. To do so, we have first to model or reformulate empirical conditions, relations, structures and processes conceptually, by redefining their particulars in abstract terms. We may then analyse their interrelations formally to separate the requisite or prerequisite items from their immediate implications or entailments, thus enabling us to re-order our conceptual equivalents of the empirical object under study by their relations of logical priority and entailment. In brief, we have to develop a method by which to translate empirical phenomena into appropriate abstractions by formulating their substantive features conceptually as principles, states or conditions, so that we may lay bare their composition and relationships and understand at a conceptual level how they articulate as principles, requisites, or as implications.

An excellent illustration of the quantitative application of such a methodology to the analysis of the division of labor by sex is that of Burton and his colleagues (1977). They were stimulated by Roy D'Andrade's (1976) qualitative requisite analysis of American ideas of common minor illnesses to quantify and compare the incidence of logically necessary relations between social conditions involved in the sexual division of labor. Later on, having outlined a scheme for the descriptive analysis of societal structures and their components in static terms, I shall discuss another way, based on the study of changing political structures (Smith 1960a; 1974; 1978), by which we may study the logically necessary relations among social units and events in both static and dynamic situations.

First, let me briefly sketch the origin of this notion of requisites, which like so much else I owe to Max Weber. In his *Economy and Society* (1978: v. 1), Weber lists the "conditions of maximum formal rationality of capital accounting". That is a beautiful piece of Weberian jargon. What does it mean? Weber was keenly concerned to isolate the essential nature, the spirit or essence, of capitalism, and eventually identified that by the "conditions of maximum formal rationality of capital accounting", i.e., the predictability of deriving expected returns from specified investments at known times in different kinds of productive enterprise operating under clearly specified conditions. According to Weber, high levels of accuracy in such predictions are preconditions of modern capitalistic enterprise. In the passage cited he listed eight conditions, which we may reduce to five, for the achievement of maximum formal rationality of capital accounting, that is, for accurately predicting production turnovers, costs and returns.

First was the complete appropriation of all material means of production, and the complete absence of formal appropriation of opportunities for profit in the market, that is, market freedom, or total freedom of market opportunities. Second came complete autonomy in the selection of management by owners, that is, complete absence of formal appropriation of rights to managerial functions. A hereditary managerial class, such as until recently the British and Soviet Russians, for instance, possessed, inhibits rationality of capitalist production, whether that is pursued privately or by the state, and so frustrates rational capital accounting. Third came the complete absence of appropriation of jobs and opportunities for acquiring them by workers, and the absence of appropriation of workers by others. In short, maximum rationality of capitalist production assumes free wage labor, that is, formal freedom of the labor market, and freedom in selection of workers. It is thus incompatible with slavery or other forms of tied labor. Clearly these are all requisite conditions of rational capitalist production, as Weber conceived it. Rational capital accounting may seem remote from these conditions, but, according to Weber, unless they obtain we cannot have a perfectly rational system of capital accounting, since it will be subject to so many irrational operating conditions. Fourth, Weber lists as necessary the complete absence of substantive regulation of consumption, production and prices, or other forms of regulation that would limit freedom of contract, or specified conditions of exchange. This requisite we may call formal freedom of contract. Here Weber makes a distinction between formal and substantive that I find very useful, and shall employ frequently below. For him substantive conditions are empirical or operational, while formal conditions derive logically from some abstract principle.

As a fifth condition Weber says we need complete calculability of the technical conditions of production, that is, a mechanically rational technology. In other words, if agriculture is not reduced to machine production, it will not conform to the model's requirements. The kind of peasant agriculture found in the tropics does not lend itself to maximum rationality of capital accounting, and for that reason among others, insurance companies will not insure peasant crops. Next comes complete calculability of the functioning of public administration and the legal order; that is, a formally rational administration and law. Predictability is the essence of rationality here. Seventh, to have the maximum formal rationality of accounting and production, the enterprise and its conditions of success or failure should be completely separate from the owners' household and other affairs. Finally, without a monetary system of the highest possible degree of formal rationality, we cannot achieve the maximum formal rationality of capital accounting, since the latter assumes the former for its calculations of profit.

Having spelt out these eight conditions, Weber says that nowhere as far as he knows have they all simultaneously been present in any economy, capitalist or other. Accordingly, they illustrate an ideal type. However, to the degree that economic systems differ in the ways they approximate this pure model of capitalism, different consequences and developments inevitably follow, thus enabling Weber to distinguish varieties of capitalism on the basis of the ways in which they depart from his ideal-type or formal model of a perfectly "rational" capitalist industrial system. What Weber does in this passage is to spell out eight essential attributes or requisites that constitute the ideal type of a formally rational system of capitalist productive enterprises competing with one another in an open unregulated market under conditions that permit accurate calculations of the costs and outcomes of production. That passage is where I first found the notion of requisites used heavily below.

To illustrate: the requisites of a unilineal descent system, whether patrilineal or matrilineal, include successive generations, agreed principles of filiation and descent, whether through the uterine or the paternal line, and an exclusive emphasis on one or other sex as appropriate for the transmission of these jural identities and rights. To localize the lineages and constitute a society of local lineages, other requisite conditions are needed which have no place in other kinship systems, such as those of the Polynesians or Eskimo. To develop a set of exogamous lineages, yet other requisites must be added. For example, there must be a number of similar lineages in the society in order that they may marry one another, since that is a requisite. No matrilineages are known to ethnography that allow mating within the matrilineage. Why is that so? Some patrilineal units, such as those of the Arabs, Pathans or Fulani, practise preferential marriage between a man and his father's brother's daughter, his FBD. That is marriage within the lineage, but nothing similar occurs in matrilineages. Why? One hardly ever hears that question, much less the answer. As a pre-requisite condition, matrilineal organization excludes intra-lineage marriage. Why is that pre-requisite? In the entire library of kinship studies in anthropology we shall not find many instances other than Robert Murphy's report on the Mundurucu, whom he labels and shows to be transitional, or Nimuendaju's Apinaye and the Akwe-Shavante of Maybury-Lewis, in which a patrilineal organization is combined with uxorilocal marriage. Why not? Operationally an endogamous matrilineage is a contradiction in terms, as parallel descent among Apinaye and Shavante indicates. Why is that so? Ask also why are all matrilineal units, clans or lineages, exogamous.

One of the things that anthropologists regularly report without pausing to ask why, and without apparently considering it a marvel, is that no society yet known has a kinship structure, unilineal or other, in which the groups or units differ in their principles of organization, or operate by different rules. In any kinship structure, whether unilineal, bilateral or other, every kinship unit must be morphologically, conceptually and operationally identical, or we shall not have a kinship system or society. In other words units of the same kind in any society must have an identity of structure and operational procedures if they are to constitute a single coherent structure together, and so maintain the society. Here again in dealing with this necessary congruence of organizational form and operation, we have evidence of the essential or requisite conditions that constitute a viable kinship system.

Suppose that we wished to constitute a society of unilineal clans, like some mythical Greek legislators, without any further division of those clans into lineage groups; but merely to subdivide the population by unilineal descent into uterine or matrilineal blocs, without entailing any form of group organisation at the local or other level. To do so it is necessary that we first conceive and then institute some principle, whether matrilineal, patrilineal or other, and then create a means or mechanism to ensure that all people of the same descent line will, however dispersed, recognise one another without difficulty as kin. The means may be a name, a style of coiffure or clothing, facial or body marks, or any item that will serve as a marker to identify all who belong to the Crocodile clan, the Monkey clan, or some other clan. Such public markers are direct or immediate entailments of the categorical clan structure, if that is to prevail in the absence of any organized collective action to enforce it. To ensure its validity we have to have some way of identifying the members of a unit. By contrast a unilineal descent group composed of aligned lineage segments presupposes some kind of genealogical scheme that allows people, fictively or otherwise, to establish collateral kinship ties and distances among themselves by tracing unilineal descent over two or more generations. If they are distributed on some other principle, such as locality or residence, this may enable kinsmen to establish fictive lineage segments as the basis for appropriate allocations of rights, resources, functions and duties between and within groups, on grounds of relative seniority or organizational scale.

The point here is that some means or set of devices to ensure that the category or group members are clearly identified or organized, according to the principles and requirements of the unit to which they belong, is an immediate entailment of the categorical or group organisation. For example to constitute an exogamous lineage, two immediate entailments are appropriate arrangements to administer and enforce the rule, firstly, by preventing in advance breaches of it, which entails control of the marriages of young people; and secondly, by devising procedures to ensure that all couples who breach the exogamy rule are sanctioned negatively by senior kinsmen on behalf of their lineage group. Without such mechanisms to monitor prospective marriages made by members of the unit, and to ensure that those who seem to contravene the exogamous rule are investigated and severely punished, the rule would soon lose its validity and collective value, and depend on individual inclination for observance.

To be incorporated into an Indian sub-caste or *jati*, since castes are endogamous and closed reproductive units, presupposes that both parents were born in the caste and properly married. Together these requisites entail descent from previous members of the caste. Even if unilineal descent comprehensively subdivides the caste, so that in practice, to be an effective member of the caste, it is necessary to belong to one or other of its lineages, lineage membership is not a requisite but an immediate implication or entailment of membership in the caste. However, if one's ancestors flouted caste norms, and were outcaste by the caste *panchayat* in consequence, their offspring would not belong to the parents' original caste, but to the newly outcaste group created by the expulsion of their ancestors. In short, besides the principle of automatic recruitment by descent from caste parents, one of the unstated requisites of caste identity is that members and their ancestors should all have performed their caste roles with credit, by honoring caste norms and observing the necessary caste rituals.

To constitute social categories such as racial, ethnic or unilineal descent categories, we need use only one criterion to specify the conditions of recruitment and delimit the aggregate or category. In such cases a single criterion is quite sufficient for purposes of unit definition and boundary closure. Among the Plateau Tonga of Zambia, who trace descent matrilineally, to prove membership in a given matriclan, such as the Crocodile clan, it is sufficient to show that one's mother was a Crocodile, and unnecessary to trace descent to her ancestresses or establish that they were also Crocodiles. Beside such "proof" of appropriate descent, observance of the necessary Crocodile taboos of incest and exogamy indicates that actors see themselves as Crocodiles. To move among the Plateau Tonga beyond the categorical organization by clan, and group clansmen into local lineages, other criteria, rules and mechanisms of group membership are necessary, such as the fictitious genealogies and positional transfers of names and social personalities, widows and other assets, without which there would be no Tonga lineage units. However, as this example shows, it is possible to organize a society categorically simply by instituting rules of unilineal descent and exogamy that establish and interlock its component clans as units of equal status with no more requisites.

To pass beyond that level of organization and re-constitute the clans or their divisions as groups, we have to institute other requisites as criteria or principles by which groups recruit their members, as we found in recruitment to Hindu castes. As groups, lineages recruit their members on two or more principles or criteria which must be culturally sanctioned as requisites for concrete structures of that type. For that to be possible, the principles of recruitment must be mutually consistent and must not obstruct, impede or contradict the simultaneous institutionalization of one another. By *institutionalization* here I mean the state or process by which the validity of a condition, rule or principle develops and is maintained by force of collective sanctions. Hence questions of institutionalization confront both requisites and their immediate implications or entailments.

To constitute social units based on three principles of recruitment, such as the localized exogamous segmentary patrilineages of the Tiv in Central Nigeria, those principles must be mutually consistent in order that the unit can be instituted as an operationally viable concrete structure in the wider society. If units of that kind are institutional features of the social order, then all descent groups will be structurally identical, as they are among the Tiv. For example, among the Kagoro, north of the Tiv, since the *kwai* or maximal lineage has several requisites, all Kagoro *kwai* have the same set of conditions. Though Kagoro society has units of other kinds besides *kwai* as maximal lineages, all *kwai* are formally the same, despite their substantive differences. A society cannot simultaneously institutionalize contradictory structures, and must therefore exclude variant forms of the concrete structures on which its organization rests. That such a rule holds universally demonstrates the most general and basic requisites of human society of every kind or level of development, namely, the fundamental requisite or principle of structural consistency which entails that units of the same kind are structurally identical and compatible with one another and with units of other kinds in the society. This requisite of structural consistency regulates the conditions under which the various principles that together constitute diverse units of the social structure may be instituted and combined together with their entailments or implications.

Let us imagine that a unit X of unspecified type is constituted or defined by certain principles, P1-4, which as requisites presuppose conditions A to N. Moreover let us assume that the requisites, A to N, of conditions P1-4 that constitute unit X have as their entailments or implications, conditions Q to Z. If that formula accurately describes the unit X as an empirical reality, and if it forms a valid logical chain, we should be able to derive conditions Q-Z from the requisites A to N; and those from the unit's basic principles, P1-4. If so, we would have a logical sequence independent of the causal or functional relations so dear to many social scientists. Right or wrong, we shall not then invoke either causal or functional relations in the ordinary sense of the words, as we discuss the logically necessary conditions for the existence or development of particular structures and the logically unavoidable entailments of those structures.

Likewise, if summarizing and translating ethnographic or historical data on a sequence of substantive changes in Unit X, we can demonstrate by analysis how the various conditions we have listed as its requisites and their entailments are associated with that process, even if together they do not describe it fully, we may perhaps initiate a study of social processes and dynamics free of all reference to cause or function.

Moreover if we can constitute a chain or series of changes in requisite conditions and their immediate entailments, we may then formulate hypotheses and test expectations derived from their implications against the empirical data. For example, if unit X based on P1-4 has A to N requisite conditions and their implications Q to Z, and if for whatever reason one of those requisites, say D, is nullified, there should be some discernible change in other conditions of unit X. This clearly follows Weber's method of ideal types. If it does, then we shall have a tool free of causal or functional assumptions and relations with which we can test systematically various hypotheses, including our own, against empirical data. We may then as necessary modify our model of unit X to improve the fit between our specifications of its principles, requisites and entailments, their empirical expression, and the unit's observable reactions to changing conditions. I shall say more on this subject later on.

CHAPTER 2

ELEMENTS
OF
SOCIETY

1. SOCIETY, CULTURE AND ECOLOGY

Before attempting to proceed further I must mention the important difference between *society* as the universal state or condition of human interactions and relations, and the concept of *societies*, which identifies each *society* as the largest empirically and analytically distinct aggregate bounded by such interactions, that is, the largest body having its unique composition and network of relations. Conceptually, the boundaries of a society coincide with the widest range in which people share and use a common distinctive stock of social units, forms of action, and modes of thought and feeling, in their relations with one another and with their environment. Empirically and objectively, as we shall see, the society's boundaries coincide with the area and time-span in which the regulatory framework of its corporate organisation is effective and valid. To its members, and to others as well, the limits of each society coincide with institutional disjunctions in the form and content of the structural frameworks by which their peoples live and maintain social relations, by which they identify themselves as separate collectivities, and are identified by others as members of distinct societies. In other words, each society is the largest aggregate having its peculiar composition and distinctive combination of social units and relations. The society is neither the population which shares this organization, though we commonly think of it so; nor is it the territory or country occupied by that population, despite our daily usage. A society is an essentially unique combination of the distinctive social units and relations of a people with one another and their material and social environments.

While each society, as the largest aggregate having its distinct structure and composition, will contain other aggregates of differing base and kind, to conceive societies as isolated, closed 'systems', as structural-functionalists have done for generations, is empirically and historically wrong. Only societies that are utterly isolated from others, and of which we therefore know nothing, are truly closed; and those are few and far between. Normally, as their members interact and intermingle, societal identifications, loyalties and boundaries are reinforced or redefined; and this may lead to some shifts of criteria or membership conditions, however slow and limited that process as a rule. Even then, most members of a common society assume its validity and closure for processes and purposes that are culturally prescribed. The fact that a society contains social aggregates of different base and kind that articulate their memberships with one another in different ways constitutes it as a unique complex of distinctive social units, relations and forms of action, and identifies its members as a distinct collectivity or people who share certain values, interests and beliefs together with their common homeland.

Since societies perpetuate themselves by reproduction and socialization they are always age- and sex-heterogeneous and include three or more generations. Territorially, most are localized within clear boundaries at any point in time. Even in nomadic societies people generally nomadize together in residential groups and bounded areas. Although initially, perhaps, all or most human societies were fully self-sustaining and produced all the goods and services their members consumed, few do so nowadays, and many depend on others for most of what they need. The more isolated the society, the more exclusively its youngest members are from infancy immersed therein, and so the more exclusive and total is their socialisation. The more open the society to external influences, the more "modern" it is, the less so. Although most societies seek to regulate their internal affairs independently, historically they differ greatly in their ability to do so, for political and other reasons. So likewise do the many diverse kinds of social unit that constitute them.

Societies also differ in their stability. Some, such as the city-states of ancient Greece, torn by incessant class struggles between oligarchs, aristocrats and plebs, or the feudal societies of Japan, early China and Europe, by the ordinary processes of their operation generate their instability. At lower levels of development and differentiation, the Anuak of the eastern Sudan, the Kachin of highland Burma, the Kaingang of Brazil, the Murngin of northern Australia, the Paktun of Swat, and Tuareg of the western Sudan likewise owe their ceaseless turmoil and change to fundamental contradictions set deep within their structures. Such variations in societal stability illustrate and presuppose corresponding differences in their structure and integration. Hence if we wish to measure and compare social integration operationally, we should not assume that it has equivalent levels and forms in all societies, but leave investigation to determine how similar they are in those respects. Finally, societies differ, sometimes greatly, in the homogeneity or diversity of their composition, that is, in the variety of peoples and cultures they contain.

Following Max Weber, I identify social relations by the mutual orientation of actors, recognising that frequently one person may be oriented towards another without the latter's awareness or reciprocity, in which case the relation is one-sided and not mutual, though it might easily become so. If we observe any busy crossroads in a city, we will notice that as pedestrians pass by, hurrying to their next engagements, two people may accidentally bump against one another. Momentarily that creates a physical relationship but not a social one, unless one then orients to the other, thereby converting the physical into a social relationship, however brief and limited. By contrast the confrontations of armies in war demonstrate their mutual orientations and intentions to destroy, and hence their social relation. In shopping for cigarettes or other trivia, we often exchange words with the clerk, following conventions that prescribe what may or may not be said on such occasions. In so doing, at each transaction we set up shallow short-term relations with the clerk. If we interact recurrently with the clerk or another over several days or weeks, the range and content of such conventional exchanges may increase, together with our awareness and expectations of one another's behavior, until informal roles gradually attach to our respective positions as customer and clerk. Even though those roles lack definitions and prescriptive sanctions, by their shared expectations of appropriate reciprocal behavior, they nonetheless constitute a social relation. In like fashion, a mother expects her infant to do certain things, while the latter soon develops complementary expectations. Though the mother may never list all that she expects her child to do, if we could compile such a list, it would probably summarize the mother's expectations.

Besides their unique complements of diverse components, which vary in their kind, number and modes of articulation with the levels of their differentiation, all societies have their own distinct territories, populations, languages, symbols and other means of communication, ecological adaptation to their habitats, specific techniques for subsistence and survival, economies, political organizations, forms of marriage and kinship, aims and ways of socializing children, and sets of normative rules, procedures and structures that regulate conduct, and ways of restraining or settling disputes. Finally, in all societies people have some set of beliefs and ideas which they hold but cannot prove about the world, nature, destiny, human nature, the afterlife, the society and its history. These ideas, assumptions and values are parts of the cultures of their communities, along with other sets of shared beliefs, norms and understandings. Inevitably such sets of collective ideas include many misconceptions and misunderstandings concerning the nature of the world, human beings, society and history, as well as that other unseen world which so many believe to permeate and regulate this one. Every human being also has his or her unique individual experience and knowledge of the societal culture, and unique combination of ignorance, insight, perception and misunderstanding. Sometimes it seems that men tacitly agree to misunderstand various processes and phenomena collectively in certain ways in order to cooperate, and that negative stereotypes of outsiders and other ethnic groups mobilise and endorse their groups in conflictual relations. Finally, since all societies, though sharing the attributes listed, differ in their social composition and organizations, their membership, histories, traditions, cultures, habitat and relations with it, and in their symbolic, technical, material and political resources, each is unique although it represents the general category, and forms a distinct variety or species which must be studied intensively to be understood, although with the same broad conceptual apparatus and procedures used to understand others.

For this reason, from the beginning social science has always been comparative in scope and method. At Athens, despite their normative priorities, this was the common foundation of the political typologies of Plato and Aristotle. It was also the method used by Ibn Khaldûn to abstract the common structure that underlay the developmental cycles of differing regimes and empires in his history of the world. Vico also grounded his 'new science' on a detailed comparison of the developmental cycles of ancient Greek and Roman culture, those being the ones he knew best. Finally, in his great work on the Laws, Montesquieu ranged widely to collate innumerable instances of the diverse aspects of legal systems from as many societies as he could. Thereafter social science has always been global in span and comparative in method, simply to secure its conclusions against errors arising from inadequate foundations.

Unlike concrete structures and other kinds of social aggregate, the ideas, symbols, values and beliefs that people share can have no memberships as such. Instead, those assumptions and beliefs about empirical phenomena form conceptual structures in the minds of men that guide their perceptions and misperceptions of one another and the world, as well as their evaluations of experience and imaginary alternatives. Together such assumptions, symbols, ideas, values, idioms of thought and dispositions constitute the culture shared by the members of each society, however unequally and imperfectly. On such bases, in interactions with one another we negotiate our understandings or misunderstandings of events, phenomena and possibilities. As outcomes of such transactions, the orientations that animate each actor are often modified by their actions, experiences of others, and social relationships. As a consequence, individual perceptions of one another and of social relations continuously develop and change, however strongly we may wish otherwise. In our social interactions, beliefs and ideas about the world, society, individuals and interests are continuously invoked, applied, tested, and confirmed or modified by experience that maintains or changes the character and content of those relations. For this reason there can be no single unilateral determinism of culture by the society as the all-inclusive action process, since such processes are themselves informed and animated by the aspirations, meanings and beliefs which express the culture. Nor are the social organization and process determined by those ideas, as Ward Goodenough, echoing Comte, proclaimed, since differences of individual belief, values and meaning generate sufficient misunderstandings and friction in social interactions to modify our perceptions and ideas continuously. Instead of either deterministic alternative, by its ordinary processes, society ensures the continuous adjustments, affirmations, and changes of collective ideas, beliefs, techniques and values, that is, of the people's culture, and simultaneously of the social structure that regulates their activities and relations.

As heterogeneous mixtures of unconscious assumptions, patterns, idioms of thought, values, orientations, ideas, apperceptions, predispositions and beliefs, cultures are heavily influenced by the language that structures thinking, perceptions, communication and experience, and vary as widely in their contents and tendencies as the societies to which they belong differ in scale and form. In consequence, hardly any social phenomena open to ethnographic observation and study do not vary in some manner or degree between societies. Even biological differences of sex and age are not exempt from such variation. Neither are the ideas or forms of paternity and parenthood, nor the basic form of the family as a group of man and woman and their child or children. Similarly, ideas and relations of kinship, affinity, descent, friendship, neighborhood, rank, property, alliance and domination or hegemony vary as widely as the social units or forms in which they appear, with the result that nowhere in the ethnographic literature shall we find any specific type of social process, activity, relation or organization that retains the same form, content and articulation in all human societies. We must therefore construct appropriate conceptions that subsume the near-infinite empirical diversity of ethnographic data in sets of formal categories based on their structurally important differences and common distinctive features. Extending such analytic concepts and constructs, we should therefore recognize that virtually without exception, every distinct kind of social relation, process or institution known to ethnography varies in its form and content as an expression of some specific socio-cultural conditions. For an example, let us briefly consider how society and culture relate to the environment and ecology.

In the study of social structure we have to deal with the social processes of people who interact, not only with one another but with their habitats, the mundane and the mystical, or supernatural. I use the word *habitat* to distinguish a people's material context from their *environment*, which in my view is the habitat as they perceive it, and so denotes how they see, interpret and use it in light of their culture. As this distinction is important, I shall illustrate it by an example from my fieldwork in Northern Nigeria.

In 1950 several culturally distinct ethnic groups inhabited the Jos Plateau, southeast of Kano. Around the mining town of Bukuru, the indigenous people were Birom, then still perhaps the most numerous, grain farmers who tilled their fields and went about their work nude, except for leaves the women wore occasionally, while men wore penis sheaths. Though Birom then seemed like a Stone Age people, they had made and used iron tools and weapons for centuries. The first newcomers to join them in this area were nomadic pastoral Fulani who moved across their land in family and lineage groups grazing their long-horned cattle, looking for water, waste land on which to graze, cattle tracks on which to move, safety for their beasts, and friendly Birom with whom to trade. Next came the British who in 1902 overran and incorporated the Plateau in their Protectorate of Northern Nigeria, and were thenceforth primarily concerned to administer the area and its peoples and to exploit its tin, columbite and other mineral resources. In 1950 when I visited Bukuru, the British used large mobile draglines and tall pylons to convey power lines, which they shifted and moved across the landscape from site to site as new mines were opened and old ones abandoned. Following the British came Muslim Hausa who were always amply clothed. At an elevation of four to five thousand feet, even during summer the Plateau was chilly in early morning. Nonetheless while the Hausa wore extra robes, and sometimes winter coats of European make for warmth, Birom would stand naked and silent in the sunlight, grasping themselves around the shoulders to warm their bodies.

The Hausa first came to Bukuru primarily to trade, since it had an excellent railhead and rail line to southern Nigeria. Hausa bought cattle from the nomadic Fulani cattle herders to transport by rail to southern

Nigeria to be sold there by their trading partners, who would then buy and send back bales of kolanuts for sale at Bukuru and Jos. With such lucrative and time-demanding trade, the Hausa at Bukuru settled compactly in a hamlet of their own away from other villages, but made no effort to farm, unlike Hausa elsewhere. At some distance from those settlements stood the labor camp or *bariki* (barracks) of a tin mine, to which came large numbers of young men from other parts of the Plateau and adjacent regions in search of wage work. In the labor camp these workers were classified by 'tribal' identity, and grouped in rows of small huts that were administered by elderly Northerners who used Hausa as the *lingua franca* and reported to the British management. Last of all to enter the area were the Yoruba and Ibo from different regions of southern Nigeria. The Ibo worked mainly as clerks and technicians in British establishments such as the provincial administration, railway workshops, stores, commercial and mining firms, schools and hospitals. Most Yoruba either practised their traditional crafts and skills, or traded between the Plateau and their homeland, since Yoruba products were highly prized and scarce in the North and in great demand.

Even if we ignore the labor camp and the ethnic and cultural diversity of the miners' labor-force, in the Bukuru district at this date there were at least five distinct peoples, speaking as many languages, having as many distinct cultures, different kinds of social organization and ecology, religions, histories, traditions, and *different environments*, though all shared the same *habitat*. Even so, since for each ethnic group that habitat necessarily included the other groups, the environment of each group differed in that respect, and in its distinctive cultural perceptions of material resources, conditions and opportunities. While Birom saw the land as farmers, Fulani did so as herdsmen, the British as rulers, merchants, miners and missionaries, Hausa as long distance traders, and Ibo and Yoruba yet differently. Thus despite their common habitat, the Birom, Fulani, Hausa, British, Yoruba and Ibo of Bukuru all inhabited distinct environments that included each other.

As that example shows, it is always necessary to distinguish sharply between the environment, which is a culturally created perception, and the habitat or raw material to which that environment refers. By doing so we shall avoid the currently fashionable idea that ecology determines culture, to which some archaeologists and anthropologists are now committed. Since a people's perceptions of their environment are culturally distinctive, even in common habitats, these environments are cultural constructs clearly different from their habitat. The simple fact that people living by different cultures in the same habitat perceive that habitat differently, and develop different ecological adaptations, demonstrates the decisive role of culture in human ecology, despite claims to the contrary. Moreover, since a people's environment includes, besides their material context, other peoples with whom they interact, their environment has both social and material dimensions.

On the relations of ecology, culture and society, Diagram 1 indicates how the society and its culture create their environment and ecology from the habitat.

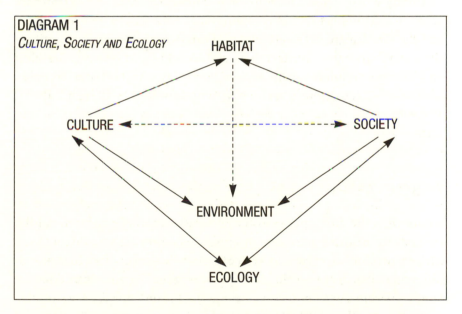

DIAGRAM 1
Culture, Society and Ecology

HABITAT

CULTURE ← - - - - - - - - - - - - - - - - → SOCIETY

ENVIRONMENT

ECOLOGY

We cannot therefore agree with Radcliffe-Brown that a people's culture, being abstracted from the behavior that we observe and from the products of such behavior, is irrelevant for the study of their social life and structure. The concept of culture is neither more abstract than such concepts as society or social structure, nor is it any less important for students of society, since by themselves neither of these concepts is independently sufficient or intelligible. Nonetheless, while freely recognizing the central role of culture in social life, unlike Talcott Parsons, I shall focus attention almost exclusively on the description and analysis of social structure, and shall incorporate therein all directly relevant cultural aspects and items, while leaving others to deal likewise with parallel aspects of cultural structures and composition. As stated above, I regard a people's culture as an especially important and sensitive dimension of their social reality, and stress the continuous process of mutual steering, reinforcement and change through which these two levels or aspects of human society, the culture and the social organization, interact. Culture, as the set of values, ideas, beliefs and assumptions by which each people creates meaning, and social structure as the particular arrangements of their groupings and relations in society, together redefine and apperceive the people's habitat and include other peoples in their culturally constructed environments. Such processes simultaneously generate and modify the understandings that distinguish a people's culture and the social aggregates, relations and units that analytically constitute their social structure. In effect then, culture and society emerge, develop and change simultaneously and dialectically through the complex continuous interactions of people with one another, with their habitat, and with members of other societies including, as they conceive it, the spirit world.

2. SOCIAL PROCESSES

To illustrate the difference between social processes of any kind and the concrete structures or membership units, let us mentally go down to the corners of Third Avenue and 47th Street or Lexington and 48th at two different times of the week: on a workday morning and at midday on Sunday. Within three minutes you will notice the difference. On a workday we shall notice that steady streams of people move purposefully along the sidewalks at each of the four corners, taking care not to bump into one another, and halting en bloc at each corner when the opposite traffic light is red and automobiles rush past followed by pedestrians. As the light turns green the stationary crowd begins to move, crossing the street to subdivide on the opposite corner, each person or small group moving on their way as briskly as they can. If we paused to watch for five or ten minutes we should notice that few people besides ourselves had remained that long in the area. In short, the corner sees a continuous flow of people moving through and across it, a process that occurs throughout the day and perhaps at different times in the evenings also. At weekends we shall find the traffic lighter and less hurried, and see that people dawdle, gazing in shop windows, and seem more relaxed. There are fewer vendors on the streets. Even on weekdays at different hours when there are fewer pedestrians and vehicles the street life changes to suit. Such oscillating volumes, rhythms and rates are features of the social process characteristic of the particular intersections at 3rd and 47th Street or Lexington and 48th, which, however small, are typical and necessary parts of New York City culture and the city's life, as that in turn is characteristic of American society. Clearly as the ebb and flow of pedestrian and other traffic at 3rd Avenue and 47th is a process in perpetual flux, we can neither conceptualize it as a concrete structure with determinate membership, nor abstract any social unit from its passing throngs. Nonetheless as characteristic and essential features of New York and U.S. society, if we wish to study either of those fully we have to bear in mind and take account of these mundane processes and others like them in our description and analysis, and to that end will have to understand and conceptualize them appropriately.

As the number of pedestrians who cross at 3rd and 48th in either direction fluctuates by the hours of the day and days of the week, it does so likewise monthly, seasonally, and sometimes in response to weather conditions, and traffic blockages or diversions elsewhere in the city. Hence to take account of those and other variations, we may have to observe traffic flows at the corner over a sufficient period at intervals.

Many other processes with comparable oscillations proceed simultaneously as routine and necessary aspects or features of the complex ongoing process of American society, much as organic metabolism, the essential criterion of life, involves consentaneous processes of circulation, respiration, autonomic nervous transmissions, digestion, and elimination as routine operations of those physiological structures. Though we often cannot identify comparable processes of social life with groups or other membership units, we cannot ignore them since they are essential conditions and aspects of the institutional order that pervades the society. Such mundane processes are structured partly by special rules, and partly by material conditions, such as the street layout and traffic lights at 3rd and 47th, and by laws and other conventional forms of conduct. By the regularities and fluctuations of their rates and volumes they facilitate and express various operational aspects of their milieu in much the same way as the diverse processes of our metabolism reflect and influence the conditions of our activities. To analyse differing processes that share common characteristics as members of the same category, we must first distinguish their essential features clearly, and then formulate a model of their common structure that we can relate to models of the concrete structures of society and other models of its analytic structures or systems such as Marion Levy, Talcott Parsons and other sociologists created by abstracting aspects of diverse social processes on functional criteria as hypothetical systems.

As an aid to exposition, to indicate the relations of the variables, criteria and categories we shall need to construct an adequate analytic framework for the study of social structure, I shall use charts and diagrams where necessary to summarize my ideas and arguments.

As stated earlier, I view society as a dynamic complex of processes, collectivities, units and relations, embedded in an empirical context which has material, cultural and social dimensions. The society interacts with differing levels and elements of its context according to the dictates and implications of the culture through which it perceives, interprets and relates to the habitat, constructs its environment and exploits the opportunities and resources available. During those processes the internal organization of the society develops and changes, partly through continuing adaptation to the context, partly through progressive readjustments and realignments of its concrete structures in the ordinary processes of their operation. The two-way relation between society and culture already discussed enables students to treat society and its processes as expressions or aspects of culture, or alternatively, as I prefer, to study society directly by subsuming culture in society. On that assumption, as shown in Chart A, the two primary categories of phenomena we have to distinguish are social entities and processes, institutional and other. Among social entities, also, we have to distinguish clearly between collectivities and social units since, as we have seen, collectivities differ from social units in lacking clear boundaries, membership status, and determinate memberships. Given those differences between social processes, collectivities and social units, in Charts B (page 64) and C (page 76) I classify the chief varieties of processes and collectivities by such analytically relevant criteria as institutional status, nature or base, recurrence, non-recurrence and duration, as discussed above. Together those three kinds of phenomena include all directly observable components and expressions of society as the frame, course and product

CHART A
COMPONENTS OF SOCIETY

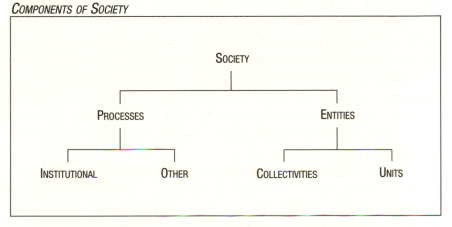

of human interaction.

Since social structure is the central interest of this text, I shall formulate concepts and criteria with which to identify and study any differences or commonalities of structure among the variety of processes and entities in a society. To that end, besides social processes I shall distinguish as social entities collectivities, social units and their relations, social structure being the condition and result of their articulations in any society. In Chart A, therefore, I set out thematically the division of society into these two categories of phenomena, namely, processes and entities, the processes themselves being further classifiable as institutional or other, that is, non-institutional; while social entities are either collectivities or units, as explained below.

The most readily observable features of society are human activities and aggregates, that is, the kinds of social processes and groupings that Marion Levy identified as analytic and concrete structures. Insofar as human beings have been socialized and enculturated since birth in their society and culture, everything they do, together or separately, will have societal and cultural roots and reference, even dreaming, memory, hermitage or suicide. (Durkheim 1951; Halbwachs 1980). Solitary activities are thus no less social than those performed by two or more persons together. Such human activities as sleep, solitary labor or travel, prayer and the like, whether or not they involve human interactions, are all in some sense social. Moreover, since most human activity is purposive, even when it simply aims to gratify and amuse the actor, we should distinguish those activities in which two or more people collaborate for personal or common purposes as collective, from others individuals undertake in isolation or separately, as for instance when they walk alone on city streets. We must also distinguish between institutional and non-institutional activities and processes, the former being regulated and supported by collective sanctions. We should recognize that while regulated, some institutional activities, such as law enforcement and adjudication, are also regulative, and are therefore "doubly institutionalized" (Bohannan 1965).

To distinguish activities and the broad social processes of which they are part by their primary purpose, we may move to Chart B which groups together as separate analytic systems all those activities and relationships that satisfy whatever criteria we adopt to distinguish such processes or activities as, e.g., socialization, education, economic, political, industrial, religious or military action and so on. As already remarked, modern structural-functionalists tend to conceive societies initially as hierarchically ordered sets of such interdependent and functionally distinguished analytic structures or processual systems, which are then broken down further into such smaller subsystems as production, distribution, investment, etc. in the economy. Since most of the activities those scholars included in their analytic structures were routine institutional features of their societies, they tended to recur and replicate their components. In consequence, being conceived as comprehensive, interdependent and mutually reinforcing, together they ensured societal continuity with a minimum of endogenously generated structural change, an unavoidable outcome that exposed the inadequacy of that theory for the study of human societies, most of which by their own operations observably generate endogenous changes as well as structural continuity. While structural continuities are outcomes of such routine societal processes as economy, socialization, social control, worship and the like, so too is social change of various kinds, cultural, demographic, ecological, ideological and so on, as well as history, which happens as the simultaneous fusion and pursuit of continuity and change, and expresses their outcome.

If we observe individuals in action long enough, we shall notice various recurrent features and forms of action, and perhaps the order in which they occur. Whether pursued separately or jointly, such observations might perhaps enable us to summarize these activities in a model that we could check, refine and develop by further observations. Such models are abstract structures of the activity processes that we observed. When the activities engage pluralities of individuals cooperating to pursue or complete particular tasks, besides the activity sequence and patterns, we are often able to develop models of the cooperating actors and their relations. Those models would describe the membership units as concrete structures in Marion Levy's sense by their membership and relational patterns. In this way we may abstract from observations of diverse mundane processes the models we construct to study family organization or community, political organisation, economic groups and activities, dispute pursuit and settlement, social control, worship and so on. If we identify the recurrent activities of membership units by careful observation, we can model those concrete structures to include the processes by which the members of those units engage and interact, whether or not those processes are institutional and collectively sanctioned. Processes defined by functional criteria that cut across such concrete structures illustrate the kind of analytic system on which Talcott Parsons, Marion Levy and their colleagues concentrated. Other processes, which do not illustrate such analytic categories, may also be isolated and discussed as social situations and subjected to situational analysis. Most of the remaining irregular processes in human society may also be understood by reference to the routine operations of concrete structures or social entities.

As Chart B indicates, society consists of a great number and diversity of social processes, some institutional and many non-institutional. Following the functionalists, the institutional ones can be classified by their function or nature as respectively, communication processes, productive processes, economic, political and ecological processes. Communication processes, as Levi-Strauss (1963) has shown, consist either in the exchange of messages, that is, speech acts between individuals; the exchange of goods and services; the exchange of women in marriage; or ritual, which communicates between the mundane and the sacred worlds.

CHART B
Social Processes

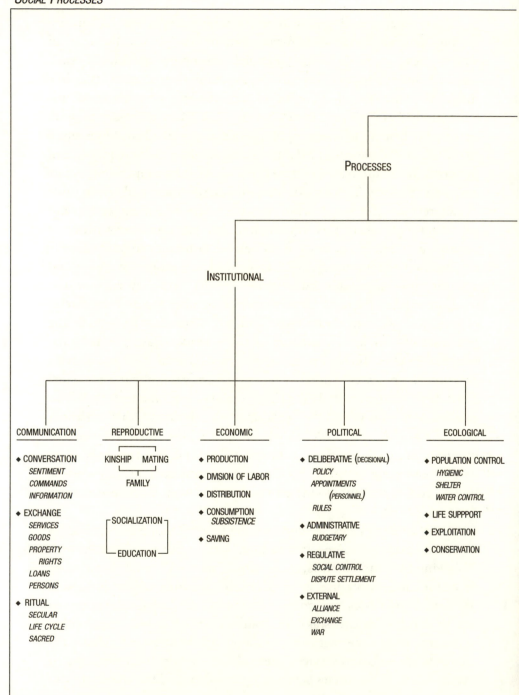

PROCESSES

INSTITUTIONAL

COMMUNICATION

- ◆ CONVERSATION
  - *SENTIMENT*
  - *COMMANDS*
  - *INFORMATION*
- ◆ EXCHANGE
  - *SERVICES*
  - *GOODS*
  - *PROPERTY*
    - *RIGHTS*
  - *LOANS*
  - *PERSONS*
- ◆ RITUAL
  - *SECULAR*
  - *LIFE CYCLE*
  - *SACRED*

REPRODUCTIVE

KINSHIP   MATING

FAMILY

┌ SOCIALIZATION ┐

└ EDUCATION ┘

ECONOMIC

- ◆ PRODUCTION
- ◆ DIVISION OF LABOR
- ◆ DISTRIBUTION
- ◆ CONSUMPTION
  - *SUBSISTENCE*
- ◆ SAVING

POLITICAL

- ◆ DELIBERATIVE (*DECISIONAL*)
  - *POLICY*
  - *APPOINTMENTS*
    - (*PERSONNEL*)
  - *RULES*
- ◆ ADMINISTRATIVE
  - *BUDGETARY*
- ◆ REGULATIVE
  - *SOCIAL CONTROL*
  - *DISPUTE SETTLEMENT*
- ◆ EXTERNAL
  - *ALLIANCE*
  - *EXCHANGE*
  - *WAR*

ECOLOGICAL

- ◆ POPULATION CONTROL
  - *HYGIENIC*
  - *SHELTER*
  - *WATER CONTROL*
- ◆ LIFE SUPPPORT
- ◆ EXPLOITATION
- ◆ CONSERVATION

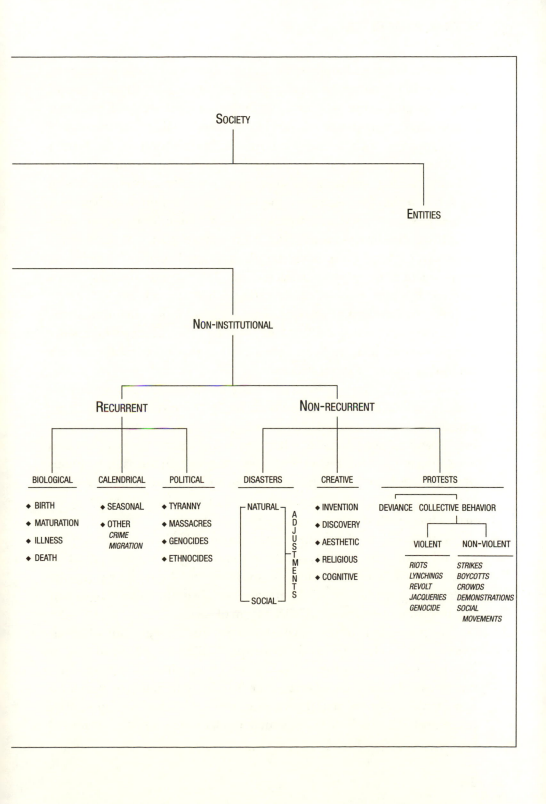

In conversational exchanges between persons, we exchange sentiments, orders or information. In other exchanges we transact services, goods, property rights, loans, and, occasionally, persons, between individuals or groups. Ritual may also be divided into secular rituals, which are mainly state functions, such as marrying outside Lenin's tomb in the former USSR, or the opening of Parliament in Britain, and various *rites de passage* of individual life cycles, and processes which seek to communicate with the sacred realm, following some sacred pattern of action. Together, these diverse processes transact the various kinds of communication and values institutionalized within society. Each sub-category, such as sentiments, orders and information, could be differentiated further by citing its purpose and most frequent characteristics. For example, property rights summarize a great body of rights distinguished in great detail at law. So do loans, transactions in persons, as wedding, adoption, manumissions, sales into slavery, and so on. We shall not enter into such detail here, since our primary focus is on those social entities that most readily allow a detailed inventory of social structure.

The reproductive processes which are institutionalized in society are frequently classified as either biological or socio-cultural, though all are equally cultural. The superficially biological processes consist of kinship, mating and family, the rest of education and socialization at all levels of development from infancy on. For those societies with formal institutions of schooling, it is also useful to distinguish education from the more inclusive and diffuse processes of socialization by its formal emphasis on instruction and learning.

At the economic level, the primary institutional processes are those of production, distribution, consumption, saving, and the organization or division of labor. Consumption may be market based, or it may be undertaken by producers of the articles for subsistence. Investment may also be distinguished as a specialized form of saving.

The political processes which have to do with the regulation of public affairs may be classified as deliberative, administrative, regulative or external. Deliberative processes being concerned with making decisions, may be classified by their subjects, as deliberations on policy, on personnel appointments, or on making various kinds of rules. Administrative processes, having to do with implementation, include the sub-category of budgetary administration which regulates both revenue and expenditure. Although, strictly speaking, all political processes are regulative, we can use that term to denote a sub-category of very widespread and formally variable processes concerned with social control, dispute settlement or pursuit, and the like, many of which are strictly interpersonal. Those political processes classified as external deal either with alliance, exchanges between units, or conflicts such as war. Ecological processes, which are very variably institutionalized in all societies, include processes of population control, life support, exploitation and conservation. Forms of population control may vary from female infanticide to exporting population, as in Polynesian societies and in ancient Greece. Life support processes include hygiene, shelter, water control, and may in the near future include climate control. Societies institutionalize processes of ecological exploitation through the practice of land tenure and land use, or the allocation and exploitation of marine, sylvan, mineral or other environmental resources. These are quite distinct from the processes of management or conservation, which include fallowing, rotation of hunting areas and times, fishing seasons, etc. These processes are all variably institutionalized in all human societies, however simple or advanced and elaborate their technology.

Non-institutional processes which are nonetheless regularly found in societies may be classified broadly as repetitive or non-repetitive. Beginning with the repetitive processes, the first category are such strictly biological processes as birth, maturation, illness and death, which each life cycle illustrates, and which occur at all times randomly. By contrast, certain recurrent processes are regulated by the calendar, as for example the seasonal processes of planting, harvest, hunting and marine or sylvan exploitation. Such calendrical processes include certain popular movements such as tourism in modern societies or "eating the dry season" (*cin rani*) among Hausa of the Central Sudan, as well as seasonal fluctuations in the incidence of certain kinds of crime, such as burglaries and robberies, which directly reflect the consumption rhythms of the social calendar. Other recurrent non-institutional processes are political and characterize those illegitimate or illegal regimes as tyranny and dictatorship. These recur despite much effort to avoid them by constitutional provisions, declaring their illegality, and by other means. Although they may mimic institutionalization, the processes by which a tyranny works its will are governed by no institutional formula or program. Nor are the purges that characterize some despotisms and illegitimate regimes. Neither are the massacres, though widespread in the 20th century in most continents, nor the genocides, ethnocides, and other atrocities, which remain such a dangerous cancer, likely to erupt explosively in all modern plural societies.

Other widespread non-institutional processes which are not repetitive include disasters, both natural and social, and the social responses they provoke. These may vary from attempted restoration of the *status quo ante* to nil when there is total elimination, as in the eruptions that buried the cities of Thera in 1628 BC and Pompeii in 79 AD beneath volcanic ash.

Another kind of non-recurrent, non-institutional social process which, though widespread, remains unpredictable, may be labelled creative. This includes processes of invention, discovery, innovation, and developments in cognitive, aesthetic and religious thought. Nowadays, however, the enormous recurrent investment in research and development increasingly delivers predictable innovations.

Other non-repetitive, non-institutional processes broadly represent varied forms of protest or reaction on the part of societies to conditions that disturb their members. These include a great variety of processes of individually deviant behavior, together with all those relatively peaceful forms of protest known to sociologists as 'collective behavior', which include strikes, boycotts, crowd phenomena, demonstrations, social and religious movements, etc.; or its more violent forms such as riots, lynchings, jacqueries, revolts, pogroms, ethnocides and civil wars. We shall have something further to say about both these categories of collective behavior, the peaceful and not-so peaceful, later on. Like the various individual behaviors we have classified as mass behavior when aggregated and reduced to rates per ten or hundred thousand of population, these different types of collective behavior specify events which are precipitated by the institutional and non-institutional processes of the society.

All non-institutional social processes listed in Chart B are empirical events, or sequences of events, unlike the five functionally defined institutional processes of communication, reproduction, economy, ecology or politics which denote analytic systems, as in Marion Levy's formulation. Nonetheless, although explicitly empirical events or processes given by the ethnography, these non-institutional processes, whether biological, calendrical, political, disastrous, creative or protesting, all relate to concrete social entities, whether persons, units or collectivities, in contrast to the analytic structures and systems by which Marion Levy distinguished institutional processes of activity.

I shall therefore describe models of empirical social processes that define relations between their components as *processual structures*, since each represents the structure of a process, whether the process is brief, simple and local like a wedding ceremony, or extensive, diffuse and prolonged, like the processes of socialization, social control or social change. This concept of *processual structure* should not be confused with the *analytic structures* we create by extracting all those activities that have a common function and arranging them sequentially. As Durkheim (1947) showed, diffuse social processes can be studied statistically as modes of mass behavior, either indirectly through their expressions and effects, or directly as structured activity sequences of great significance and interest.

I first became aware that such processes as structural change had their own structures while studying the political development of the Hausa emirate of Zazzau or Zaria in Northern Nigeria, when I found that relations between the elements of that processual structure prescribed the order of change (Smith 1960a:298-314). In that case, having reviewed the historical development of political institutions at Zaria under successive Hausa, Fulani and British rulers from 1800 until 1950, to analyse those developments I compared those differing political regimes and summarized their common and dissimilar features in a single set of seven categories. Being abstract and formal, these categories were easily ordered by their relations of logical priority in a series descending from the first and most general to the last and most specific, as follows:

(1) Status differentiation.
(2) Offices differentiated as perpetual statuses.
(3) Differentiation of office by status conditions of eligibility.
(4) Kingship as the most senior office.
(5) Rank organisation of offices.
(6) Role differentiation of offices.
(7) Organization of offices with similar status of qualifications in exclusive promotional series.

The order of logical priority that aligned these formal categories is the logically necessary order of their creation and succession, since we cannot conceive or formulate later categories in the series without assuming successively each antecedent category of that logical order. With this tool I examined the history of political change at Zaria to see whether there were any incidents in which such changes proceeded in any sequence except the order of logical priority that aligned these formal categories. My hypothesis was that by virtue of its logical structure,

> "the revision and redefinition of a system of categories arranged in an order of logical priority can only proceed by a sequence which repeats the order of logical relations holding among the categories themselves. Moreover, revision of any single category in such a system presupposes certain changes in the content of the categories which precede it. In consequence, the order in which categories change will be identical with that in which the system as a whole undergoes revision." (1960a.:300)

Historical analysis found no instance of structural change in the polity of Zaria during its successive transformations under the Fulani and the British which differed structurally from the order of logical priority that aligned the common formal categories of its three successive regimes, Hausa, Fulani and Anglo-Fulani. However, it was only several years later that I realized that the series of formal categories represented the *latent structure* that underlay the concrete structures of those political regimes in much the same way that the *concrete structure* itself underlay the *analytic structures* of political and administrative relations which, following Marion Levy's example, I had isolated by functional criteria in my search for substantive regularities in the process of political change (Smith 1978:440-442; 1960a:298-314).

3. COLLECTIVITIES

To formulate a scheme for the analytic and comparative study of social structures or entities, we should first specify the criteria on which we shall construct and classify them. Besides being few and clear, the criteria chosen should together lay the basis for a discriminating and comprehensive analytic classification of social entities of all kinds, namely, collectivities, corporations and other kinds of membership units. To that end we only need four criteria, of which three are primary, being prerequisite for the fourth. These are respectively the closure, size, institutional status, and corporate or non-corporate attributes of concrete structures.

To have members, *social units* require criteria or boundaries that exclude non-members. Membership in any social unit is a position or status which entails conduct that observes and supports the unit's rules. As boundary markers a social unit can use a variety of criteria that may simultaneously serve as the principles, conditions or means by which it recruits its members. Not all social aggregates are bounded thus, or have such mechanisms and criteria; but without them those aggregates can have no determinate membership since they lack the criteria to recruit members and the means to formulate rules of conduct. It is thus essential to distinguish clearly such weakly bounded aggregates from those whose unity and membership rules assume their boundaries. I shall therefore describe those aggregates with unclear boundaries and membership as *collectivities*, and refer to those with determinate membership and that status based on their criteria of recruitment and closure as *social units*. To illustrate, I attach a summary classification of the principal varieties of collectivities in Chart C (page 76), which may be compared with that of social units (Chart D, page 120), and discuss both below.

Social entities are of two kinds, collectivities and social units or concrete structures. By a social unit I mean a social entity of any kind that has its own membership or personnel, that is, a concrete structure having determinate membership, as contrasted with analytic structures abstracted from social processes by the analytic criteria adopted by scholars, which are really model systems. Thus, whereas analytic structures are conceptual artefacts that differ in their content and range with the criteria on which they are based, even when abstracted from the same social processes, concrete structures are objective ethnographic realities that, together with their internal and external relationships, constitute the society as the most inclusive social unit of which they are part.

As bounded entities whose members are aligned by their statuses, roles, and interrelations, social units articulate with one another in diverse ways, as units, and by relations between their members. Together with their interrelations, the differing kinds of social units and collectivities in the society constitute its concrete structure. Successive units in Chart D denote corresponding levels of the hierarchy of social units that order their categories by increasing specificity as we proceed from the higher levels of the diagram towards its base.

Concrete structures in human society vary vastly in the nature and status of their memberships. While some, such as a role, office or a person conceived as a social entity, can only have one member, others such as the West African Poro, the religions of Islam, Roman Catholicism, Marxism or Buddhism, are transnational in range. Moreover, while many, and perhaps most social entities are institutionally defined, regulated and sanctioned, others are not, or at best weakly so; and some are opposed to the prevailing institutional order of society and anti-institutional. In addition, while many concrete structures are corporate and regulatory, in any society most are not. Perhaps the most important difference among social entities, however, is that between those that are closed or firmly bounded and those that are not. By a firmly bounded membership unit I mean one, such as a school or a club, which has clearly defined and routinely enforced rules of recruitment and exclusion. The individual family is a fine example, being familiar to all. Families generally begin after the marriage of their principals. Lacking offspring, a couple are not a family until the birth of their first child, following which their family grows as other children appear. In most cultures families, based on the marriage of their principals, emerge and recruit other members by birth. Universities, factories, bureaucracies or armies recruit their members very differently, as do Christian churches, Islamic *tariqa* or orders, Freemasons, Marxist parties, social clubs, chambers of commerce, and the Soviet labor camps described by Solzhenitsyn. In all cases the unit's rules of recruitment or inclusion operate also as rules of exclusion, thus segregating its members from outsiders or non-members, and at least for certain purposes regulating their relations. However, as mentioned above, not all social entities are clearly and firmly bounded, either because they are temporary, *ad hoc* collectivities such as crowds, mobs, audiences, passengers on a bus or train, or shifting throngs of vendors and purchasers in a West African market; or because, even if permanent, the *collectivities* are not bounded by clear criteria and lack procedures to exclude non-members. Such loosely bounded and perduring collectivities include social or economic classes such as peasants or petite bourgeoisie, racial stocks, many ethnic or linguistic 'groups', social 'regions', neighborhoods and dispersed 'communities' and such loose categories as the rich and poor, rural and urban, young, old and middle-aged, or the wed and unwed.

This distinction between social units having determinate memberships, and other entities that do not, has many important implications. As Marx perceived after he had subdivided industrial societies into economic classes, being analytic, those categories contained inchoate collectivities without identity, self-consciousness, membership codes, organization and leadership, and could only come to act as purposive groups or *classes-for-themselves* by revolutionary transformations. Of these, the most fundamental converted the 'working class' into a militant proletariat by self-consciously adopting criteria and mechanisms that transformed them into self-conscious proletarians, excluded all others, and gave them their own inclusive organization, leaders and procedures to coordinate their common action. As Marx, and later Lenin, saw, without such developments it is not possible to convert such inert categories as classes, unaware of their collective boundaries and interests, into social units able to recruit, organize and direct their members to undertake collective action. Without such boundaries and organization, neither regional populations, neighborhoods, dispersed communities, nor such broadly occupational and socio-economic categories as peasants, workers and petite bourgeoisie, nor such age grades as the youth, elderly and middle-aged, or racial and ethno-linguistic stocks, despite their permanence and societal extent, are capable of positive social action. Neither, as loosely defined and poorly bounded collectivities, can they acquire institutional status without prior closure of their boundaries and membership.

In all societies, and especially in the larger highly differentiated industrial nation-states of modern times, there are many extensive collectivities whose incapacities and non-institutional status directly reflect their ambiguous identities and obscure boundaries, and hence their indeterminate populations and membership. Besides social and cultural classes, regional populations, neighborhoods, dispersed communities, age-grades and income brackets or divisions in population, collectivities include such occupational groupings as peasants, racial, linguistic and ideological categories, personal kindreds, some kinds of networks, political, religious and social movements, followers or supporters, crowds, mobs, demonstrations, and such other ill-defined aggregates as the rural, urban, commuter, educated, progressive or deviant, wed or unwed, in modern societies. Though by no means the only examples of non-institutional collectivities, these are perhaps the most familiar and best studied.

Even though observers may agree that the majority of people in most or all of the large *collectivities* do "belong" or "fit" there, and thus that they may have members, given the ambiguous criteria that define their boundaries, sufficient uncertainties surround their self-placements, and the placement of others, to indicate the structural implications of such ambiguous identities and boundaries for membership. As a specific status having specific roles, membership in any social unit differs radically from places in such weakly bounded collectivities as crowds, classes, mobs, age-grades, etc. In consequence, unless transformed, those collectivities can neither have definite membership nor membership status, and cannot therefore act as coherent inclusive units on behalf of their members by coordinating their resources, manpower and skills. Since these differences of organization and capacity are fundamental, though both are concrete structures, those loosely bounded, inchoate aggregates are distinguished as *collectivities* from the bounded *social units*, whose closure is the source of their unity, membership and capacity for institutional action.

Let us now look at Chart C. We first distinguish those collectivities that are *ad hoc* and shortlived from others that are not, and in either division between aggregates and categories, that is, such aggregates as regional areas, and such categories as social or economic strata, age grades, income and property classes that are perduring features of their societies. While many perduring collectivities are societally extensive, some, such as neighborhoods and dispersed communities, are not, and many extensive collectivities, such as modern mass media audiences, are *ad hoc* and very short-lived. Strictly speaking that category should also include such smaller groupings as kindreds, personal networks, and patron-client clusters, which are loosely bounded and egocentric by definition, but which often operate as quasi-groups when mobilized and coordinated to pursue specific ends by the central individual to whom all others are linked, directly or otherwise. Though loosely structured, such quasi-groups are treated as social units in the following discussion. Finally there are such short-lived collectivities as crowds, mobs, demonstrations and other forms of public protest which are either unrelated, or which occur as incidents in the course of a social movement. Lacking institutional bases, patterns and sanctions, such occasional forms of collective action are manifestly non-institutional, or at best, as in certain modes of audience reaction, weakly institutional. Sociologists generally discuss such brief outbursts of public protest and concern as *collective behavior,* since they express the joint action of non-institutional collectivities. Though often providing peaceful demonstrations of public support for some feature of the institutional order, this category also includes strikes, boycotts and certain other forms of industrial action, crowds, riots, marches, lynching and other forms of mob violence, including revolt, which express opposition. However, unless temporarily mobilized for such events, the "members" of collectivities normally pursue their affairs separately or in small groups. Hence to determine their characteristics, we must often study their individual behavior, and compare the actions and opinions of representative samples of unrelated individuals drawn from two or more collectivities. As the occasions for collective behaviour are brief and rare, such rates of public opinions and mass behavior are sometimes used by observers to indicate and compare the less evident characteristics of different collectivities, being the most readily accessible expression of their aggregate patterns.

Social entities, or various kinds of concrete structure that constitute a society's structure, are either collectivities or social units, and differ in their capacities in consequence of their differing nature and bases. As clearly bounded entities, whatever their form or size, all social units, institutional or other, recruit and regulate their members by criteria and procedures that exclude non-members, while collectivities lack those qualities, and can neither recruit any members nor regulate those they include. Age-grades, social classes, neighbourhoods, and certain kinds of economic, regional and ethnic aggregates illustrate these differences between collectivities and social units. Such aggregates are neither firmly bounded nor adequately defined by clear criteria. They are therefore incapable of common action and have no common identities. Though often permanent and sometimes coextensive with their societies, being loosely defined, ambiguously bounded, and without adequate social bases, they are all non-institutional and lack determinate memberships and

CHART C
COLLECTIVITIES

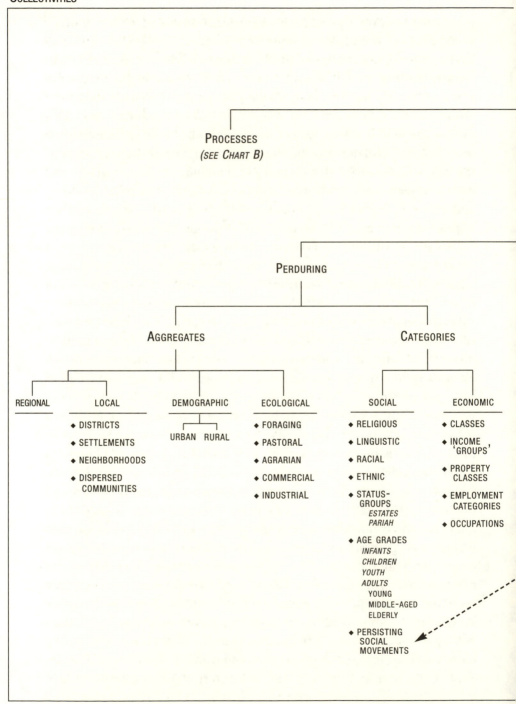

PROCESSES
(SEE CHART B)

PERDURING

AGGREGATES

CATEGORIES

REGIONAL

LOCAL
- DISTRICTS
- SETTLEMENTS
- NEIGHBORHOODS
- DISPERSED COMMUNITIES

DEMOGRAPHIC
URBAN RURAL

ECOLOGICAL
- FORAGING
- PASTORAL
- AGRARIAN
- COMMERCIAL
- INDUSTRIAL

SOCIAL
- RELIGIOUS
- LINGUISTIC
- RACIAL
- ETHNIC
- STATUS-GROUPS
  ESTATES
  PARIAH
- AGE GRADES
  INFANTS
  CHILDREN
  YOUTH
  ADULTS
    YOUNG
    MIDDLE-AGED
    ELDERLY
- PERSISTING SOCIAL MOVEMENTS

ECONOMIC
- CLASSES
- INCOME 'GROUPS'
- PROPERTY CLASSES
- EMPLOYMENT CATEGORIES
- OCCUPATIONS

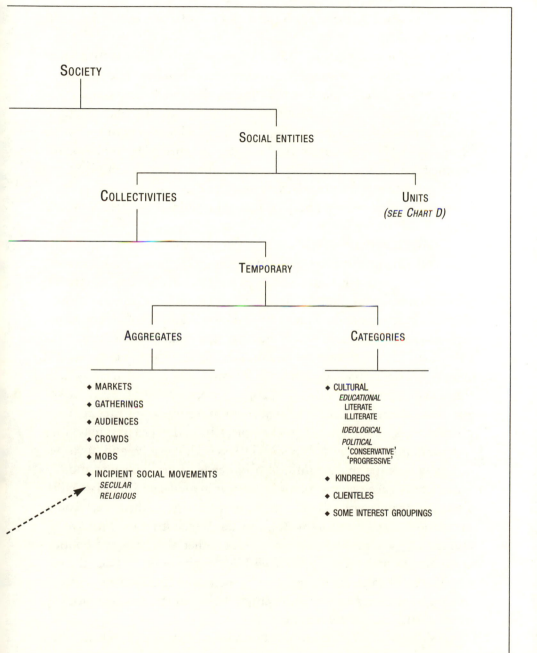

SOCIETY

SOCIAL ENTITIES

COLLECTIVITIES

UNITS
(SEE CHART D)

TEMPORARY

AGGREGATES

CATEGORIES

- MARKETS
- GATHERINGS
- AUDIENCES
- CROWDS
- MOBS
- INCIPIENT SOCIAL MOVEMENTS
  SECULAR
  RELIGIOUS

- CULTURAL
  EDUCATIONAL
  LITERATE
  ILLITERATE
  IDEOLOGICAL
  POLITICAL
  'CONSERVATIVE'
  'PROGRESSIVE'
- KINDREDS
- CLIENTELES
- SOME INTEREST GROUPINGS

corporate status. To distinguish them as a class from social units, I call them collectivities.

It is useful to classify social units irrespective of their institutional status by relative size, distinguishing micro units that have one or at most two members, intermediate units of limited size and duration, and those of greater extent as macro, all units of the two latter classes, whether group or category, being classified as aggregates, and all that are not corporate being set apart from those that are. Though distinguished from social units by their ambiguous boundaries, recruitment criteria, implication, indeterminate membership, lack of unity, and non-institutional status, *collectivities* may be either very large or of intermediate size. None are miniscule.

Its largest and most extensive non-corporate entities are among the most perduring distinctive features of a society. Besides local communities, such aggregates include many regional divisions, age grades, social classes, castes, industrial, occupational and professional classes, religious, linguistic and ethnic units and racial blocs. Though perduring and unique, as previously stated, these aggregates differ from social units in lacking adequate closure and determinate membership, since the several criteria that define them do not bound them clearly, so that in many cases the "class" or aggregate in which people properly belong on grounds of age, occupation, income, ethnicity, religion, residence or race remains obscure and ambiguous. For example, since the criteria may vary independently, people define social classes differently, and since we normally lack the precise information needed to classify one another accurately by such criteria, it is often unclear in modern societies to which class many people correctly belong; and so too as regards their age, income, occupation, ethnicity, provenience, and, less frequently, their race. We are also often unsure and uninformed of one another's religious and political convictions which often fluctuate with issues and context. Nonetheless, even if most aggregates distinguished by such loose criteria are ambiguous in their boundaries and "membership", their character, persistence and extent ensure their social significance.

Besides those large and weakly bounded collectivities which are often co-extensive with their milieux, we have also to deal with others of lesser size and significance that vary in their bases, such as factions which differ widely in size, composition, duration, membership conditions, organization, openness, as well as leadership structures, interests, goals, contexts and modes of operation. Such loose congeries of gangs as currently contest control of the drug trade in American inner cities may be structurally similar. Among the Muslim Hausa of northern Nigeria, leading candidates for political offices at different levels within the emirates were each supported by a *kunjiya*, or loose body of supporters composed of kin, allies, servants and clients, most of whom had their own dependents and supporters. Individuals likewise may mobilize their personal networks of kin, friends, associates, colleagues, neighbors and others as action-sets to contest elections for local office, or to assert or defend certain interests and rights. If such loose groupings are mobilized recurrently, despite their situationally changing membership, they may operate more and more like factions. However prominent, extensive, permanent and pervasive they may be in societies, lacking closure, membership criteria and procedures, collectivities lack the essential preconditions for the institutionalization needed to define their memberships, recruit their members and collectively regulate their relations.

Like action-sets and personal networks, kindreds are egocentric groupings of an individual's consanguineal kin traced collaterally through either parent as far as these are known. Besides their imperfect boundaries due to those limitations, such kindreds differ as genealogical clusters and mental constructs from the groups of kin that periodically contribute to or assemble at ceremonial events for that individual. Like kindreds and personal networks, neighborhoods are also loosely bounded egocentric units that differ in their composition and boundaries as we move from one household or family to the next with the result that, unless institutionally closed and regulated, such groupings lack both membership status and codes of neighborly behavior.

However, to illustrate the structural aspects of cultural variation, in the miniscule Caribbean island society of Carriacou, neighborhoods are bounded social groups. For a range of historic and ecological reasons Carriacou neighborhoods cooperate annually to clean and repair the local ponds on which they depend for water during the long dry season, since the island has no streams, wells or rivers. Though households conserve the seasonal rain in tanks and cisterns, they cooperate to clean and repair the communal ponds that provide water for their cattle. So at some point during the dry season all who use a common pond turn out and work together for the day to clear and repair that pond for their common good. Likewise when the local seine nets more fish than its crew can handle, at the sound of a conch shell all able-bodied men from the neighborhood turn out in their boats to help take in the catch. When a hurricane hits the island, people in Carriacou neighborhoods join together to commandeer the building materials they need from local lumber yards, builders and hardware shops, and simply set to work in neighborhood groups to repair their roofs and damaged buildings as quickly as they can, moving from one house to the next in turn. Later on, when the repairs are done, the materials used on each house are listed, costed, and added together to calculate the amounts owed by the neighborhood group and each of its households for those supplies. In like style when houses are built or schooners launched, Carriacou neighborhoods and communities celebrate the event with a Nation Dance to the Big Drum (Smith 1962).

Although in most societies neighborhoods are loosely bounded, egocentric overlapping collectivities, in some cultures they are social units, being firmly bounded and entrusted with special tasks and common resources. Unlike the wards in Hausa villages or the barrios in Central American towns, the settlement patterns and population density in modern cities define their neighborhoods as egocentric, amorphous and variable. Rural populations having dispersed settlement patterns are not dissimilar, since they too lack clearly bounded neighborhoods, ward organization and such structures as local associations, councils and headmen characteristic of compact communities.

On the basis of his materialist analysis of capitalist society, Karl Marx expected its transformation through revolutionary action of the proletariat or working class, but was acutely aware that, as an amorphous collectivity, the proletariat lacked the necessary preconditions of collective action. Accordingly he devoted much thought and effort to effecting those changes. As indicated by the fluid, flexible boundaries and ambiguous relations of *proletariat* and *lumpenproletariat* in the works of Marxist scholars, even in that particularly critical category, individual membership often remained so ambiguous and obscure that, however defined and delimited, that class lacked the requisite conditions for comprehensive group organisation, and therefore could not easily change from the analytic category of an observer into a self-conscious militant group capable of undertaking collective action to pursue its common interests.

Thus in C, which follows the distinction between social processes and entities that informs B, I first distinguish collectivities from units, and then, with the exception of those social movements which persist, the perduring from the temporary collectivities. Next, of those which are perduring, some are clearly aggregates, or "groupings" similar to groups; while others, although aggregates, are clearly categorical. Of aggregates that are similar to groupings but not fully groups, some are regional and others local, the latter being illustrated by districts, settlements, from neighborhoods and dispersed communities. Other aggregates are demographic, namely, the urban and rural divisions of modern societies, and yet others ecological, such as foragers, pastoralists and collectivities that depend on farming, commerce or industry for their livelihoods.

Of the categorical collectivities, Chart C distinguishes the social from the economic. It may be argued that a more important distinction is that between the secular and the religious, both the social and economic categories being subdivisions of the secular. However, if we follow Chart C, then religious groupings are simply one division of the social collectivities, others being linguistic, racial, ethnic, age grades, and what Weber called status groups, that is, the estates and social orders of ancient and medieval societies, or the pariahs and 'under-classes' in our own. Subdivisions of population by age, as infants, children, youth, young adults, middle-aged and elderly, are sufficiently imprecise to illustrate their nature as social collectivities. As mentioned above, perduring collectivities include those uninstitutionalized social movements that persist over time.

So too are the economic classes of modern and transitional societies, which are often defined imprecisely by measures of socio-economic status as income groups and property classes, together with their occupational and employment categories. Being imprecisely bounded and defined, these and other economic subdivisions of societies such as the proletariat, the peasantry, the petite bourgeoisie etc., although extensive and perduring, are equally imprecise in their placements of individuals. For these reasons, although beloved of ideologues who delight in manipulating the criteria that define them and elaborating the consequences, these economic classifications of a society are difficult to work with.

Like perduring collectivities, those of a temporary or transient kind also subdivide into aggregates and categories, the former being those collectivities localized in a given time and place such as markets, gatherings, audiences, crowds, mobs, marches, riots, etc. Categorical collectivities, by contrast, are those distinguished by some criterion or criteria, such as education, ideology, political orientation, relationship to an individual, as consanguine or client, those with shared interests, and, but only in their initial stages, social movements, both religious and secular. Like the various forms of collective behavior already discussed, these transient and temporary collectivities depend heavily on the institutional processes of social life for their genesis, shape and development.

4. ELEMENTS OF SOCIAL STRUCTURE

Before proceeding further I shall outline the conceptual framework I have developed for the descriptive analysis of social structure.

By social structure I understand the set of social collectivities, units and relations within and between them which gives a society its characteristic and perduring form, boundaries, organization and processes or modes of operation. Structure in this sense is a summary model abstracted from the processes of social life and interaction by observation and analysis. The elements of social structure are the most elementary components of that framework. Hence, if the framework is intended to apply to all societies, its elements must be equally general and abstract. They should also be sufficiently discriminating to enable us to construct appropriate models of the structure of any human society. We should therefore discuss with care the necessary and sufficient concepts for that purpose.

Ideally the most elementary units of social structure, such as *status* and *role*, terms I shall define later, should be irreducible and indivisible. In practice, however, as we shall see, even those elementary units are analytically divisible. Roles are anchored in statuses, and ideally both are institutionalized, as for example, the status and roles of mother and son, husband and wife, physician and patient. Institutional social relations are reciprocal roles that link their respective statuses. Institutionalization is the process and condition that defines and endows such units of status and role with social sanctions and indicates their appropriate relations. Institutional norms prescribe appropriate behavior and validate appropriate sanctions. Most institutionally established units of status-and-role are integrated into larger social units which are also institutionally defined and sanctioned. These elementary units of social structure therefore enter as essential components into larger units; and in many cases those units are themselves components of larger bodies and of such institutional structures as the market, the polity, or the kinship system. We shall therefore have to deal with social units of differing kind, scale and level, ranging from the individual status and role to societies as wholes. However, since all components of social structure are not equally institutionalized, we must also consider its variable institutionalization and non-institutional features.

Institutional units fall into four major classes. At the micro-level, besides status and role, there are persons and dyads. In society individuals become *persons* and therefore differ through the statuses they hold and the roles they play. At any moment an individual's *persona* or social *identity* consists in the total set of roles and statuses that he or she holds, even though (s)he rarely enacts more than one set at a time. At the most elementary level social relations are interpersonal and dyadic. Institutional *dyads* may either appear independently, or as components of larger institutional units. However, in many societies various dyadic relations are not institutionalized, for example, those between friends, lovers, rivals or enemies. Whether institutional or not, dyadic relations may link together to form chains or such open-ended structures as networks and action sets.

Such transitory units as families, kindreds, work-teams, peer-groups, cliques or sets represent a class of social units of intermediate level and complexity. Being impermanent, none are corporate; and, although most are groups, some like kindreds and social networks are not; but all intermediate units consist of dyads, institutional or not, that is, of relations between actors identified by status and role.

The last kind of institutional unit that occurs frequently in social structure is the corporation, of which there are four pure varieties, namely, corporate groups, corporate categories, colleges and offices. A fifth 'impure' type of quasi-corporations called commissions, of which there are three kinds, is discussed below.

In studying a society it is necessary to distinguish the macro, intermediate, and micro levels of its institutional and non-institutional structure, to examine the composition of each, and analyse their interrelations. Besides corporations, the macro structural level includes such societally extensive collectivities as age-grades, social classes, castes (*varna*), racial and ethnic categories, religious, regional and loosely defined ideological collectivities, and social sections or segments in plural societies, while the micro-level consists of elementary statuses, roles, persons and dyadic relationships. The intermediate level of institutional and other structures includes such impermanent, complex and universal groupings as families, kindreds, neighborhoods, networks, schools, factions, work-teams, etc., but neither extensive collectivities nor corporations.

Besides their institutional components and processes, all societies generate and exhibit various non-institutional modes of behavior as routine features of their operation. These events are frequently described as *collective behavior*, a loose term that includes audience reactions and such phenomena as crowds, mobs, riots, demonstrations, strikes, boycotts, social movements, and revolutions. It also includes the manifestations of different kinds of *mass behavior* such as communal rates of migration, marriage, reproduction, mortality, suicide, crime, social mobility, voting, conversion, income distribution, occupation, literacy, etc. As such patterns of mass and collective behavior affect and reflect the forms and processes of collective action in the society's institutional structure, dialectical relations holding between them and the institutional forms of social structure regulate their nature, form and distribution.

As the generic term for all membership units, then, the concept of social unit is highly elastic and includes at one extreme those that consist of social persons or roles and at the other entire societies. Yet so long as a social entity has an identifiable member or members, we can study its bases, form, mode of articulation, membership criteria and rules as a unit, together with its relation to other social units of the same and different kinds. As we shall see, that is no less true of the role than of an inclusive society, since as an empirical entity every social role has its own personnel, namely, the individual who actually holds it. Even though that individual may in due course abandon the role, unless it is eliminated by some process of change, it will continue to exist as a unit to be filled by others.

Though individuals are the ultimate agents of social action, as anthropologists we lack the skills necessary to investigate the bases and dimensions of human individuality, or to understand how our peculiar biological and psychological qualities reflect or affect our social experience. I shall therefore not attempt to discuss individuals and individuality, but concentrate instead on the conditions, composition and structure of their society. However, since human societies are aggregates of people whose individuality we cannot ignore even though we cannot adequately deal with it, to include individual actors in our study we shall follow Radcliffe-Brown (1952) and conceive them as *persons* whose social identities at any moment in their lives consist of the combination of statuses, roles and social relations in which they are then engaged. Thus as individuals change their statuses, roles and relations in the course of a lifetime, so likewise do the content and structure of their social identities and personalities, without any necessary or corresponding changes of their individuality. While some of the statuses and roles that everyone holds will be based on such biological characteristics as sex, generation, age, race and health, others may reflect their education, present and past occupations, nationality and political status, beliefs, residence, economic position, property, career, reputation, kinship, marriage and family, membership in formal and informal associations, and so on.

Social units that are not microscopic like persons and roles are either categories or groups. Though many human aggregates have the organization necessary to facilitate their joint action, others do not. Only those that have such organization and capability are *groups*. By a *group* I mean any aggregate of three or more members having the organization necessary to combine and act together. By a *category*, I mean any social aggregate whose members share one or more attributes and lack the organization and ability to act together. Analytic categories depend on the individual analyst, being artificial constructs, while others like social classes are objective cultural constructs that denote perduring realities of social structure. Such social categories as women are concrete units, being bounded aggregates, institutionalized by the society on the basis of the criteria that define them. Other categories, such as racial and ethnic stocks, such economic classes as the workers, peasants, rentiers and landlords, children, the middle-aged, elderly, slaves, serfs, and colonized populations, are more puzzling. While some social categories are firmly bounded by unambiguous criteria, such as sex, or legal status as free, serf or slave, those based on age, class, and income source are not, and yet others, such as racial and ethnic categories, are often ambiguous. In consequence while the closed categories, being each a unique and presumptively perpetual division of the society in which it occurs, have determinate memberships by virtue of their closure, and are corporate, such loosely defined social categories as the aged, young, wealthy, poor, workers, lower working or middle class, bourgeois, ethnic or racial stocks, which have ambiguous boundaries, lack the status of membership, and despite their presumed perpetuity and distinctness are *collectivities*, and neither institutional nor corporate.

As students we may often subdivide populations into analytic categories by our own criteria. For example, in studying witchcraft we may distinguish reputed witches, suspected witches, their accusers, those who judge the accusations, and others who punish 'proven' witches, from others who take no active part in the proceedings. To classify populations by levels of educational attainment, we may distinguish those with postgraduate degrees from those with first degrees or equivalent professional qualifications, those with advanced technical diplomas or equivalent certificates, those with five or more years of secondary school attendance, others with less, those whose education ceased in primary school, and those who never went to school. However, unless the society to which these classifications refer explicitly recognises and incorporates such divisions in its structure as collectivities or units, they are clearly *analytic categories* created by students, and should not be confused with those *social categories* which are objective components of the social structure.

Besides groups and social categories, which always have three or more members, we must also take account of quasi-groups, that is, units whose members need have no direct relations with one another, but who may nonetheless act together for common ends. An individual's personal network of kin, friends, allies and dependents becomes a quasi-group when the central ego mobilises others as an action set to help him or her pursue some end, each doing what he can on his own (Mayer 1966). Given the unit's lack of central organization and ambiguous boundaries, its members, being normally heterogeneous, may change during the activity, and are only connected indirectly through their diverse personal links with the central ego rather than one another. For the occasion the unit is therefore neither a collectivity, a group nor a category, but an action-set or *quasi-group*. So too are personal networks, individual kindreds, fractions of factions, clienteles or sections of them, and other *ad hoc* aggregates which, though dispersed, can readily be mobilized for common action by those persons to whom the others are linked directly or indirectly.

Groups, categories, quasi-groups and all social units with three or more members are aggregates; but not all pluralities are groups, categories or quasi-groups. The modern industrial city encloses many social aggregates of differing size that are neither groups, categories nor quasi-groups, but simply physically adjacent congeries of people whose families, workshops, factories, and offices use its roads, railways, sewerage systems and other facilities. The collectivities demarcated by the regional subdivisions of most countries are aggregates of the same kind, since their populations lack any binding common interests or organization, and therefore cannot act as units. So likewise are neighborhoods in most cultures and such short-lived *ad hoc* collectivities as parades, markets, trading fairs, or at sporting events, in shopping centres, polling divisions, postal or electoral districts and constituencies, all of which, being inchoate collectivities and not units, are incapable of autonomous joint action.

Although many societies are genuine groups because they have the inclusive or representative organization which is prerequisite for common deliberation and action, many others lack such co-extensive organisation and are therefore incapable of mobilizing their members or resources for common action. If their identities and membership criteria are clearly defined, such societies are therefore aggregates of a categorical kind. Since their cultures and institutions normally identify their members and exclude non-members, these societies represent corporate categories of the same general kind as women, slaves, serfs, colonial and other populations, whose recruitment criteria define their boundaries, identify their members and prescribe their membership norms. Thus bounded and self-reproducing, their collective identities are each unique and presumed to be perpetual. Such acephalous segmentary societies as the Nuer, Tallensi and Tiv illustrate the type, as do other acephalous and polycephalous societies such as the Trobriands, Anuak, Australian Aboriginal tribes, New Guinea Highlanders, populations of hunters and gatherers, and most Amerindian societies north of Mexico, which lacked the organization essential to convert categories and other inert aggregates into groups capable of united common action. Since all distinct societies that have inclusive organizations have unique identities, their own rules of recruitment and closure, regulate their memberships, and are assumed to be perpetual, all are therefore distinct corporate groups. As such, besides the requisite organization and regulatory procedures, each has a set of exclusive common affairs, which includes its organization and procedures, together with the autonomy it needs to manage those affairs and carry on its collective life.

As ethnography demonstrates, the overwhelming majority of simple, weakly differentiated societies, many of which lack the organization they require to be groups, and to have the capacity for joint collective action that groups enjoy, owe their boundaries and internal order to the common institutions shared by their people. Wherever recognized, the boundaries of such acephalous societies coincide in the minds of their members and outsiders nearby with important institutional differences of language, religion, economy, kinship, marriage or law between adjacent populations. Those institutional differences generally coincide with discontinuities in the corporate organizations of different adjacent communities, since corporations are the most elaborate institutional kinds of social unit.

As Malinowski stressed, people who share common institutions thereby share common values, goals, rules and forms of behavior, as well as common beliefs and ideas, modes of action, grouping and organization, since social institutions integrate beliefs, ideas, values, rules and forms of social relation that regulate behavior, interaction, motivation, and the choice of goals to pursue. Accordingly, members of those societies that have been overrun, subjugated, exploited and often substantially destroyed by larger, more powerful groups, owe their internal order, collective identity and cultural coherence to the common institutional systems they share, which simultaneously distinguish their community and sanction their interpersonal and intergroup relations. Thus, by virtue of their institutional homogeneity, even acephalous societies, which lack the organization necessary to coordinate and regulate their relations, routinely exhibit the shared common beliefs, ideas, values, rules, and modes of action, as well as social processes, relations and forms of grouping, that illustrate their distinct identity and common culture. As a consequence of their shared cultural institutions, members of an acephalous society generally enjoy sufficient consensus and common understandings in their routine activities to ensure internal peace and unity. Accordingly when two or more dissimilar collectivities, whether acephalous or organized, are incorporated in a single society, their institutional differences initially divide that society into as many culturally and socially different 'groups.' To distinguish such societies from those whose members share a single common set of institutions, following J. S. Furnivall (1948), I shall describe them as *plural societies* in contrast to the simpler institutionally *homogeneous societies* studied by anthropologists (Smith 1960b; 1984; 1991) and discuss their difference later. At this stage however, it is sufficient if we recognize that many societies are not institutionally uniform but plural and institutionally heterogeneous. Indeed with few exceptions almost all the nation-states in which mankind now live incorporate various kinds of plural societies, very few of those societies being institutionally homogeneous.

5. INSTITUTIONAL STATUS

To facilitate social structural analysis, as related above, we must first classify collectivities and social units by their size, durability and organization. Such minimal entities as person, dyad, status or role that constitute dyadic relations represent the distinct kinds of micro-unit. Human societies differ in their cultures, histories, and demographic, social, economic, ethnic and political composition. However, while some aggregates are organized as groups, for example, families, lineages, work teams and peer groups; others such as personal networks, kindreds or action sets, are quasi-groups; and yet others distinguished by one or more criteria are clearly categories, that is, segments of the wider population such as women, serfs, clans, those of middle income, Blacks, atheists, physicians, athletes, etc. To study social structure we must therefore define such basic concepts as status, role, relation, group, category, aggregate, corporation, dyad, collective and mass behavior, and thereafter use those terms and concepts consistently.

To distinguish them from *dyads* I treat *triads* as groups, since each consists of three constituent members. As a result of their superior complexity triads differ structurally from the simpler dyads. Moreover, to distinguish social units having three or more members from dyads and such elementary units as persons, statuses or roles, I shall describe them as aggregates, even though the memberships and activities of some aggregates may be coextensive with their societies, while others such as the family, work groups and clubs, are units of far smaller size and span.

The third criterion needed to classify concrete structures, that of institutional status, is considerably more complex and will require discussion. By the term institutional status I mean broadly, whether or not a given practice or structure has the character and attributes of an institution, and if imperfectly, how and to what degree. Thus, besides distinguishing institutional from non-institutional bodies, we have also to deal with those that are anti-institutional. To indicate the appropriate institutional status of social entities, we therefore need sound criteria of institutional status that presuppose operationally clear conceptions of institution, institutionalization, the institutional order in societies, and anti-institutional activities. Neither are all social phenomena equally institutionalized, nor does that always imply the same mode. Despite the social theories of Durkheim and Parsons, we have to deal with diverse anti-institutional, non-institutional and variably institutional social forms.

Under the influence of Talcott Parsons in 1950 certain American sociologists tried to list the functional prerequisites of human society, as they perceived them. Their list began with the essential prerequisite of adequate survival relations with the environment, followed by role differentiation and assignment, adequate communication within the population, shared cognitive orientations, a shared articulated set of goals, agreed normative regulations of means for their pursuit, regulation of affective expression, appropriate socialization, and effective control of disruptive behavior. That list, which was extended within two years by one of the group, Marion Levy, was later superseded by Talcott Parsons' set of four functional requisites, namely, adequate adaptation to the environment, (A); goal definitions, articulation and pursuit, (G); integration, (I); and latency, or cultural maintenance and renewal, (L). Although their order lacked any demonstrable basis of relations of logical priority among its four components, according to Parsons, those four essential dimensions or aspects of any institutional form or process of social action always recur in the same sequence of phases, namely A-G-I-L.

Even before that publication, the Parsonian structural-functionalists had treated roles and other forms and modes of social action as institutional processes regulated by shared cognitive, normative and other orientations and adequately supported by the prevailing sanction structure of social control. On those grounds, in light of their list of functional prerequisites they conceived roles as structures entailed by those combinations of cognitive and value orientations which members of a society shared and regarded as instrumentally and normatively valid, thereby restricting their attention to institutional roles. Having assumed that everyone in a society shared the same set of cognitive value and other orientations, choice of goals and means, and so forth, the Parsonians concluded that all roles are institutional, and are regarded as normatively and instrumentally valid by their holders and others in their society. In consequence those scholars tended to regard non-institutional modes of behavior, like those that were positively anti-institutional, being opposed to the prevailing institutional order, goals and supporting set of cognitive and value orientations, as deviant and potentially disruptive. With such conservative inclinations, having postulated shared values, cognitive orientations, and choice of goals and means as functional prerequisites of society, they excluded dissensus. Hence, to validate the implication that all roles are institutionally prescribed and assigned, those theorists assumed that social behavior would be effectively regulated by the institutional authority, and that any social behavior inconsistent with its norms would be suppressed, thus ignoring collective forms of protest, including marches, strikes, demonstrations, as well as riots, civil wars and revolutions.

If, however, we recognize that social roles are variably institutionalized and sometimes loosely defined, but always attached to some status, we shall avoid many of the problems created by those Harvard sociologists who sought to treat societies as normative and cognitive consensual systems, although their institutional goals and structures did not include the full range of their social processes and interactions. A fundamental weakness of this general theory is apparent in its stress on regulation as a functional prerequisite of social order, given the earlier assumptions of common cognitive, normative orientations and goals throughout the population. Only if those shared cognitive and normative orientations particularly emphasized law and order Would such collective regulation be essential or legitimate. Perhaps for that reason Parsons later shifted his emphasis from regulation to integration and latency in the set of four functional requisites, A-G-I-L.

However, conceiving his general theory as one of social action, Parsons defined roles as distinctive forms or programs of individual interaction that are the most strategic and appropriate foci for theoretical study. By thus disconnecting roles from the specific statuses to which they attach, Parsons compounded the problem of accounting for them in all their variety. He tried to deal with that problem, first, by assuming the equivalent institutionalization of roles; and then, by restricting his concern to such institutional units; thirdly, by treating institutional roles as manifestations of cognitive and value orientations that underlay the system of social action at the cultural level; and fourthly, by dismissing as anomalous or deviant all roles that did not fit his scheme. Thus, by ignoring the specific status to which each role is bound, and by restricting attention to adequately institutionalized roles, Parsons and other action theorists freed themselves to treat societies as self-created and self-regulating action systems whose essential elements are institutional roles that owe their existence, scope and effect to the functional requisites of the institutional systems of which they are part, much as those systems express the prerequisites that underlie society.

Since roles are their key components, Parsons and his colleagues accordingly identified the system of social action they regarded as society almost exclusively with its institutional structure which, being shaped by the functional prerequisites they had identified, ensured the integration and persistence of the social order with minimal change. In that way those scholars shackled themselves with the unnecessary and spurious problem of accounting for change, which they found intractable, having vainly excluded the dynamism inherent in the anti-institutional and non-institutional aspects and sectors of social orders. In such conditions and by such means, women now try to redefine the roles and identities they have inherited from their mothers, and set about constructing new kinds of status and social relations, not only with men and with one another, but with their society and culture at the ideational and institutional levels, as well as those of action and organization. In so doing, women sometimes generate changes in a wide range of social conditions and structures, the ramifications of which will spread at different rates and in differing degrees and ways throughout the social order.

By excluding similar unprecedented forces and processes from their models of social systems as anomalous, Parsonians identified social change as problematic forms of deviance from the appropriate institutional order. They therefore treated diverse alternatives to institutional forms of correct action as equally deviant, thus ignoring the great difference in the ranges of social behaviors and relationships that are weakly, if at all, institutionalized, non-institutional, and/or anti-institutional. To treat any departure from some vague, ideal, presumptive norm, and therefore any instance of change, as deviance, is clearly misleading since that classifies variation, which is statistically normal, as deviant. In that sense we are all in different contexts, ways and degrees inevitably deviant. If that were not the case we should all behave like soldiers on parade or ants in an anthill and enact roles of every kind uniformly, irrespective of differing circumstances, differing individual endowments, and other conditions. Fortunately that is not so, human beings are not ants, nor are societies armies. People inevitably exhibit and expect the variety and differences of individual abilities, opinions, wishes and experience without which human society of any kind is inconceivable. Thus, however "functional" the structural-functional model of society as a self-perpetuating functionally integrated institutional system may have seemed to its creators and champions, in practice it is highly disfunctional since it deviates so widely from the reality for which it was developed. At the core of these problems lies Parsons' presumption that the essential and sufficient elements of action systems are individual roles conceived as fully institutional forms.

As indicated above, the term institution is polysemic. The Concise Oxford Dictionary (Sykes 1976:560) interprets it as an "established law, custom or practice (colloq., of person etc.), familiar object", and defines an institution as a "society or organization for promotion of scientific, educational, or other public objects; or a building used for this." In the last sense we often describe central banks, colleges, hospitals, legislatures, courts, prisons, museums, military academies, and such celebrated organizations as the Yankees, the Baseball League, the Olympic Games, or the Middlesex Cricket Club, as institutions, together with the buildings or premises that house them. This meaning of the term corresponds closely with Malinowski's idea of institution as an organized group, as well as the colloquial use to denote a 'familiar object'. In social science, however, the term generally refers to the "established law, custom or practice" of a society or community. The distinction is important, since in plural societies, differing communities or populations customarily practice different forms of the same institution, and sometimes observe different laws, ordained by their differing religions or political status.

In the sense preferred by social scientists, an institution is an established law, custom, or form of action, that is, either a collectively sanctioned authoritative rule of conduct, or the standardized form of behavior practised by a people. However, neither are all the customary practices a population regards as right or necessary prescribed by its 'established law', nor are all laws equally 'established' or habitually followed as right and proper by those to whom they apply. For example, in the U.S.A. the prohibition laws were widely ignored as ill-conceived and inappropriate, as were the Consolidated Slave Codes annually passed by the Legislature of Jamaica, but routinely ignored by the planters who enacted them, and by their agents. Likewise in the Southern U.S., despite Federal and State laws to the contrary, for decades Negroes were lynched without redress, forbidden to register or vote, and generally deprived of those civil rights and liberties guaranteed by law. Besides "established law", we therefore have to deal with "dead-letter laws" which, lacking popular support, may routinely be set aside with impunity and breached by sections of the population. In much the same way, while some customs are routinely practised by all or most of a people, others are not, but vary widely in popular observation and esteem, being regarded by some as morally right and binding, but not by others. In short, besides the dictionary's implicit distinctions between institutional and non-institutional rules and modes of action, we have to recognize and deal with variable degrees of institutionalization of rules and customs.

By 'established', the dictionary means "routinely effective authoritative, or generally accepted and observed rules or forms of action." Such authoritative and generally accepted rules and behavior patterns are commonly treated as normatively valid and proper forms of conduct; but the criteria behind them are not absolute. Quite often people ascribe normative values to such conventional patterns as the rules of language, arithmetic, buildings, farming, and so on. Conversely we often treat normative principles and rules as if they are existential realities, like the laws of gravity. How and when culturally the 'is' becomes the 'ought', or the normative existential, remains one of the least studied and most important problems in empirical social science, though it subsumes a variety of forms of social and cultural change by processes that de-institutionalize formerly valid rules or practices, and replace them by others having different social and cultural implications.

When rules and customs are firmly established people generally take them for granted as the normal and appropriate patterns to follow in making decisions, pursuing interests, and interaction. Thus the institutional is essentially something a population takes for granted as the right and proper thing to do, and is commonly sanctioned by some form of collective action to punish contraventions (Radcliffe-Brown 1952). That which is taken for granted, including the idea that twice two is four, is typically regarded as right and legitimate, as well as being most efficient and aesthetically desirable, in contrast with that which is unusual, unfamiliar, or foreign to the prevailing mores and culture. *Institutionalization* may thus be described as the process by which forms of behavior or rules of conduct gradually acquire sufficient popular acceptance, currency and observance to be adopted as normatively correct, legitimate, and enforceable by public sanctions. *De-institutionalization* is thus the contrary process by which formerly valid rules or forms of behavior lose general acceptance, normative status and collective sanction, whether abruptly or gradually, as through changes of fashion, technology, ideas, and such processes as urbanization, monetization, defeat and subjugation, or the like. From one perspective, social and cultural history may be seen as the process of simultaneous and progressive deinstitutionalization of pristine rules, customs and forms of social organization and the abrupt or gradual institutionalization of others to replace them.

Our tendency to take for granted the elements of the institutional order under which we live, endows that order and all its components with an illusory stability, permanence and validity, illusions that are necessary to ensure sufficient consensus for peaceful interaction and collective observance of the order. When institutions cease to be taken for granted by sufficient numbers of people, to recover the popular support on which their authority depends, they must either be modified and adapted, or lose their validity, lapse and be replaced by other rules or patterns, even though, as we normally take our institutional order and its components so much for granted, we may rarely examine or criticize their elements. Social science illustrates this nicely by its prolonged failure to address the gross, pervasive civil inferiority of women in Western and other societies, despite its explicit commitment to value neutrality and freedom from cultural bias in research and analysis. Often, however, since some routine forms of social behavior may lack legal validity and collective sanction, while many prevailing laws are inadequately enforced and widely ignored, the institutional status of specific rules and forms of behavior is difficult to determine or disentangle from the complementary processes of institutionalization and de-institutionalization that they may illustrate.

While institutionalization denotes the process by which a particular rule or pattern of social conduct, set of ideas, activities or social relations, including roles, becomes clearly defined, widely known and accepted within a population as normatively desirable and collectively sanctioned, it also connotes the condition or state of affairs that is the effect of that process. The evidence shows that not all statuses or roles that people hold are equally institutional, even when they occur as elements of institutional units. Likewise our data show that neither are social units all equally institutional, nor are all their elements. While some social units are so heavily institutional that as organs of state and other regulative corporations, they serve as both a source or agent and subject of legal sanctions, a wide variety of units, relations and activities are weakly institutionalized or variably non-institutional. Moreover such perduring, non-institutional features of society as classes, races, or age-grades are both universal, and facilitate the internal adaptations of its social units, being more labile and flexible than its institutional components. Accordingly, such non-institutional patterns enable internal developments to permit or express the changes required to accommodate pressures, and allow people to adopt new ideas, goals and patterns of action. Clearly, the least heavily institutional elements of social structure are the most likely to generate endogenous pressures for change, or to express, experience and respond to external pressures. To some degree, therefore, the resilience of a society, that is, its ability to absorb and adjust to change, whether exogenous or endogenous in origin, depends on the nature, proportion and relations of its strongly and weakly institutional components, as well as the non-institutional ones. Conceivably, a perfectly institutional, functionally coherent and closed societal structure such as Parsons theorized would have great difficulty in adjusting appropriately and with the necessary speed to abrupt important changes in its environment, or to the cumulative effects of internal changes in its demographic structure, population distribution and economy, whereas a more loosely institutional structure may adapt more flexibly to such changing conditions.

6. THE ALTERNATIVES

In addition to weakly institutional and non-institutional social units, there are the loosely bounded collectivities already mentioned that differ from social units in lacking clear boundaries, institutional status, membership statuses, and determinate memberships. We must also take account of those units and activities which are either overtly or covertly anti-institutional, being opposed to the basic rules, values, and organization of the prevailing institutional order. In my usage, anti-institutional activities or groupings are those that seek to subvert the institutional order and its preconditions, or to challenge and overthrow some important part of it and destroy its legitimacy. In certain contexts, we may find problematic collectivities such as the hippies of the sixties in the U.S.A., aggregates that are neither militant nor overtly hostile to the dominant institutional order, which they nonetheless repudiate and reject. In others, we shall find groups having explicit commitments to disrupt or destroy various regulative institutions, so that they might destabilize the social order and replace it by something radically different, on political, religious or other grounds. Activity of the latter sort is clearly anti-institutional, and in its most extreme form, terrorism, violent.

Terrorist activities are generally carried out by small, tightly closed and secret groups which have great dedication and internal solidarity. However, when used by such states as Iran or Libya to harass their enemies or to export revolution, terrorism may involve much larger programs of training, deployment, communications and control, over a wide area and several years. In recent years some rogue states have openly undertaken terrorist activities beyond their borders, while others have done so surreptitiously or indirectly through proxies. We should therefore recognize both the variety of social units that actively promote terrorism, and the corresponding range of those units and activities. As the rise of Nazism and the state of Israel show, if a terrorist program has local leaders, personnel and aims, and if its attacks on the institutional order and its representatives win sufficient support, its anti-institutional emphases may reduce and recede as the movement wins wider support and approaches its goal, namely, the seizure of social power. In such a process, even if terrorist groups persist, the movement of which they are part, having won mass support, may change its character and develop a more open, accessible organization, public leaders, and explicit programs for publication. These developments also marked the Fascist path to power in Italy under Mussolini, unlike the history of Bolshevik rule in Russia.

Terrorist groups, secret societies such as the Mafia in Sicily, the Camorra of Naples and Calabria, or the IRA in Ulster, like certain ideologically motivated revolutionary groups, may be morally indifferent to all else except their goals and operational validity. In my terms all such units are anti-institutional, being hostile and actively opposed to the dominant institutional order of their society. Though each has its own code of conduct to guide its members, and may even punish their disloyalty by death, however effective and binding within the group, such codes, role definitions and sanction structures lack the character and status of institutions, of which they are not a caricature, but the opposite, being known and accepted as valid only by those within the group, but otherwise explicitly illegal and illegitimate.

Unlike terrorists, Mafiosi and similar groups, even during the heyday of their movement, the hippies of California were neither violent nor militantly hostile to the dominant American institutional order, which they repudiated individually and collectively. They objected, briefly, to the institutional culture of white middle class America, the "silent" or "moral" majority from which most hippies derived, having dropped out of their families or marriages, universities, communities, churches, schools, jobs, political parties, and most aspects of the "great American rat-race", as they perceived it. As social and cultural drop-outs, the chief aim of those hippies was to abandon middle class America, its ethos and culture, and to withdraw rather than challenge or confront it by militant action. However, given their theory, to Parsons and his colleagues the hippie movement and such militant protests as the students' and civil rights movements, were simply modes of deviance, not unlike the Mafia, internal terrorism, and the KKK. To classify such a wide diversity of social movements of radically differing kinds, goals and bases as forms of deviance clearly raises many problems that expose the flaws in their theory.

Quite different from terrorism, though potentially and in certain contexts and modes far more disruptive, is the variety of non-institutional activities which sociologists generally discuss as *collective behavior*. Perhaps 'misbehavior' might seem a more appropriate term, since its most prominent forms are mobs and crowds, riots, demonstrations, strikes, revolts and revolutions, protest movements of differing scale, duration, intensity and methods, racial or ethnic *jacqueries*, as recently in Azerbaijan, Rwanda and Burundi, or gang warfare, as in some American cities. These illustrate the kinds of phenomenon of which Durkheim spoke when referring to currents that swept across the collective conscience and social order, sometimes represented by men on white horses riding through capitals at the head of mobs threatening to overturn the state. In large complex democratic societies like the USA, several less violent social movements of differing nature, scale, complexity and duration, such as the student movement, the civil rights movement, the anti-war movement, and the female liberation movement may proceed simultaneously or serially in swift succession, generating, feeding on, cross-cutting and reinforcing one another to produce appropriate changes and reorientations in the society and culture.

Yet another kind of collective behavior, one variety of which Durkheim studied in his monograph on suicide, differs so widely from those collective events that it is now studied separately as *mass behavior*. The difference between collective behavior as sociologists use the term and mass behavior is that collective behavior is the behavior of collectivities acting together, whether it be crowd behavior, riots or revolts, audience behavior or social movements, all of which involve aggregates acting together. Mass behavior on the other hand is the aggregated behavior of individuals acting separately or in small groups to do such things as getting married, committing suicide, delivering babies, emigrating, or having accidents, i.e., of individuals or small groups going about their personal business. When we add the number of times that members of a common society, category or group do the same thing in a month, year or other period of time, and treat this total statistically, we can calculate the rate or incidence of that behavior per thousand or per hundred thousand adults or people, for specified units of time, and then study those rates comparatively to see what they reveal. Such studies show that the average rate for any specific behavior that occurs at random tends to be fairly stable as long as the social situation and prevailing institutional conditions persist.

Being unscheduled and optional, the celebration of marriage, whether for the first or some subsequent time, in modern societies involves mass behavior; but among the Kagoro of Northern Nigeria, not long ago people who were expecting to get married for the first time all had to do so on a certain day called *tuk pirung*. Kagoro had a highly sophisticated view of marriage, which without recognizing divorce allowed adults of both sexes, once they were initially married, to make new marriages at any time. However, to do so for the first time, they all had to marry on *tuk pirung*. It should therefore be possible to count all first marriages for the year on that day, and so to calculate the tribal rate of all Kagoro first marriages that year. In modern countries, by contrast, people choose freely when to get married for the first, second or third time, and no day is institutionally prescribed. The marriage rates of modern societies accordingly vary by season as well as age, sex, education, class and other conditions. These rates, which summarise the number of individuals or couples who have acted independently in the same way provide the kind of data now referred to as 'mass behavior', since they enumerate the behaviors *en masse* of individuals acting separately in a society. Defined thus, mass behavior is characteristic of all societies from the simplest to the most advanced, but its study in simple societies has so far received less attention than the institutions that regulate their characteristic activities.

Anthropological studies of collective behavior have been mainly concerned with cargo cults, such other nativistic movements as the Ghost Dance in North America which followed the Civil War, or separatist religious movements such as Kimbanguism in Zaire, the Rastafarians of Jamaica, the Harris church of the Cote d'Ivoire, and the African churches in the Republic of South Africa. Historians have recently begun to study comparable phenomena in earlier periods (Cohn 1957; Rudé 1964). Though as yet anthropologists have paid less attention to collective behavior than sociologists studying more advanced differentiated societies, recent studies of peasant revolt (Wolf 1969), industrial strikes

(Epstein 1958) and other forms of collective action indicate its value and promise.

Together mass and collective behavior represent certain kinds of social processes which are either non-institutional or anti-institutional, and impossible to institutionalize without transforming their nature. Most people in the U.S.A. may use Colgate's toothpaste, or some other kind. Whether that is so and how many do so can only be learnt *post facto* by systematic surveys. As no institutional rule obliges anyone to do so, the aggregate amounts purchased of different varieties of toothpaste really summarize so many free individual choices, rather than any institutional pattern of behavior.

Collective and mass behavior arise how, when and where they do, with the frequency and significance that they have, as more or less direct expressions of the routine and antecedent operation of the institutional order. In short, the non-institutional, anti-institutional order and the institutional order of the social process are dialectically related. Widely perceived inadequacies of the institutional order in its immediate context provide the bases for many of the non-institutional and anti-institutional developments that emerge within it. The women's movement, student and civil rights movements, which together inundated America in the sixties, all addressed widely perceived inadequacies and inconsistencies of American culture and society. Although formally committed to uphold human equality in law and the state, by its pervasive racism and sexism, that society discriminated against Negroes, Amerindians and other non-whites, women and students, and generated these responses by violating these constitutional and legal commitments that large sections of its people hold dear. In the small-scale societies that anthropologists study, in response to foreign influences or otherwise, a people sometimes lose faith in the capability of their traditional culture to fulfil routinely their modest traditional expectations of fertility, successful childbearing and rearing, health, weather, harvests, trade and the like. Prophets may then emerge who proclaim new doctrines and kinds of ritual to handle the harsh new problems of daily life, and often direct the people to repudiate and reject the traditional cults and their taboos, to destroy their ritual objects, holy places and shrines, and proclaim new cults that enjoin radical reorientations of the society and culture. Such explosive incidents of collective behavior arise when, as and where they do, as a people's response to their experience and perception of the inadequacies of their traditional institutional order.

We are all continuously aware, directly or indirectly, explicitly, overtly, critically and otherwise, of the social orders we inhabit and share; and when we find fellow-spirits, we communicate with them to exchange and discuss our views. By such small steps, three or four people may create informal groups to discuss issues and interests of common concern. Social movements often begin thus, and emerge when a variety of such small, isolated units, each with its own leaders and personnel, its own priorities, perceptions of social problems, and preferred solutions, come together to exchange ideas and share their skills and experience in order to act effectively together. Appropriate definitions of the central problem, and proposals to resolve it, appropriate organization and campaign strategies must then be developed by the members of those units and others who join them, until the original diversity of their opinions flows together to become a common ideology.

The social movement, if it persists and grows for several years, in order to survive will gradually institutionalize appropriate working procedures to discuss, agree, organize, plan and coordinate the strategies, campaigns and programs its participants advocate. Eventually, if successful to some degree, the protest movement may become an institutional part of the ongoing social fabric it has helped to shape, as, for instance, happened to the labor and birth control movements, mass democracy, and the enfranchisement of women, which were gradually institutionalized in the USA and Western Europe during the last two centuries, in response to public pressures against popularly perceived inadequacies of their prevailing institutional orders. Such dialectical processes are perhaps the chief means by which society adapts to changing circumstances, renews itself, and avoids the institutional paralysis and senility that afflicted Ancient Egypt and imperial China after resisting change for millenia. To divert, arrest and prevent these processes of collective renewal from challenging, strengthening and developing the social order by enhancing its adaptive capacity, a society requires a powerful repressive apparatus, such as those of Stalinist Russia, Maoist China, Ancient Egypt or imperial China; but even then it cannot arrest the tides indefinitely.

The alternative may be calamitous. If conditions of repression are efficiently institutionalized for two or three generations, as in the USSR,

Romania and Marxist China, the population they regulate may lose their independent capacities to reform or replace the social order, and become dependent upon it. If so, the society and culture will tend to petrify, losing vitality and direction, while repeating old patterns that fail to solve its endemic problems, which simply accumulate. When the institutional order finally breaks down, as recently in the USSR and Yugoslavia, there may then be prolonged turmoil before the people identify their society's problems and start to rebuild a new social order.

There are two points to note about collective behavior in this context. Firstly, since such behavior is not institutionalized, without appropriate adjustments, techniques of institutional analysis do not apply to them directly. Secondly, when social movements, whether political or religious, gain strength and grow, as an operational requisite of their persistence and coherence, unless forbidden by their ideology or by material conditions, they generally develop a directive organization. That can be studied using the schema discussed below, to reveal its process of growth and to determine its coherence by analyzing the congruence of the conditions, procedures and means by which leaders and followers co-ordinate their resources and activities to pursue common goals. As social movements are particularly significant modes of collective behavior for students of social structure and change, it is essential to develop appropriate instruments for their systematic analysis and comparative study.

Novel forms of collective behavior emerge as popular responses to events or circumstances that seem to their participants to require some immediate and unusual reaction which cannot realistically be expected of institutional structures. Such novel collective behavior is often, and perhaps always, a spontaneous popular response to developments and changes in the circumstances of a society that clearly require responses beyond the capacity of its institutional structures. In such situations, popular perceptions of the inadequacies of their traditional institutions underlie and generate the social movements that seek to change or replace them. Accordingly, to understand the forms, development and conditions of such collective behavior, we must first examine and compare the initial and the changed circumstances of the society, and then analyse the processes of change and institutional inadequacies in the changing situation that provide the basis for comprehension. To that end, having analysed the antecedent institutional structure, we may identify those modifications in its ecological situation that destabilized it, and stimulated novel forms of collective action. To do that, as explained below, we should list and examine the conditions assumed and entailed by the antecedent institutional structure in order to identify precisely those factors that ensured its inefficacy, and so provoked collective responses to redress and stabilize the situation. At that stage some of the concepts and procedures used to analyse institutions may be useful, provided that they also apply to non-institutional dimensions of society.

7. STATUS AND ROLE

Social units, then, are empirical units that have clear boundaries and membership, the smallest units being the status and role which are both quite complex, and the person, which summarizes the social aspect of an individual, that is, his or her current statuses and roles or social attributes, sometimes described as the individual's 'social personality.' While the role concept clearly hails from the theatre and denotes the part that a person plays or performs in a particular context, which may be brief or prolonged, status is the Latin word for 'position', and like such other terms as corporation has entered social science from the law. Unfortunately, although lawyers commonly identify such statuses as those of husband or wife by their respective rights, duties, privileges, immunities and liabilities, the term status is also used more widely to denote a person's position or rank in the community or society to which they belong. However in many societies, and especially modern ones, that usage does not denote a person's rank by a specific set of rights and duties which is common to all who hold that status. Thus, since the familiar meaning of status as rank differs from that derived from law, the two distinct meanings of the word should be separated clearly. I shall therefore distinguish the two alternatives as social and institutional status respectively. By *institutional status* I refer to a position in an institutional unit or structure, such as that of husband, wife, mother, father, daughter or son in the family, judge, juror, prosecuting or defending counsel and clerk of court in courts of law, head teacher or principal, assistant teachers, parents, governor, council, technicians and pupils in relation to a school, and so on, these all being different kinds of institutional structure. In contrast, a person's *social status* is his or her general position or rank in the community or society to which they belong, that is, what we often describe as their social position or class. While institutional status always involves institutional roles, social status lacks such roles in many societies, including modern industrial ones. Moreover although an individual, or rather a person, since the individual holds many statuses, may only enact a single social status at any moment, he or she will have as many institutional statuses as the institutions in which they take part. However, while many statuses that we hold as individuals are institutional, not all of those statuses are equally institutional, and some are not, since several, such as friend, neighbor, lover, gossip, recluse or half-caste, occur outside institutional contexts and lack collective sanctions. To accommodate those situations we should therefore broaden our distinction between social and institutional status to contrast an individual's social status or 'general' position with his many distinct 'specific' positions, institutional and other.

Unfortunately that is not the end of the matter. Max Weber, seeking to analyse the complexities of social stratification in modern society, distinguished three separate interrelated scales, namely, the economic, which is indicated by an individual's relations to the market; the political, which indicates the individual's relative power (*herrschaft*); and the scale of prestige or social honor as expressed in codes of conduct, style of life, connubium and membership in some status group. To denote the scale of social honor or rank, Weber used the German term *stande* (i.e., standing, rank, meaning social status), which his American disciple, Talcott Parsons, identified with status, but translated as prestige. Thus for Parsons in sociology the primary meaning of status is an individual's position in society, which he equated with prestige, as it lacked a distinctive set of rights or duties.

Ralph Linton, who introduced concepts of status and role to anthropology, linked them as reciprocals in his definitions, without distinguishing between the social or general and institutional or specific meanings of status, as I have done above. Talcott Parsons however, having identified status with Max Weber's *stande* as general position or prestige, rejected Ralph Linton's unhappy definition based on its legal meaning as "a collection of rights and duties" (Linton 1936:113-114). In Goodenough's words (1965:2), while for Linton a status is a collection of rights and duties, "a role, the dynamic aspect of status, (is) the putting into effect of its rights and duties."

Among the problems created by Linton's linked definitions of status and role are their apparent redundancy, even though the concept of status is emphatically static while Linton identifies the role with action. Secondly, as already noted, without distinguishing institutional from social status, Linton identifies the concept with specific sets of rights and duties. However, neither is that true of general social status, nor of non-institutional statuses, since rights and duties are socially sanctioned and enforceable claims and obligations that distinguish institutional from non-institutional positions. Accordingly several authors such as Southall (1956), Banton (1965) and Nadel (1957) have chosen to follow the lead of Talcott Parsons who, translating Weber, equated status with prestige or social standing in the wider sense, and have redefined role in terms of expected behavior.

In Parsons' definition of roles, as in Linton's, behavior or action is essential, but no more important than the normative expectation of the particular kind of conduct. Having omitted to anchor those patterns of expected behavior in discrete social positions or statuses for the reasons stated above, Parsons sought to account for them by stressing their normative and cognitive components, which he seemed to regard as logical entailments and combinations of certain cognitive and value orientations or 'pattern variables' that pervaded the culture and regulated institutional behavior within a society. On those assumptions, the roles that Parsonians theorized and discussed were all firmly institutional, being socially sanctioned and prescriptive. Accordingly, societies were assumed to share the common cognitive and value orientations, norms and instrumental priorities that constituted the roles under discussion, endowed them with validity, and ensured their public acceptance, regular performance, and congruence with the prevailing system of social action.

In thus redefining roles as expected patterns of behavior, Parsons abandoned Linton's restrictive conception of roles as action that fulfils duties or exercises rights, broadening it to include other socially significant forms of behavior expected of actors in different positions. What the Parsonian scheme signally failed to deal with is the fact that different expectations and perceptions of behavior attach to differing social positions, institutional and non-institutional, and are held by those who occupy them. We do not normally expect teachers to behave like policemen, pastors like soldiers, singers and dancers like research scientists, parents and children like bureaucrats, presidents and prime ministers like thugs, judges like bandits, or the reverse. The problem then is why, given the generality of shared cognitive and value orientations presumed by Parsons throughout societies, are those behavioral expectations so constructed and specific to the persons holding those different positions, some of which such as teachers, policemen, judges, research scientists, require long training and superior professional performances before appointment, while others such as parents, presidents or prime ministers generally presuppose conditions of eligibility that often include previous tenure of specific institutional positions. In short, we cannot adequately list, classify or understand any set of differentiated social roles without firmly anchoring each of them in some specific status, institutional or other. Moreover as history shows, societal status structures often perdure substantially despite such sweeping cognitive and value re-orientations as the Protestant Reformation, the feminist movement, or the rise and triumph of capitalism, political democracy and nationalism in Western Europe and the USA. We surely need therefore to segregate the status structure that constitutes the society as a distinctive array of specific positions to which differentiated role behaviors and expectations attach, from the prevailing set of cultural orientations, cognitive and other. This is especially necessary since the structure of institutional statuses in any society neither encompasses its totality of discrete positions or their accompanying role behaviors, nor subsumes and reflects fully its prevailing cultural orientations.

Following Ralph Linton's introduction of the role concept and Talcott Parsons' reformulation of it, Robert Merton's essay on role sets is perhaps the most important contribution to the development and efficient use of the concepts in empirical research. As Merton (1949) shows, to teach in schools, teachers have to interact and cooperate with one another, with the school head or principal, with the pupils, often with their parents, sometimes with the school governors, and with the wider community. Members of all those categories occupy different statuses and differ in their relations with teachers correspondingly. They also hold differing expectations of the teacher's appropriate behavior, much as he or she does of theirs. Such a set of structurally diverse role behaviors and expectations associated with the different statuses to which the role relates, Merton calls a role-set. Seen from the teacher's central role, it represents the behavioral manifestation of those statuses, since the situations of all who occupy the same institutional status are essentially similar. For example, in football a full- or quarter-back has to relate effectively to the rest of his team, its opponents, and to heed instructions from his captain and colleagues as well as the referee and club officials. Each player also has diffuse unstructured relations with fans and others who support and follow the game, including journalists of press, television and radio, and their respective audiences. As in the school-teacher's role-set, each of the diverse categories with which the player interacts represents a different status and has differing expectations of his behavior. For the player to perform his role fully, he therefore has to take account of those differing categories and respond appropriately to their diverse expectations. In much the same way husbands and wives are inevitably involved in elaborate role-sets with one another's kindred, colleagues and friends. As children appear, those role-sets generally expand to include various others in their community, many of whom hold different social positions as clergy, laity, neighbors, health workers, officials, and so on.

In effect, by holding an institutional status, a person is inevitably involved in a set of reciprocal role relations with others whose similar or different statuses articulate with his or hers. The same is true of most if not all non-institutional statuses, at least contingently. Thus friends or lovers, however private their relations, almost inevitably come to know one another's acquaintances, colleagues or kin, and may well become involved in diverse relations with several such. Perhaps the hermit alone has no interacting role-set, whether his status is institutional or not. We should therefore always recognize that, whether institutional or not, a position or status, being simply one of several such units, some similar, others different, inevitably engages its occupant in reciprocal role relations with several others. The more important a status in the society's affairs, the more numerous and diverse its relations with other status categories, whether directly or indirectly; the less extensive and differentiated the status-set attached to any specific position, the less important its role performance for the social order. Since any individual simultaneously holds a plurality of differentiated statuses, the complexity of the status sets and role relations through which individuals participate as persons in social processes and interact with one another routinely or occasionally, increases with the number of statuses and roles that they actively hold.

Having recognized the ambiguous meaning of status in Linton's usage, Ward Goodenough (1965:2) decided to retain Linton's legalistic definition of status, but tried to distinguish the specific collections of rights and duties from the positions to which they are attached by calling the latter 'social identities'. In Goodenough's scheme, "the formal properties of statuses involve (1) what legal theorists call rights, duties, privileges, powers, liabilities, and immunities, . . . and (2) the ordered ways in which these are distributed in what I shall call *identity relationships*" (his emphasis). Goodenough then points out that as thus defined, every individual has several social "identities" at any point in time, and accordingly has to choose behavior appropriate to each of these diverse "identities" in different contexts of social interaction. He regards each institutional status as a social category that confers a distinct identity on those who hold it, ignoring the fact that as rank, social status subsumes and denotes the individual's identities in all their institutional and non-institutional positions. Moreover since for Goodenough the statuses that define an individual's social identity consist in "what legal theorists call rights, duties," such non-institutional positions and relations that an individual may have as lover, friend, celebrity, poet, philanthropist etc., can play no part in his or her social "identity."

Goodenough then develops the concepts of identity and identity-relationships, and constructs hypothetical scales based on distributions of rights and duties between people holding different statuses in different dyadic relations. However interesting, the value of Goodenough's scheme is compromised by the error on which it rests. As indicated below, those "properties of status", classified as rights and duties by lawyers, are not formal, as Goodenough claims, but substantive entitlements and obligations. They are thus neither intrinsic nor essential features of status, but extrinsic, conditional and contingent on the reciprocal "identities" involved in social relations, among other conditions, as his hypothetical status scales indicate. In short, what Goodenough regards as a 'status relationship' (1965:8) corresponds closely to a role relation in Linton's terms.

As Goodenough (1965:2) perceived, social positions differ from the specific set of rights and duties ascribed to them at any point in time, since the positions often persist as formal units despite changes in those substantive rights and duties. For example, history records substantial change in the substantive rights and duties of the English monarchy over the past eight centuries without corresponding change in its formal position. This is equally true for the American presidency and governorships of American states. Among the Ashanti of central Ghana at the start of this century, the mother's brother had juridical authority to pledge his sister's son as a pawn at will. Since Ashanti practise matrilineal descent, the mother's brother (MB) was head of his sister's family, and thus the *pater* of his sister's son (ZS). As such he could place his ZS in pawn or temporary serfdom, simply by borrowing money, land or anything of value from someone else, and depositing the young man in care of the lender as security for the loan. If gravely displeased with his sister's son, the mother's brother might leave him for years in that situation as pawn to his creditor. After subduing the Ashanti at the turn of this century, being committed to abolish slavery and misunderstanding this transaction, the British abrogated the traditional right of the Ashanti mother's brother to pawn his sister's son, along with other traditional forms of "slavery" in Ashanti. Thereafter the rights and duties of the mother's brother vis-à-vis his sister's son in Ashanti changed abruptly without corresponding changes in those positions, since both before and after the British decree these statuses in the Ashanti kinship system remained formally the same, despite substantial changes in their reciprocal rights and relations. Thus, although the juridical contents of those statuses, i.e., their respective rights and duties, changed abruptly and dramatically by colonial decree, as formal units the statuses themselves remained unchanged, and so too their formal relations. In Western Europe and North America parallel developments have occurred during the past generation in the relations of women and men. During this period, several important aspects of husband-wife relations have changed without any formal revision of those statuses, or of the more general statuses of men and women, despite considerable pressure to that effect. Similarly, despite continuous changes in its substantive power and influence, rights, duties, privileges, powers, liabilities and immunities, as well as policies and personnel, as a status the office of president, in the U.S.A. as in other countries, persists in its constitutionally prescribed relations without formal change.

In Ashanti, besides their respective rights and duties before and under British rule, there were many other non-juridical aspects of the relation between MB and ZS which, as Parsons saw, were widely expected and often sanctioned diffusely by public opinion, though not by law. However, if we identify roles with the enactment and pursuit of jural rights and duties attached to reciprocal statuses, we shall exclude such behavior patterns despite their popular expectation and sanction, although they clearly form important parts of the role as popularly conceived and practised. These implications are so inconsistent with social practice as to destroy the concept's utility. We must therefore set aside the ideas of status, role and their relationships advanced by Linton, Parsons, Goodenough and others in favour of something more appropriate.

In my usage, a status is any social position in a set of related positions, which may be filled either by an individual or by a social unit qualified to hold it. At the individual level, the positions of full- and quarter-back in football teams, or mother's brother and sister's son in kinship systems nicely illustrate this concept of status. So too do such positions as those of teacher, policeman, juror, judge, councillor, physician, nurse, pastor, parent, student, engineer, friend, rival, lover, colleague, partner and so on. At the collective level, such corporations as lineages, clans, universities, states, churches, incorporated firms and certain other associations may for various purposes in their specific social contexts have the qualities requisite to occupy a status.

In any social context relations between the holders of similar and different statuses generally involve interaction, whether occasional or routinely recurrent. To ensure their satisfactory orientation, such relations are generally patterned so that each party can reasonably expect a certain predictable range of behavior from the other. Such patterned modes of interaction between status-incumbents correspond to Talcott Parsons' roles or role-expectations as expected forms of behavior. In many status relations, those behavioral expectations may and do include legally enforceable rights, duties, privileges, powers, liabilities and immunities, as Goodenough perceived; but with the sole exception of public office in certain cultures, in no case can the behavior expected of any status-holder consist exclusively of such rights, duties and other juridical attributes. No list of legal rights and duties, however exhaustive, can ever adequately describe the behavioral patterns expected of one who holds a particular status, since such rights and duties, privileges, immunities and liabilities are inert capacities, incapable of independent self-expression or enactment.

On those grounds therefore, I regard roles as culturally appropriate sets of behaviors expected of persons who hold particular statuses in their interactions with specific others, and recognize that such behaviors often involve the pursuit or exercise of rights and claims as well as the fulfilment of duties. Popular and scholarly definitions of particular statuses in terms of duties and rights merely illustrate the misplaced concreteness that pervades collective symbolism in societies. Rights and duties ascribed at any point in time to a particular status are historically and culturally specific to that context and are not intrinsic to the status, but extraneous and contingently ascribed to it. In consequence, their range, development or elimination normally leaves the status as a formal unit among other units in its structural context, quite unchanged. In short, neither is a role ever fully reducible to the set of legal rights and duties identified with the status that it expresses, nor can those substantive rights and duties, and/or the specific role performance, ever constitute a status, since the latter is a strictly formal unit. As substantive concepts, like expected role-performances, such rights and duties have contingent relationships with the statuses they manifest, and not logically necessary ones, as Linton thought. While in many situations and cases, the empirical linkage of the status and its role-contents may seem very close, that linkage is always contingent, and will vary with prevailing historical and cultural conditions. In Ashanti society formally, the mother's brother remains the pater of his sister's son, whatever their juridical rights and obligations and their interaction.

As noted above, although an individual can only have a single general or social status at any time, he or she generally has as many institutional statuses as institutions in which they take part. Most of the statuses or positions we hold are usually of this institutional kind; but not all of those individual statuses are equally institutional, since several, such as those of friends, lovers, drop-outs, neighbors, rivals, and half-castes or 'mixed-bloods' occur outside of institutional contexts, and lack collective prescriptions and sanctions.

In their imperial heyday the British used to classify Far Eastern elite males as "Worthy Oriental Gentlemen" or WOGS in contrast to wops, dagoes, yids, coons and other whatnots, terms that distinguished outsiders of differing kinds as status categories. The specific behavioral expectations and contents of those terms remain obscure, and show that the status of a pejorative residual category often lacks commensurate behavioral patterns or roles. Celebrities, though highly esteemed, are not dissimilar, since that status lacks any institutional basis, duties or rights, sanctions, and expected behavior.

Such social relations as those of pedestrians who first meet on bumping against one another on a street, or customers and clerks at shop counters, soldiers in battle, or mother and child illustrate dyadic relations between persons whose behavior reflects their statuses. Even the pedestrians who bumped into one another at 47th Street and 3rd Avenue have the status of strangers. However the content and significance of status-structured relations increase as we move from such incidents on the street to the shop counter, and so to the infant's cradle. In short, dyadic relations differ widely in their scope, significance and duration as implications of the statuses that they articulate, the dyad being both the minimal social unit in any social interaction, and an essential element of larger units such as the family, work group, clique, church or club. Family groups articulate dyadic relations between family members, husband and wife, mother and child, father and child, and between siblings. In primary or face to face groups, dyadic relations constitute the organization that enables the plurality to act as a unit continuously or at will.

As these examples show, dyads also vary in their degree of institutionalization. For pedestrians in New York the relevant rules prescribe their mutual non-interference and observance of traffic regulations. For shop customer and clerk, social conventions regulate interaction and standardize acceptable patterns; but on the battlefield elaborate codes and punitive sanctions regulate the conduct of soldiers. The mother-child relation is also heavily surrounded by legal, religious and other social sanctions that apply asymmetrically and diffusely to the mother throughout the child's minority. Whenever dyadic relations are institutionalized by collective definitions, norms and sanctions, their essential components, the statuses and roles through which their principals relate, are equally institutional. However, many different kinds of dyadic relations evidently lack institutional status and sanction, for example, those between shamans and members of their clienteles. People who approach them generally expect the shamans to decide whether, when and how they will shamanize. Teachers employed in most public schools lack similar freedoms, being obliged to observe the expectations that regulate their role-performances to avoid reproof and win approval. The prescriptions that regulate the conduct of judges, jurors and other legal personnel in their juridical role are even more stringent. We must therefore recognize that role-performances and dyadic relations vary widely in their stringency and latitude as functions of their institutionalization, and take systematic account of such variation.

When roles and relations are institutionalized weakly or not at all, those engaged are left to develop and shape them as they wish within the limits allowed by law and circumstance. Friends, lovers, rivals and neighbours have such weak or non-institutional relations, colleagues variably so. The relative freedom that most actors enjoy to shape and develop their relations reciprocally is likely to diminish when those relations are enclosed within larger units such as triads or groups. Clearly, to the degree that dyadic relations lack institutional definition and sanction, their inclusion in larger units will entail corresponding gaps in the latters' institutional validity.

In various societies individuals may establish institutional relations of formal friendship as bond friends or blood brothers with one another. Such relations are strongly sanctioned and carry specific rights, obligations and privileges that bind the participants reciprocally, sometimes for life. Even when such institutional ties lack legal sanction, their validity and observance are assured by their clear definition, cultural value, and by community support. By contrast, in Western society since the nature, form, content, duration and basis of friendship are left for friends to determine themselves, the relation allows people to define it freely and apply implicit sanctions of reciprocity to one another, to ensure that each fulfils the other's expectations without any institutional prescriptions of form, content or limit.

Comparable reciprocities characterize patron-client relations in certain societies, although those reciprocities are usually asymmetrical. In the societies of feudal Europe, patron-client relations were heavily institutional, unequal and sometimes elaborately extended by placing the vassal of a vassal under the liege lord of his lord, thus generating pyramidal structures of political accountability and authority. In other societies, though institutional, asymmetrical and culturally sanctioned, patron-client relationships are less formal and legalistic. In much of Latin America patron-client relations seem pervasive, even in such officially impersonal structures as the bureaucracy and army. In many other societies, such personalistic relations may also interfere with an organization's commitments to impersonal and efficient operation. Most patron-client ensembles are strictly quasi-groups, since the various clients only associate indirectly with one another and are coordinated in action by virtue of their common allegiance to the patron; but not all such quasi-groups are equally reliable units, since the other loyalties and interests of their members may conflict. Nonetheless when mobilized and directed by the patron for limited periods and specific goals, they are often effective action-sets. Action-sets of a different kind and base appear vividly in football games, as groupings of players emerge and dissolve to exploit or create opportunities for their teams. Like kindreds, patron-client action-sets are egocentric quasi-groups of people linked indirectly to one another by direct individual ties to some central person. They illustrate the variable institutionalization of roles and dyadic relations in intermediate units of differing base and kind.

Intermediate units are essential elements of every society; but the statuses and roles that together define the dyadic relations of their members, whether institutional or not, must be sufficiently consistent for the intermediate social unit they constitute to be structurally viable. Likewise the operational requisites and entailments of that intermediate unit, whether institutional or not, should be consistent with the requisites and entailments of the society's corporate organization which includes and regulates it. If not, either those structures will conflict, or, being incompatible and inconsistent with the society's corporate organization, the intermediate unit will be either anti-institutional or non-institutional. That presently seems to be the situation in many and perhaps most modern societies which have so many incompatible commitments that they are institutionally torn and disharmonic; for example, Italy, torn between the state, the Catholic church and Mafia; or Iraq and Iran, in opposing directions; Israel, Britain, the USA, the ex-USSR, Yugoslavia, Brazil, much of Latin America, India and most "developing" Third World societies. In preindustrial society, comparable inconsistencies can be seen in the institutional orders of ancient Greece and Rome, among the Kachin, the Murngin, the Swat Pathans and Tuareg, the Kaingang, Tiv, Tallensi or Ibo, as well as feudal society in Europe, China and Japan.

To retain validity and perpetuate itself despite such anti-institutional structures and processes, given their mutual contradictions, the society's corporate framework must either suppress, neutralize or destroy the anti-institutional units mobilized against it, or accommodate them without losing control, as the U.S.A. has for generations accommodated the KKK, Mafia, Communist Party, and other organizations committed to subvert its institutional order. In short, for a population to constitute a society having a valid and inclusive framework of corporate organization, social units at all differing levels of structure, from the micro level of status, role, person and dyad through the intermediate to the macro level, both corporate and non-corporate, must have sufficient structural consistency to allow them to co-exist and operate routinely and efficiently together. For that to be possible, the requisites and entailments of different kinds of social units included in the structure must be sufficiently consistent to exclude those contradictions and oppositions that would either dislocate or disrupt and frustrate the satisfactory articulation of other structures. Such requirements indicate the limiting conditions that together define the fully harmonious society as an ideal type.

Just as the roles and statuses integrated in dyads must be compatible for those units to operate, so the dyads included in triads must be minimally congruous for those triads to be viable. So too must the various kinds of intermediate unit, group or quasi-group to which those dyads and triads belong, as well as the society's macro units, non-corporate and corporate, that coordinate and subsume the intermediate units and their components, directly or otherwise. While a perfectly consistent or integrated societal structure would exclude endogenous change, the tensions and problems produced by structural inconsistency stimulate adjustments and developments within societies that generate their accommodation and internal change as well as external adaptation.

Just as the lesser units that constitute them presuppose the cultural and structural consistency of their components, the status-role complex, dyadic relations and intermediate units, so too the diverse kinds of macro unit in which the population is enrolled, to be viable, must also be consistent, not only with one another but also with the overarching framework of corporate organization that provides the regulative order.

While some macro units have organizations to coordinate their members and resources for common action, others such as age-grades, income groups, social classes, dispersed communities, regional, ethnic or racial divisions do not. Yet others such as political parties, trade unions, professional associations, occupational groups and various religious congregations, have the extensive organization required to mobilize their memberships and pursue common courses of action. Aggregates that have such organization also have the other attributes of corporations, and so form part of the corporate organization that regulates the society. To discuss these further, it is first necessary to review the distinctive features of corporations and the conditions of corporate organization. Having already published much on those topics, I shall try to do so briefly.

CHAPTER 3

MAPPING
SOCIAL
STRUCTURE

1. SOCIAL UNITS

Like the preceding diagrams, Chart D uses the genealogical framework
familiar to anthropologists to align the principal categories we shall use
to classify the different kinds of membership units that constitute societies
whatever their levels of complexity, development and differentiation.
While Charts A to C illustrate the upper rows of Chart D, the lowest row
lists some instances of each sub-class. Briefly, Chart D indicates the
hierarchic order of analytical categories that we shall use to classify and
study social units of all kinds.

Within the category of social units the primary distinction is that
between corporations and non-corporate units, as shown in Chart D. At
this stage it is sufficient to distinguish corporations from other kinds of
social unit by the following requisites: their presumptive perpetuity,

CHART D
Social Units Grouped By Size and Institutional Status

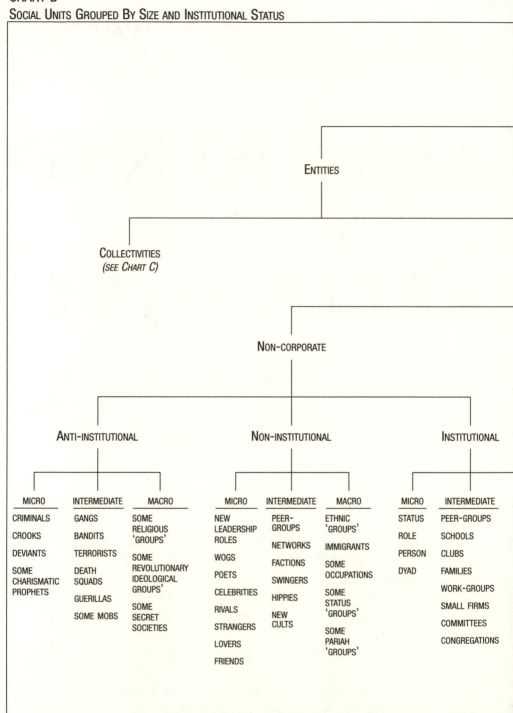

ENTITIES

COLLECTIVITIES
(SEE CHART C)

NON-CORPORATE

ANTI-INSTITUTIONAL

MICRO	INTERMEDIATE	MACRO
CRIMINALS	GANGS	SOME RELIGIOUS 'GROUPS'
CROOKS	BANDITS	
DEVIANTS	TERRORISTS	SOME REVOLUTIONARY IDEOLOGICAL GROUPS'
SOME CHARISMATIC PROPHETS	DEATH SQUADS	
	GUERILLAS	SOME SECRET SOCIETIES
	SOME MOBS	

NON-INSTITUTIONAL

MICRO	INTERMEDIATE	MACRO
NEW LEADERSHIP ROLES	PEER-GROUPS	ETHNIC 'GROUPS'
WOGS	NETWORKS	IMMIGRANTS
POETS	FACTIONS	SOME OCCUPATIONS
CELEBRITIES	SWINGERS	
RIVALS	HIPPIES	SOME STATUS 'GROUPS'
STRANGERS	NEW CULTS	
LOVERS		SOME PARIAH 'GROUPS'
FRIENDS		

INSTITUTIONAL

MICRO	INTERMEDIATE
STATUS	PEER-GROUPS
ROLE	SCHOOLS
PERSON	CLUBS
DYAD	FAMILIES
	WORK-GROUPS
	SMALL FIRMS
	COMMITTEES
	CONGREGATIONS

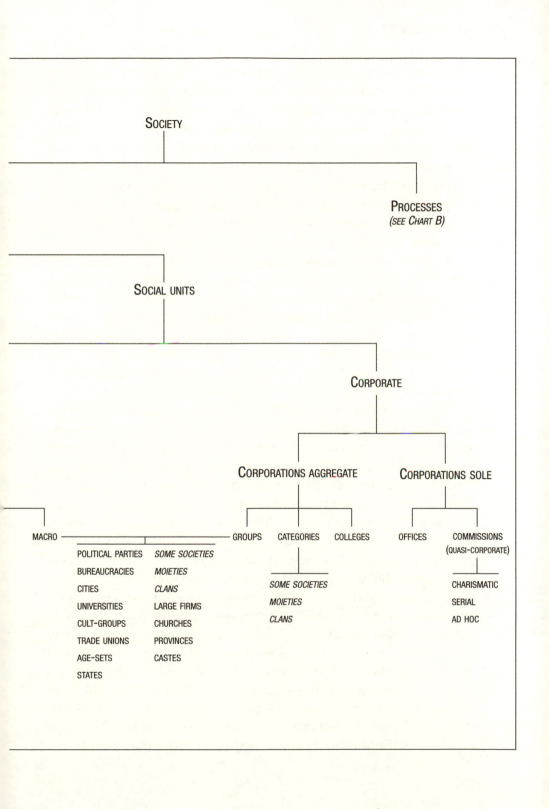

SOCIETY

PROCESSES
(SEE CHART B)

SOCIAL UNITS

CORPORATE

CORPORATIONS AGGREGATE   CORPORATIONS SOLE

MACRO   GROUPS   CATEGORIES   COLLEGES   OFFICES   COMMISSIONS
                                                             (QUASI-CORPORATE)

POLITICAL PARTIES   *SOME SOCIETIES*
BUREAUCRACIES   *MOIETIES*   *SOME SOCIETIES*   CHARISMATIC
CITIES   *CLANS*   *MOIETIES*   SERIAL
UNIVERSITIES   LARGE FIRMS   *CLANS*   AD HOC
CULT-GROUPS   CHURCHES
TRADE UNIONS   PROVINCES
AGE-SETS   CASTES
STATES

closure, unique identities, and determinate membership at any point in time, four characteristics that together presuppose their institutionalization. All corporations are therefore institutional units, excluding the quasi-corporation that best represents the antithesis, namely, the unique, unprecedented and self-authenticating charismatic leadership identified by Weber, which however can only perpetuate itself by transformation into the institutional status of an office. With the exception of that anomaly, all corporations are explicitly institutional. Nonetheless, since such units as the IRA, the Mafia and the KKK, being corporate, are also institutional, despite their pronounced anti-institutional character and activities, it is best to distinguish the class of corporations and quasi-corporations from other kinds of social unit, as well as collectivities, which being uniformly non-institutional, are polar opposites of corporations. As the double alignments in Chart D indicate, several large or macro institutional units, such as cities, castes, trade unions and states, are also corporate groups, while others, such as clans and moieties, are corporate categories; and some societies are corporate groups, while others are categories.

Of non-corporate social units, while many are firmly institutional, others lack institutional status, definition and collective sanctions; and yet others are so opposed to the prevailing institutional order or some sufficient sector of it as to be clearly anti-institutional. These distinctions are indicated at the next level of the chart, along with those between corporations aggregate and sole, which are discussed below.

I shall treat pluralities with three or more members as groups or aggregates, in contrast to dyadic pairs and such elementary units as persons, statuses and roles; but while some aggregates have large extensive memberships and spheres of operation, sometimes transecting an entire society, others, such as the family and work-group, though highly important, are units of lesser size and span. To take account of those differences, I shall classify non-corporate units of any institutional status by their relative size and span, as micro-units, i.e., those with one or at most two members, as intermediate units of limited size, duration and span, and macro-units of greater size and range, the two latter sub-classes being aggregates. Accordingly at the next level of Chart D, non-corporate social units of anti-institutional, non-institutional, and institutional kinds are sub-classified further by size and span as micro, intermediate and macro, while the categories of quasi-corporations and corporations aggregate and sole are subdivided respectively into groups, colleges and categories, offices and commissions. As aggregates of people who share common and distinctive characteristics, the social categories like clans, moieties and Nuer age-sets which are closed, presumed to be perpetual, and have unique identities and determinate membership, are corporations, in contrast to other social categories, such as classes or age-grades which, being collectivities, lack both closure and determinate membership, unlike those social categories which, though perduring structures, are non-institutional, all corporate categories are fully institutionalized. For lack of organization, both corporate categories and social categories are unable to act in unison. For convenience, Chart D lists examples of both the anti-institutional and non-institutional aggregates before the institutional, since many of the largest institutional units are corporate groups and categories, as it indicates.

The lowest level of the chart lists various examples of each preceding sub-category of non-corporate social units, institutional or other, citing statuses, roles, dyads and persons as institutional micro-units; families, peer groups, work groups, schools and clubs as units of intermediate size; and certain organizations like firms and trade unions, cult-groups, churches, age-sets and castes as institutional macro-units, before listing comparable examples of micro, macro and intermediate units of non-institutional and anti-institutional kinds, thus completing our classification of the differing kinds of non-corporate social unit or bounded concrete structure we shall find in human societies, both historic and contemporary. Examples of large institutional units which are either corporate groups or categories include political parties, universities, bureaucracies, cities, provinces, states, societies, moieties and clans. This dual identity or status is indicated by their alignments in the chart. However, given their variety and structural significance, Chart D does not provide a comparable list of corporations, since those are best discussed separately. Neither does the chart attempt to list all the various events whose incidence or rates indicate prevailing patterns of mass behaviors, such as natality, marriage, divorce, mortality, crime, suicide, bankruptcy, literacy and migration, or other quantifiable modes of mass behavior that can easily be made to yield rates per annum and per thousand of population.

These comprehensive typologies of corporate and non-corporate social units, the latter reclassified as micro, macro and intermediate on one hand, and institutional, non-institutional or anti-institutional on the other, are regrouped and aligned differently in Chart E. That chart presents the conceptual structure of the classification as a matrix created by the variable institutionalization of social units on the one hand, and by their variable size on the other, the different classes of social units being distributed on the chart according to their size and institutional status, which excludes collectivities together with all kinds of "mass behavior".

Chart E classifies social units of all types and size, corporate and non-corporate, micro, macro and intermediate, by the intensity of their institutionalization in four levels, namely, heavily institutional, normally so, and weakly so, non-institutional, and anti-institutional. At the heavily institutional extreme, the chart places those units that generally have the strongest structure of positive and negative collective prescriptions and sanctions to regulate the activities and relations of their members. At the opposite extreme it places various statuses, relations and groupings that, despite their prevalence in many societies, formally lack institutional prescriptions and collective sanctions. In between the chart places those units that differ in the intensity of their institutional prescription and enforcement. However, the chart also indicates that units of several different kinds vary widely in the levels of their institutionalization in different social contexts and periods as an expression of cultural differences.

Some examples of intermediate units with such features, most of which are not true groups, are included in Chart E; for example, kindreds and other egocentered aggregates of consanguineal kin. While inactive and marginal in many societies, such units are firmly institutional in others. However, when the diverse relations of close kin with the central ego are not coherently aligned, expectations of their several rights and obligations may generate conflict between them, as Jules Henry found among the Kaingang of Brazil, due to inadequate definition and resulting inconsistencies of their kinship roles.

As examples in Chart E illustrate, excluding corporations, social units of the same general kind may differ widely in their institutional status, or in the intensity of their institutionalization in different societies, in the same society at different points in time, and in differing social contexts.

CHART E

SOCIAL UNITS BY SIZE AND INSTITUTIONAL STATUS

UNITS	INTENSITY OF INSTITUTIONALIZATION				ANTI-INSTITUTIONAL
	INSTITUTIONAL ←---------------------------→ NON-INSTITUTIONAL				
	VERY STRONG	STRONG	WEAK	NIL	
MICRO	←------- OFFICES* -------→			Celebrity	Witch
		←-- AD HOC* --→	←----- Poet	Heretic
			←--- CHARISMATIC* ------------→		Atheist
		COMMISSIONS*		Dropout	Deviant
				WOG	Crook
		←--- SERIAL* --→		Coon	Criminal
	←------- Statuses -------------→			Friend	Swindler
	←------- Roles ----------------→				Black marketeer
	←------- Dyads ----------------→			Lover	
	Blood Brothers				
	←--- Clientage -----→			←-- Person --→	
	←--- Kin -----------→			←-- Colleagues --→	
	←--- Affines -------→			←-- Prophet -----→	
	←--- Partners -----→				
INTERMEDIATE	←--- COLLEGES* ---→			←--- Networks ---→	Gangs
		←------ Kindreds -----------→			Outlaws
	←--- Family --→				Guerrillas
			←--- Peer groups -----→		Terrorists
			←--- Cliques ---→		
		←--- Work-groups --→			
				←--- Communes ---→	Lynching parties
		←--- Teams -------→			Death squads
	←---- Schools -→		←--- Quasi-groups --→		Some mobs
			←-- Audiences --→		Hippies
		←----- Factions -----→			
	←--- Small firms ----→				
	←-- Thrift clubs --→				
MACRO	CORPORATE CATEGORIES*	←-- CLANS ---→			Organized crowds
		SERFS			Organized mobs
	←------ SLAVES ------→				Rebels
	←--- SOCIETIES ----→				Revolutionary groups
	←----- CASTES -----→				
	←--- AGE-SETS ---→				Some secret societies
	CORPORATE GROUPS*				
	←--- ARMIES ----→				MAFIA
		←----- LINEAGES ---→			IRA
	UNIVERSITIES				Triad
	←--- GUILDS ----→				
	←--- TRADE UNIONS ---→				
	←--- RELIGIOUS ORDERS --→				
	←--- POLITICAL PARTIES --→				Infidels
	←-- LARGE FIRMS --→				
	←--- STATES ---→				
	←--- CHURCHES ---→				

*Upper-case denotes corporations. For other examples, see CHART G.

For example, while some local communities are constituted as closed perpetual corporate groups, others are not; while some quasi-groups have institutional status, however weak, others have none; and some are even anti-institutional. The same point holds for public demonstrations, some of which are institutional and positively sanctioned while others are not, and some are anti-institutional. In other words, in differing cultures, and even in the same society in different contexts, social units of the same general kind, such as occupational or religious groups, may differ in their degrees and kinds of institutional status.

As schematic representations of the institutional status of different kinds of social unit, Charts D and E ignore the different processes of mass behavior and forms of collective behavior. However, both charts cite various forms of collective behavior which are anti-institutional phenomena at intermediate or macro level. These include events that may either express group action or collective behavior, for example, crowds, mobs and riots, demonstrations, marches, social movements, revolts and certain categories of industrial action.

2. CORPORATIONS

Of membership units, as we have seen, the most firmly institutionalized are corporations. Accordingly in Chart D corporations are set apart from all other social units, some of which are non-institutional and others anti-institutional, even though they differ importantly among themselves in the degrees and modes of their institutionalization.

As a class of social units, corporations have several essential and distinctive features. Even though in human society nothing ever is perpetual, they are presumed to be so by the population. Except in moments of grave social breakdown, in all societies men presume the perpetuity of certain social units, structures and conditions, including that of the society itself and the state, if there is one. For example, most persons now alive as well as everyone in the U.S.A., presume that the American state will continue indefinitely, i.e., that it is perpetual. So likewise, this university is presumed by its members, the city and the community at large to be perpetual. In its day so too were the Roman Empires in both the East and West, though time has proved otherwise. History is the great waste-basket of such "perpetual" structures as societies, empires, states, regimes, churches, dynasties, universities, legal, economic, and almost every corporation. Nonetheless, as Plato and Malinowski saw, men need such myths or postulates to create and order their societies, so they may live in peace and security. Perhaps the most necessary of such essential myths is the presumption that the society, its corporations and major regulative units are perpetual, despite all the historical evidence against it.

For any social unit to be the object of such presumptions, we must first know its distinct identity, especially if it is one of a class of similar units. Hence, to presume the perpetuity of such corporations as the state, a medieval guild or an African patrilineage, each unit must be conceived as unique, having its own distinct identity, much as the American presidency or the presidency of this university is unique, despite being members of classes of similar units. However, for any item to be unique it must first be bounded or closed. Hence, if the unit is social, despite the mortality and mobility of its members, it must have modes of recruitment that guarantee an assured continuity and, at any point in time, a determinate membership. Together these are the four formal requisites of corporations of all kinds. Their closure, by the rules through which they recruit their members and automatically exclude all others, identifies their members as a definite body which is collectively unique. People may presume or deny and reject the perpetuity of such units; but if they are endowed with corporate status and regulative authority as sources of those norms and sanctions on which the institutional order depends, collective assumptions of their perpetuity are an essential prerequisite for the validity of their culture and social order.

To illustrate: the U.S.A. elects a president every four years, one of two final candidates. Each election ends a cycle of the process by which the country recruits its president, who, in due course, takes up that office and is its sole incumbent for the years of his presidency. As a concrete unit, like any other office at any time, the presidency has only one occupant, one member, though being presumptively perpetual, over the centuries it has had many more, the current president being merely forty-second on the list. Interestingly, like other offices, this office is embedded in and identified with two much larger corporations or corporate complexes, the American state and the American society, of which it is the supreme executive. Outside the state, which cannot exist outside the society, the presidency has no existence. Other societies and states may have their presidents or other kinds of heads of state; but many societies lack both the state or any alternative institution or supreme executive such as that of paramount chief, and differ accordingly from groups in lacking the organisation prerequisite for common deliberation and action. Though corporate units, such societies are not groups but aggregates of another kind, namely, categories, since their people share a common culture, institutional framework, name, locus, history, identity, boundaries and normally a common language. African segmentary lineage societies, like Australian aboriginal societies, with their complex marriage systems, are familiar examples of such categorical societies without the state.

Chart F classifies corporations by their memberships and their attributes, as corporations aggregate and sole, and as perfect or imperfect corporations, using those terms to mean complete and incomplete as in Latin. The second diagram sets out the essential four formal properties or requisites of all corporations, *perfect* and *imperfect*. It lists the four substantive properties or requisites of all perfect corporations, that is, of all that are capable of acting independently as units on their own. The first classification in Chart F distinguishes those corporations that have all the formal and substantive requisites or properties listed as 'perfect' or complete, from others, like the corporate category and the commission, that lack one or more of those eight attributes, and differ accordingly. Indeed, properly speaking, although they generally operate like corporations, all three varieties of commissions are properly speaking *quasi-corporations*, since neither can claim the perpetuity requisite for corporations, and one variety, the serialized commission, also lacks uniqueness. Nonetheless, given their regulatory positions and roles, and the ease with which they are transformed into perfect corporations by acquiring the necessary substantive attributes, I discuss commissions and corporate categories together with the various kinds of perfect corporation, the office, group and college. As anomalies, they demonstrate the structural adaptability of corporate organization as the essential foundation of social order and cohesion.

Social science inherited from common law the old distinction between corporations aggregate, that is, between those with two or more members, and corporations sole, that is, those having only one occupant at a time, typically such offices as the papacy, presidency or kingship.

CHART F
REQUISITES AND TYPES OF CORPORATIONS

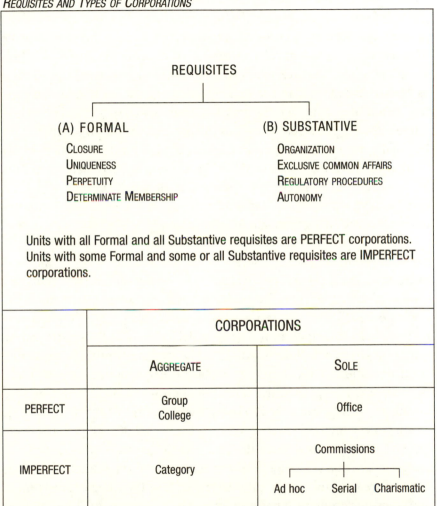

REQUISITES

(A) FORMAL
CLOSURE
UNIQUENESS
PERPETUITY
DETERMINATE MEMBERSHIP

(B) SUBSTANTIVE
ORGANIZATION
EXCLUSIVE COMMON AFFAIRS
REGULATORY PROCEDURES
AUTONOMY

Units with all Formal and all Substantive requisites are PERFECT corporations. Units with some Formal and some or all Substantive requisites are IMPERFECT corporations.

	CORPORATIONS	
	AGGREGATE	SOLE
PERFECT	Group College	Office
IMPERFECT	Category	Commissions — Ad hoc / Serial / Charismatic

Following Maine (1861) and legal practice, for generations social scientists wrote as if there were only two varieties of corporation, namely, offices and corporate groups. However, in his wide-ranging review of types of political organization, Max Weber isolated a third kind of perfect corporation, the *college*, to describe such perpetual councils or standing committees as the Congress of the USA, Parliament in the United Kingdom, the Roman Senate, the Athenian Ecclesia, the College of

Cardinals or councils of aldermen, elders, lineage heads, and *panchayats*, all of which deliberate public issues and help to regulate the corporate groups of which they are part. These three kinds of perfect corporations have all eight formal and substantive properties, and are therefore capable of such continuous or discontinuous independent action as their situations allow However, to appreciate fully their structural significance as the basic framework and central regulative agencies of human societies, we should also consider the two varieties of imperfect corporation, namely, the corporate category and the commission, both of which may be rapidly converted into perfect corporations as groups or offices either by their own independent actions, or alternatively by heteronomous investment with the necessary powers and attributes. They may with equal ease be created by actions that revoke or suspend the relevant attributes of extant corporate groups and offices.

Besides categories, corporations include such presumptively perpetual *groups* as lineages, states, local communities, guilds, churches, universities, trade unions, political parties, many other kinds of secondary groups, and such *offices* as the papacy, presidency, crown, and numberless lesser positions. *Colleges* as a variety of corporations are illustrated by parliaments, municipal councils, the judicial benches of supreme courts, senates, legislatures, church synods, and other presumptively perpetual regulative councils or committees. Colleges such as councils of elders are the deliberative organs of the corporate groups to which their members belong, the college membership being always a minority of the corporate group from which it is drawn. While all colleges, offices and corporate groups have the formal requisites that constitute corporations, *corporate categories* are in a sense the purest instance of the type, since those four features are their only corporate attributes. Like the category, the college and corporate group each has several members, whereas an office can have only one at any time. Unlike corporate categories, colleges, offices and corporate groups have comprehensive organizations, regulatory procedures, exclusive common affairs and the autonomy required to administer these affairs. The organization that distinguishes them from corporate categories is their common internal requisite, since it gives each of them as a unit capacities for continuous or discontinuous positive action. Its organization is therefore the most essential and inalienable central common property for each of these units, and the most common important affair it has to administer. To administer their organizations and other common affairs, the college, office or corporate group all require appropriate procedures, autonomy and other essential resources.

3. COMMISSIONS

Having briefly described the four varieties of corporation, let us now review the important class of quasi-corporations, which contains commissions of three kinds. The kinds of commission illustrated by the officer ranks in modern military or civil bureaucracies consists of regulatory public roles that are neither unique nor perpetual, being instituted hierarchically and allocated to individuals explicitly as substitutable units of identical scope and form in one or other of the organization's ranked strata, each of which, like the structure as a whole, is conceptually of indefinite duration and extent. The hierarchic aggregate of such ranked indefinite series constitutes a distinctive kind of corporate group, perhaps best represented by modern armies and national bureaucracies.

To illustrate: when someone is commissioned as a captain, lieutenant or major, that commission is formally unique in that it attaches exclusively to the individual who receives it, but only as long as he continues to hold that rank. If he leaves the force or is promoted to some higher rank, that commission lapses as the holder gives it up and takes a new one; but while he holds it the officer is expected to undertake and perform all the duties required of that rank in any part of the organization to which they apply, the essential principle being to assure the mutual substitutability of all who hold commissions of the same rank, since such substitutions are frequently required in battle and other exigencies. However, unlike the office which persists after its holder leaves it, whatever the reason, these military commissions lapse when those to whom they were given cease to hold them. Hence, being prescriptively equivalent and substitutable, they are neither presumptively perpetual nor individually unique. They certainly neither claim perpetuity nor are so regarded, being dispensable elements in a hierarchic and essentially bureaucratic organization which, to implement the elaborate code that regulates its members' activities, organises them in ranked strata of diminishing autonomy and responsibility, and prescribes the equivalence of all who hold the same commission or rank. Simultaneously, it ensures that those appointments can be multiplied and extended indefinitely as necessary without compromising the organization's structure or efficiency. The civil services of modern states all employ this kind of organization, as do universities, which commission faculty as lecturers or professors, the ranked strata of modern judiciaries, and so on. So do the managerial staffs of multinational or transnational corporations and other large firms, the Roman Catholic Church, the West African Poro society, the Communist party of the former USSR and other Marxist-Leninist parties with their *apparatchiki*, and so on. In short this variety of ranked serialized commission is the essential element in the structure of all large-scale perduring modern bureaucratic organizations which have to coordinate large populations and diverse operations through centralized rule-regulated hierarchies of commissioned personnel. Of all three varieties of commissions, being the essential elements of centralized bureaucratic organizations, those that constitute ranked series of identical units are the most precisely defined and systematically rule-regulated. Their significance in the bureaucracies of which they are part is neatly indicated by the distinction between the commissioned officers and non-commissioned ranks of armies, between the established and other posts in a civil service, and between priests and lay brethren in a church.

There is a second type of commission which may or may not be unique, but which is not presumed to be perpetual. Commissions of this category are illustrated by such charismatic capacities as prophecy, sainthood, shamanism and other exemplary modes of leadership. Unlike the military or bureaucratic commissions discussed above, which are established by institutional procedures within a major corporate structure, these commissions are always self-assumed, often anti-institutional, and most often self-created and self-authenticating. Often also these novel, self-authenticating commissions provide the leadership and catalysts of major upheavals such as the French or Russian revolutions, or proclaim and lead new religions, cargo or messianic cults, ceasing to be anti-institutional as they institute the new order. They are therefore of special interest to students of change at collective levels of social organization, and frequently convert collectivities into institutional social units.

Finally, in centralized societies, governmental bodies endowed with appropriate authority may create unique commissions when necessary to undertake specific tasks, after which they cease to exist. Such commissions as presidential or parliamentary commissions of enquiry differ from the two preceding types in their uniqueness, self-liquidating character, the authority to devise their own working procedures, and their typical constitution as committees. Moreover, as we shall see, in many societies private persons may also create commissions for certain culturally approved purposes. We should therefore distinguish such public or privately appointed commissions from the self-assumed charismatic variety that figures so prominently in both traditional and modern societies.

Commissions of this third category are created by those having the authority to deal with specific situations or problems that need urgent attention or resolution. Typically in centralized states, the public agencies authorised to create such commissions are the supreme executive or legislative bodies at the national or relevant administrative level. Such presidential commissions as the Warren Commission that investigated the assassination of President John Kennedy, and the Royal or Parliamentary Commissions that undertake special assignments and investigations for the British Parliament and government, are familiar examples. So too are those papal envoys commissioned to investigate or deal with some specific situation or problem of the church, commissions appointed by municipal councils or state governors in federal polities to deal with local issues, and the agents assigned responsibility by paramount chiefs in traditional societies to deal with specific exigencies.

In some societies that lack such central structures and tribunals to settle disputes peacefully, men engaged in disputes that could lead to open conflict were culturally authorized to commission one or more others to investigate and arbitrate the disputed issue to avoid recourse to violence. Among the Yurok Indians of California, according to A. L. Kroeber, disputants selected men of good repute to act as "Crossers", so called since they had continuously to "cross" between the disputants to gather and investigate their accounts of the affair they had to arbitrate. Each disputant having commissioned his Crosser, the two Crossers would gather, sift and discuss the relevant evidence, and then jointly decide where the fault lay and what should be transferred as damages to compensate the injured party, when and how. Having been freely chosen by the disputants to settle their dispute, the Crossers' decision could not be challenged by either party. Once the decision was announced and implemented, their task having been performed, their commissions lapsed. In like fashion among the Ifugao of Luzon in the Philippines (Barton, 1919), another acephalous society based on dispersed groups of bilateral kin, to settle their disputes and avoid violence, men would frequently select and commission someone with sufficient power and influence to investigate and decide their case, and enforce the decision. They did so by relating their grievance and telling their story to the man they had selected, the *monkalun* as he was called, asking him to administer the dispute. Having adequately investigated the other party's version of the dispute, the *monkalun* would declare his decision and levy such fines or damages on the offender as he deemed fit. If those payments were not made by the set date, the *monkalun* would then lead his followers against the debtor's home to collect the debt himself. Having transferred the compensation to the injured party and so completed his commission, the arbitrator ceased to be *monkalun* until someone else in due course reinvested him with that status.

Among the North American Indians, outstanding braves who wished to raid their enemies would announce when they planned to set out, and set up their standards in some public place where those who wished to join their war party could assemble. Once the group set off, the man who initiated the raid had final command and responsibility as the group captain, having been invested with that commission by the warriors who joined his troop. On returning from the raid, the war party dissolved and with it the captain's military commission. Like the Ifugao *monkalun*, the raid leader immediately resumed his former status. Acephalous and centralised societies both have appropriate institutional machinery to create *ad hoc* commissions to deal with exigencies that need prompt attention and action. Sometimes, as with the Yurok Crossers and the Warren Commission, the task is entrusted to two or more persons who act as a single unit. In Western societies when private citizens make wills and appoint executors to ensure their performance, those chosen have been explicitly commissioned for that task. Sometimes, as happened to the group initially commissioned to plan and supervise the restoration of fertility in the Tennessee Valley, when the task for which a commission was created is recognised as chronic, it may be perpetuated by conversion into an office or college to continue its work indefinitely. In short, *ad hoc* commissions to deal with specific matters or problems occur at various levels in society and are institutionalized by culture in diverse ways, being created to handle both personal and public political emergencies.

In different cultural contexts, such as ancient Rome and feudal Japan, successful military and political leaders, having generated their own commissions and power by their achievements, appointed themselves chief servants or supreme executives of their divine emperors. In Renaissance Italy, strife-torn city states that sought internal peace, order, and security sometimes chose celebrated *condottieri* to govern them as *podesta*, following the custom of the Roman republic where in moments of great crisis the senate would commission some distinguished man to act as dictator and "save the Republic", as Cicero did from Catiline. Like the self-created charismatic variety, such *ad hoc* commissions occur in centralized and acephalous societies alike, irrespective of their developmental levels, but unlike the charismatic commission, these *ad hoc* ones are always legitimate when appointed by those with the authority to do so. However, being elements of large stratified bureaucratic or hierocratic corporations, commissions organized serially in hierarchic strata such as military ranks, cannot occur in acephalous societies that lack such structures.

4. CORPORATIONS AND CHANGE

I classify these three types of commission as quasi-corporations, and group them with corporations, since these various types of unit between them exercise all public regulatory powers, and they are all reciprocally reversible. While most commissions lack two, and all at least one, of the essential formal requisites of perfect corporations, in their constitution and operation alike, they approximate the latter so closely that it is appropriate to treat them as quasi-corporations, and to consider both kinds of unit together, in order to determine their similarities, differences, and relations with other parts of the corporate organization and the non-corporate social structure.

As indicated in Chart F, charismatic self-created commissions are one of three kinds of commission that differ in various ways but share several important attributes, namely, all are regulatory, though in different spheres and ways; all are closed by their specific requisites, and so have a determinate membership at any point in time; but while some, such as the commission of the Shehu Usman of Gobir and Sokoto, like those of prophets and outstanding political leaders such as Mahatma Gandhi, Adolf Hitler, Winston Churchill and Napoleon Bonaparte, are clearly unique, others differ, except that each commission, being ascribed to a given individual, is uniquely identified with that person and, at least initially, is therefore not presumptively perpetual.

Thus, of these seven kinds of unit, the office, college, corporate group and category, and the three varieties of commission, only corporate categories lack positive regulatory capacities. However, precisely because they are defined negatively by rules that regulate their members' conduct with one another and with outsiders, such units are highly significant for collective regulation. Moreover, as we shall see, both corporate categories and self-created charismatic commissions are often pivotal to revolutionary structural change.

As indicated above, the critical difference between a group and a category is the latter's lack of the essential organization without which its members can neither plan nor undertake coordinated activities together on any regular basis. In consequence, whereas groups, whether corporate or not, are the principal agents of collective action at all levels of human society, categories, whether firmly closed and corporate or not, are incapable of collective action as units, even though some of their members may form groups and act together. Accordingly relatively small numbers of men organised as groups can easily overrun and dominate much larger populations that lack such organization and therefore cannot offer united resistance. That difference has enabled relatively small numbers of Europeans to overrun and govern much larger numbers of people in various continents. In the Caribbean slave colonies those differences also enabled small numbers of white slave owners and free men to dominate slave populations many times as large. However, for such regimes to persist, as the *sine qua non* of minority rule, the subordinate category must be denied any inclusive or effective organizations. Thus, when the Roman plebs transformed themselves from a category to a group by appointing their ten tribunes and creating a council, the patrician minority who had formerly governed Rome, though challenged, did not directly confront them, but thereafter took care to cultivate plebeian support and avoid their united opposition, so long as Rome remained republican. That event laid the basis of the divided imperium in republican Rome between the Senate and *Concilium plebis.*

According to Titus Livy, in 439 BC, the Roman plebs, having suffered long and severely from the patricians who monopolized political authority and public offices in the Senate, and who reserved for themselves access to the patrician Law of the Twelve Tables which regulated everyone, convened at their temple on the Aventine Hill and swore a collective oath to establish a council of ten tribunes, whom they promptly elected, each authorized independently to veto senatorial decrees and other official decisions on behalf of all. By that act the Roman plebs simultaneously created and instituted the tribunate, a college of ten offices filled by periodic election, to review and uphold their interests. They thereby independently converted their collectivity from a corporate category or section of the Roman people, distinguished by the political and legal disabilities mentioned above, into a corporate group endowed with the substantive requisites of group action, namely, organization, exclusive common affairs, appropriate regulatory procedures, and the requisite autonomy. The Roman plebs, having been earlier constituted as a presumptively perpetual division of the Roman people, like a caste, by patrician prohibitions against their citizenship and intermarriage, common worship or political and legal status, following that historic meeting on the Aventine to elect and authorize their tribunes, had formally under their council the same corporate status as their patrician rulers organized by their senate. Both were corporate groups.

In unusual circumstances, self-created charismatic commissions may also be transformed by their holders into offices. However, efforts by others to achieve such transformations after the charismatic leader's death often fail, as happened with Oliver Cromwell, Benito Mussolini and Adolf Hitler. An example of the successful transformation of a charismatic commission into an office occurred at and with the foundation of the Sokoto caliphate by Usuman dan Fodio (Othman ibn Fudi), a Fulani religious leader of Gobir in what is now Northwestern Nigeria. Over many years, by his teaching, personality and various miracles, Usuman had created for himself a unique commission as the outstanding religious leader of his age in the Central Sudan, and accordingly had a large following of devout Muslims, to the annoyance of the Hausa chief of

Gobir. In 1804 A.D. when the inevitable confrontation developed, in a public assembly of his followers, the Shehu appointed himself Caliph of the Believers (*Amir el-Mu'munin*), much as Napoleon crowned himself Emperor. He thereby converted the commission he had created into the presumptively perpetual office of caliph, which persisted until 1903, when the British overran the caliphate of Sokoto. By assuming the office of caliph, the Shehu simultaneously reconstituted his amorphous community of followers, or *jema'a*, hitherto an amorphous collectivity and as such non-institutional, into the corporate group or community of Muslims.

In an opposite style and with strictly secular juridical authority, President Roosevelt in the thirties converted a committee set up by the Federal Government to oversee the conservation and development of the Tennessee Valley into a statutory corporation, the Tennessee Valley Authority, with perpetual responsibilities for the area's ecology. In the Americas, Africa and elsewhere, European conquest and colonization provide many examples of the opposite kind of conversion process by which populations previously organized as corporate groups under such rulers as the Sapa Inca, the Aztec emperor, King of Dahomey, Emir of Zinder or the Asantehene, the supreme chief of the Ashanti, were abruptly decapitated and transformed into corporate categories by the abolition of their central supreme offices and simultaneous elimination of the essential organization without which the people could not act as a unit on their own to manage their common affairs or pursue their common interests. In similar fashion, the Sokoto caliphate which the Shehu Usuman had founded, ceased to exist and split into its various parts, when defeated and overrun by the British in 1903.

Together corporations furnish the bounding collective structures that order social life, societies themselves being merely the most extensive types of corporations aggregate, sometimes constituted as corporate groups, sometimes as corporate categories. Moreover, in all cases the boundaries between societies coincide with differences in the structures of their corporate organization. In short, to analyse continuities or change in societal macro-structures, we can usefully employ these conceptions of corporations, particularly since their presumptive perpetuity identifies such units as the primary and indispensable persistent concrete structures of all societies. Any changes of their type, bases, properties or articulations may therefore entail significant structural changes in the units affected and in the societies of which they are part.

Corporations are therefore especially strategic foci for studies of major processes of social change; firstly, because they provide the central contexts and instruments of collective regulation and include all regulatory social structures of maximal range, duration and scope; secondly, because, being explicitly established as perpetual units with immutable properties or estates, their bases, scope, autonomies and articulations together provide the most salient and reliable data on the society's macro-structure, and the most obvious indicators of its continuity or change. Thirdly, as corporations incorporate individuals and regulate their interactions, by distributing them in differentiated statuses and roles, their internal articulations can be analysed at the appropriate level as complexes or networks of dyadic relations among members who hold the same or differing statuses. Thus, methodologically uniform analyses of corporations, intermediate social units and such micro-units as roles should enrich and complement one another. Together they should therefore enable us to examine all levels and aspects of societies as "systems" and social units, corporate and other.

Societies endowed with such central regulatory structures as chiefship, kingship or presidential office and senates, parliaments or congressional bodies, are thereby constituted as perfect corporate groups able to act as units at any time. The central offices and/or colleges of such societies provide their essential organizational resources, being their supreme executives and deliberative bodies. We shall never find any office or college, however humble or exalted, that is not rooted in some corporate group as its executive or deliberative organ. Accordingly, when the Roman plebs established the tribunes and *concilium* as their representatives and executives, they simultaneously converted the plebeian order from a category into a corporate group.

Until then the plebs had remained a corporate category in the Roman state under the rule of the patrician senate and its officers, the consuls, praetors, aediles and others. At that early period the plebs were an order, a corporate category within a corporate group, the Roman state, in much the same way as women have constituted a corporate category in all human societies, having never had an exclusive comprehensive organization of their own through which they could all contest the conditions of male dominance. Besides women, who are probably the oldest, largest and most universal corporate category in human history, all societies, whether constituted as corporate groups by their organization or as corporate categories by their lack of it, often contain other corporate categories. Such are the Blacks, Hispanics and Amerindians in the USA, the serfs and villeins of European feudalism, unenfranchized majorities in preindustrial oligarchic states, slaves, native peoples and colonials in colonial America, Africa and the Far East, the Untouchables and Tribals in contemporary India, and Palestinian Arabs in Israel. Conversely, in any corporate category that has a large or scattered population, we shall frequently find local segments organized as corporate groups as, for example, were the serfs on a manor, slaves on a plantation, or the localized groups of clansmen among the Plateau Tonga of Zambia. In the heyday of the civil rights movement, Martin Luther King and his assistants in CORE, SNCC and other civil rights agencies nearly succeeded in bringing the many Black communities throughout the USA into a common organization and so uniting them. In consequence of the failure to do so before Dr. King's assassination, to this day the large dispersed population of Black Americans remains a corporate category incapable of exercising influence on public affairs commensurate with its size or need.

Since offices, like colleges, cannot exist outside the context of corporate groups, all aggregates that have a regulatory office, such as a chiefship or headship, are corporate groups. Corporate categories can never have an office, since that would automatically reconstitute them as corporate groups by providing the requisite organization. At most, then, members of a corporate category may group themselves locally or otherwise into discrete, unarticulated units, corporate or other, each with its own members and leaders. Alternately, for the guidance and leadership their members need, corporate categories may rely on such self-commissioned leaders as the Big Men of Melanesia provided for their communities, or the shamans of Siberia and North and South America for theirs. Such leaders achieve public recognition and influence by various means, but mainly by the unusual actions, secular or mystical, that endorse their self-created commissions with popular support. Typically, in acephalous societies having such institutions, at any moment we shall find several self-commissioned Big Men, shamans or military heroes competing for public support, so that while some enhance their personal renown, others lose favor and decline. Such was the situation of seers in ancient Israel, unlike prophets, who as the sole authentic religious voices of their age succeeded one another *seriatim* at intervals in contexts of crisis. Each of these outstanding spokesmen proclaimed and demonstrated their charismatic qualities as spokesmen of God, in much the same way that the Shehu Usuman dan Fodio, thirteen centuries after the Prophet Muhammad, created his unique commission among the people of Gobir and its environs by proclaiming and preaching Islam.

Offices, as perpetual statuses having only one occupant at any time, recruit the holders and regulate their performance by established rules and procedures, unlike those commissions that outstanding individuals create independently by their actions and the public faith in their abilities, which often repudiate authority and are clearly not subject to rules, being autonomous manifestations of their holders' charismatic powers. In like fashion the scope and range of a commission's activity, as well as the frequency and continuity of its exercise, are less predictable and regular than those of offices. Among the Masai, Kipsigis and other East African Nilo-Hamites, and in many pastoral Islamic societies, the most capable descendants of outstanding mediators may be informally selected by diffuse public choice to inherit and exercise the commissions created by their ancestors as *sa'ids* or *laibonak*, and so help those who seek it. Often also when a supreme royal office has been usurped or suppressed, as its legitimate heir, the claimant or pretender will exercise an unqualified commission among his people to recover and restore the office with their help. When commissions are transformed into offices and so perpetuated as unique statuses, the procedures, means and criteria by which their holders will be recruited, and the particular ends they must pursue, will reflect the primary aims, attributes and charismatic deeds of their creators as closely as the social context permits.

However misleading analytically, the anthropological contrast between centralized and acephalous or stateless societies reflects the differences between societies constituted as corporate groups by virtue of their central regulative organisations, namely, a supreme office and/or directing college, and others which, lacking such coextensive organization and regulative central authority, are corporate categories by virtue of their institutional, territorial, historic and other qualities, that is, unique and presumptively perpetual aggregates that have determinate memberships and distinctive common attributes. Nuer, Tallensi, Tiv and Gusii are familiar African examples of acephalous societies constituted as corporate categories. So too are such polycephalous societies as the Tikopia, Kachin, Trobriands and others whose populations, though sharing common institutional cultures, are politically subdivided by those institutions under two or more leaders. Just as women, youth or slaves, lacking the organization prerequisite for coordinated action, can undertake no common project and form corporate categories within societies, so too societies constituted as corporate categories by their institutional closure, presumed perpetuity, common characteristics and lack of coextensive organization, are unable to undertake common action, or even deliberation when threatened with enslavement, dispersal or extinction. Faced with such threats, the patrilineal Nuer of the Southern Sudan were unable to develop the organization prerequisite for common action, and were only mobilized above the level of their tribal divisions by a succession of charismatic prophets who emerged as in Israel at intervals, in response to acute recurrent societal crises and need.

In short, the typology of corporations and quasi-corporations embraces the various kinds of public regulative structures we shall find in societies of any kind, ecological base or developmental level. It also explains the basic differences between acephalous and centralized societies, namely, that the former are, by their lack of any inclusive or representative organization, constituted as inchoate corporate categories, while the latter as corporate groups are capable of autonomous activity to regulate their own affairs, and act aggressively or defend themselves against outsiders. The essential mechanisms through which collective action is planned, administered and implemented by societies organized as corporate groups or states are, separately or together, either their central executive offices or senior colleges, whereas, however occasional, the major organizing agencies of the acephalous societies are such unique charismatic commissions as those created by prophets in ancient Israel, among the Nuer, and in Gobir just over 200 years ago by the Shehu Usuman dan Fodio.

5. STRUCTURAL CONSISTENCY

To indicate the great variety and fundamental importance of corporations in human societies at all levels of development, in Chart G I have listed examples of the different kinds of corporations sole and aggregate, namely, offices, commissions of the types discussed above, and corporate groups, colleges, and corporate categories. While these examples are only a fraction of the universe, they should indicate the ubiquity, variety and value of corporate structures for the organization and operation of society.

In Chart G, corporate groups are classified by the principal criteria on which they are based, as local or residential, groups based on descent, shared beliefs, on occupation and other economic factors, or residually, those based on political and other factors. Perhaps we should also classify separately corporate groups based on status, education, age or other criteria. However, since most corporate groups are based on multiple criteria and have several interests, such classification merely illustrates their protean variety, diverse bases and differing concerns. For that reason on no account should the recruitment criteria by which these units are classified be interpreted as evidence of their functional specificity, since, as indicated above, all corporate groups are multifunctional, though all do not discharge the same set of functions equally and routinely as Parsons' A-G-I-L analysis of social action implies. For example, while lineage and family engage in physical and social reproduction, schools, monasteries, banks, factions, armies and other kinds of corporate groups do not. However, since societies cannot persist unless their functional requisites are maintained by the processes of their routine operation, given the highly variable distribution of such functional inputs among their structural units, instead of misdirecting our enquiry towards such functional aspects, it is more useful and rewarding to analyse the societal structure to determine the articulation and mutual consistency of its concrete components, since its elements and recurring processes should be mutually compatible for its structure to be operationally viable.

The overriding requisite of structural consistency among the components and processes of a common society is sufficiently broad to accommodate various discordances within the range of inconsistency its structure can tolerate as friction without disruption or decline. We must therefore determine the nature and limits of that range for each kind of

CHART G
CORPORATIONS BY TYPES AND BASES

CLASSES	TYPES	EXAMPLES

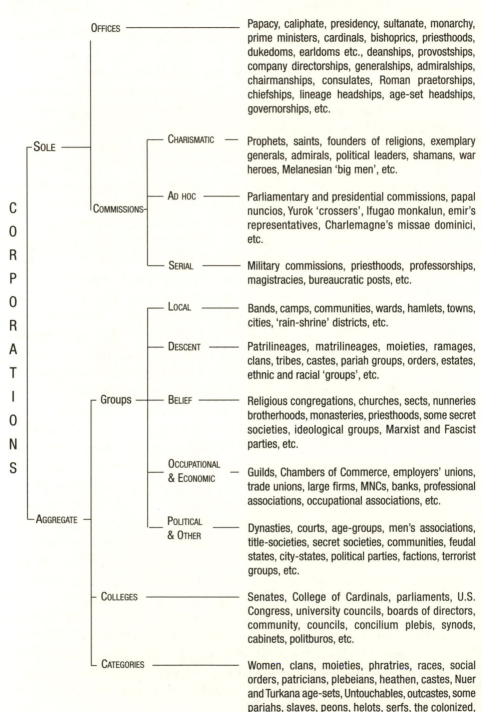

OFFICES — Papacy, caliphate, presidency, sultanate, monarchy, prime ministers, cardinals, bishoprics, priesthoods, dukedoms, earldoms etc., deanships, provostships, company directorships, generalships, admiralships, chairmanships, consulates, Roman praetorships, chiefships, lineage headships, age-set headships, governorships, etc.

SOLE

COMMISSIONS

CHARISMATIC — Prophets, saints, founders of religions, exemplary generals, admirals, political leaders, shamans, war heroes, Melanesian 'big men', etc.

AD HOC — Parliamentary and presidential commissions, papal nuncios, Yurok 'crossers', Ifugao monkalun, emir's representatives, Charlemagne's missae dominici, etc.

SERIAL — Military commissions, priesthoods, professorships, magistracies, bureaucratic posts, etc.

LOCAL — Bands, camps, communities, wards, hamlets, towns, cities, 'rain-shrine' districts, etc.

DESCENT — Patrilineages, matrilineages, moieties, ramages, clans, tribes, castes, pariah groups, orders, estates, ethnic and racial 'groups', etc.

C O R P O R A T I O N S

Groups

BELIEF — Religious congregations, churches, sects, nunneries brotherhoods, monasteries, priesthoods, some secret societies, ideological groups, Marxist and Fascist parties, etc.

OCCUPATIONAL & ECONOMIC — Guilds, Chambers of Commerce, employers' unions, trade unions, large firms, MNCs, banks, professional associations, occupational associations, etc.

POLITICAL & OTHER — Dynasties, courts, age-groups, men's associations, title-societies, secret societies, communities, feudal states, city-states, political parties, factions, terrorist groups, etc.

AGGREGATE

COLLEGES — Senates, College of Cardinals, parliaments, U.S. Congress, university councils, boards of directors, community, councils, concilium plebis, synods, cabinets, politburos, etc.

CATEGORIES — Women, clans, moieties, phratries, races, social orders, patricians, plebeians, heathen, castes, Nuer and Turkana age-sets, Untouchables, outcastes, some pariahs, slaves, peons, helots, serfs, the colonized, the disenfranchised, acephalous societies, etc.

concrete structure in its social context. Familiar examples will illustrate the point. The structural resilience of some modern industrial democracies enables them to sustain their normal rhythms and organization despite such major developments as the civil rights movement, students' movement, female liberation and feminist movement, economic recession and severe unemployment, military defeat and internal or international terrorism. To survive such powerful strains and stresses separately and together, a society's regulative structures must be able to respond positively by guiding those movements and repercussions sympathetically, and by harnessing popular support to create new opportunities, objectives and structures for those involved, while protecting or enhancing its capacity for further growth.

Since corporations provide the perduring units and regulative structures in all societies, by their relations they constitute the corporate organization that coordinates their macrostructure. Accordingly the corporate components of those societal frameworks must be mutually consistent. They should also be each sufficiently compatible with such diffuse non-corporate units and processes as family, cult, market, the division of labor and mode of production, to facilitate their institutionalization and provide effective sanctions.

Given the consistency of a sufficient variety and number of non-corporate units and processes with the requirements of the society's corporate organization, and especially with the requisites of those corporate units that enrol most of its people as members, the corporate framework should easily withstand endogenous social movements and various kinds of external influences such as ideological subversion, terrorism or natural disasters. However if, for whatever reason, the population ceases to believe in the operational adequacy and normative validity of the structural framework and its complementary institutions, as happened to many Indian tribes when the United States put them on reservations following the U.S. Civil War of 1861-65, new beliefs, ideas and faith may be needed to provide the basis for a new social order.

In the preceding review of corporations of various kinds I have cited several combinations that differed in their structural consistency. Among corporations aggregate, while at societal or sub-societal levels a corporate category may include a number of corporate groups lacking the necessary links to organize the inclusive aggregate as a single corporate group, corporate groups likewise often include corporate categories within them. We have also noticed the ease and speed with which, in favorable circumstances, corporate categories may be transformed into corporate groups, or commissions into offices and *vice versa*. Given their central inability to act as units, however numerous, corporate categories are rarely able to withstand or overthrow the corporate groups of lesser size that dominate them. We have also seen that when created, offices and colleges automatically reconstitute the corporate categories in which they are based as groups capable of continuous effective common action. Not all corporate groups need or have offices and/or colleges to coordinate and regulate their affairs, those sufficiently small and egalitarian, such as the Pygmy or Bushman band, being normally able to do so through direct group discussion. By contrast, in most corporate groups of moderate or larger size, collective regulation and coordination are provided by central offices or councils. Accordingly in such units where they co-exist, the office-holder and the council will often be locked in political struggles to preserve or enhance their respective autonomy, influence and power against one another.

To become the chief regulative agencies in human societies, corporations must first regulate their members and ensure their routine observance of rules and norms, and then protect their own and their members' rights and autonomy against trespass by units of like or differing kind. In consequence, political and administrative relations within as well as between corporations are pervasive and critical for the ability of each corporate unit to perpetuate itself by ensuring the necessary conditions for persistence in its current form, without loss of its resources, autonomy or scope. If most members of a society belong simultaneously to two or more corporate units of diverse base, scope and type, their rights and duties as individual members in each must therefore be mutually consistent in order that they may perform their diverse membership roles in the wider society routinely and efficiently. In that case the corporations to which they belong will form an integrated and coherent society. To achieve such conditions, not only must the specific interests, resources, autonomies and rights of the various kinds of corporation be clearly established and known. The relative priority of their respective claims on the loyalties of their members in all recurrent situations where such claims may compete or conflict must be so predetermined by their membership conditions and articulations that either such potential dilemmas do not occur, or they are resolved smoothly without impairing the corporate scope and autonomy of either corporation, or straining the loyalty of their members.

Alternative arrangements that avoid such corporate confrontations are nicely illustrated by certain African societies that traditionally incorporated their members simultaneously in patrilineal descent units, age-sets and local communities, but defined and distributed the rights and obligations of those corporations differently, to ensure their mutual consistency and smooth articulation.

While each of these different corporations, the age-set, descent unit and community, autonomously regulated certain resources, interests and activities, and to those ends had unchallenged authority over its members, their scope and autonomy had to be mutually compatible to avoid the recurrent conflicts that would divide their members' loyalties. Among the pastoral Nuer and Karimojong of the southern Sudan and northwestern Kenya, local communities disperse and come together at different seasons of the year, as the annual floods advance, recede, and leave the land free for grazing. Nuer are celebrated for their segmentary unilineal groups which incorporate everyone, provide most of their material and social necessities, and prescribe the rights and obligations of traditional life. Nuer also had a structure of male age-sets which were periodically constituted in each tribe by ceremonies that initiated adolescent youth in the most junior set. Unlike their patrilineages, which were territorially anchored and divided Nuer tribes territorially by unilineal descent, the age organization, being tribally co-extensive, incorporated in each age-set all males of approximately the same physiological age. Unilineal descent provided men with their political identity, civic rights, property, and a home district which they defended collectively when necessary in inter-lineage feud. While descent regulated marriage, widow inheritance, and relations with non-kin, within a tribe the age organization served primarily to align men of different lineages as age-mates, seniors or juniors, and to restrain violence between them by subordinating their lineage loyalties to the solidarities of agemates, and the authority of seniors over juniors. Nonetheless, in contexts of feud, Nuer men sided with their lineages, and, while taking care not to injure their age-mates, fought members of the feuding lineage in other age-sets. Thus restricted by the rule of age-mate solidarity, lineage loyalties had priority over other age-set bonds in situations of feud. While patrilineages were the dominant corporate groups in Nuer society, their age-sets were *de facto* corporate categories whose members, though recognizing their mutual obligations of solidarity and assistance as age-mates, were never fully mobilized for joint action. Among the Karimojong pastoralists southeast of the Nuer, local communities also disperse seasonally, but, lacking effective organization, age-sets rank below lineages in their claims on individual loyalty whenever the two conflict. As among Nuer, Karimojong age-sets are corporate categories, while the patrilineages that provide all Nuer and Karimojong with their civic identity, kin, home, economic and political rights, property, marriage partners and insurance against destitution, are their basic corporate groups.

By contrast, among the pastoral Kipsigis of Kenya, who are Nilo-Hamites, unilineal descent, though important, neither constitutes segmentary corporate groups, nor endows individuals with their primary identities and civic rights, even though it supplies their social and economic needs, Kipsigi descent units being exogamous categorical patriclans, rather than corporate lineage groups. In their more hospitable habitat, the Kipsigis elders and women and children occupy their homesites continuously throughout the year, while younger men herd the cattle away from the settlements. The age-set organization provides Kipsigis with their most effective regulative structures, and excludes violence irrespective of descent and local loyalties. Indeed, the effectiveness and primacy of age-set loyalties and regulation over these alternative corporate structures made it almost impossible for Peristiany, their ethnographer, to find any instance of homicide in the tribe within living memory. Traditionally, Kipsigis initiated new age-sets every fifteen years, each set containing five sub-sets, incorporated at three yearly intervals during the interim. After initiation a man's primary loyalties and relations lay first with the age-mates of his sub-set, and then with his set as a whole; but since men of the same or successive age-sets are forbidden to fight and obliged to assist one another, and since, as always, juniors must obey men of senior age-sets, in traditional times the Kipsigi age-organization guaranteed peace, order and cooperation throughout the tribe, by excluding lineage conflict between men of different communities and patriclans. Fighting originally in troops based on local communities,

Kipsigi age-sets raided their enemies for cattle and defended their localities. However, following a defeat by the Gusii in the last century, to increase their field forces, elders of the oldest age-sets devised a new structure of four age-regiments that cut across the traditional age-sets and the tribe's four territorial divisions and recruited their members patrilineally, regrouping them for action by age-sets within the regiment. The new regimental organization was mainly used for large-scale raids, and for defence against such nearby peoples as the Masai and Gusii, while local divisions of age-sets continued to raid and defend their herds and villages.

Thus among Kipsigis, as among Masai, the social organization gave structural primacy to age-sets by constituting them as corporate groups whose members' identities and loyalties took precedence and political priority over their kinship ties. Likewise, though organized in troops by local communities, being tribal in their range and membership, age-set bonds transcended local loyalties and gave all men a common solidarity and status. Broadly similar alignments of age organization, descent and local communities prevailed among the Galla or Oromo of Ethiopia, who based the elaborate organization and procedures of their tribal governments on their *gada* age-sets; but differing structural arrangements of descent, community and age organization prevailed among the Gusii of Kenya and Ibo of Southeastern Nigeria. Quite literally, Gusii encapsulated the age organization in their large, modally monolineal local communities, which incorporated a new set each year by initiation rituals separately, and divided them in each lineage into sub-sets by local communities. This eliminated in advance any possible conflicts of loyalty, by subordinating age-sets to their segmentary lineage organization which forbade internal violence, while leaving each monolineal community free to use its age-sets against other Gusii lineages, as well as neighboring peoples.

Among the Ibo of Southeastern Nigeria, local communities were also formally monolineal, but each village group was nonetheless divided by locality and descent into two exogamous coordinate halves for various social and religious purposes. The age-sets, constituted annually in each exclusive local community, incorporated men from both segments of its dual organization to provide the village with large organized groups of young men for its defence and public works, while enabling either half of the community to call out its own age-sets as its elders decided. Since Ibo age-sets forbade violence between age-mates and between juniors and seniors, being coextensive with the divided local community, their age-organization provided effective mechanisms for the restraint of internal violence, for peaceful settlement of local disputes and the regulation of public affairs by each half of the village separately, or jointly for the regulation of their common affairs through a hierarchy of village councils or colleges and supporting male associations.

As these examples show, the differing societies developed a range of alternative arrangements by which age-organizations, unilineal descent groupings, local communities and other structures, including chiefship, councils, tribunals and men's associations, were aligned so as to minimize the structural conflicts that would otherwise occur between them, and provide a variety of efficient regulative frameworks. Together these examples also illustrate the flexibility with which corporations of such differing kind and base as descent, age and locality can be accommodated to one another within diverse but structurally consistent frameworks by adjusting their respective forms, bases, claims, resources, scope, autonomy and range, and their external and internal articulations. Such differences in the bases and forms of those corporations, and in their internal and external articulations, entail corresponding differences in their scope, resources, range, autonomy and capacities. The diverse macro-structures of these African societies illustrate the capacity of corporate organization to adapt and develop a variety of differing viable adjustments. They also demonstrate how essential it is that the various kinds of corporation should be operationally and substantively congruent with one another to exclude the conflicts that would otherwise occur between them, and to provide the society with a stable structural framework. Examples of structurally inconsistent and therefore internally disruptive societies include such ancient Greek city-states as Corcyra, the feudal polities of ancient China, medieval Europe and Japan, the Tuareg of the southwestern Sahara, the Kaingang of Brazil, the Kachin of highland Burma, highlanders of Papua New Guinea, and Murngin of Northern Australia; but undoubtedly we lack information on many societies that have failed to survive the disruptive conflicts generated within them by the structural inconsistencies of their inappropriately constituted and articulated corporations.

Since corporations aggregate are the perduring units that organize and coordinate the members of a society, the greater their number and variety, the greater is the structural complexity of the society. The greater the complexity of a society, the more urgent its dependence on the harmonious articulation of its corporate categories, groups, colleges, offices and commissions with one another, with its collectivities and non-corporate units, institutional and other; and the greater the capacity of its structure to absorb internal pressures for change without destabilization. As the Nuer, Gusii, Kipsigis and Ibo illustrate, in different societies corporations aggregate of the same general kind, such as age-sets, may differ in their form as groups or categories. They may differ also at base in the specific ways and conditions by which they recruit their members, for example, as local, descent or age units; and in their internal and external articulations. The greater the number of corporations aggregate or sole that recruit their members on differing bases or conditions, the greater the complexity of the corporate organization that provides the macrostructure of that society. In consequence, the simplest societies should be those with the fewest kinds of corporate units, the least variety. Today these are best illustrated by the few remaining groups of hunter-gatherers in Africa, the Philippines, North and South America, and Southeast Asia, the Australian Aborigines being structurally quite atypical of populations with such rudimentary ecologies.

In societies of foragers, bands are the prime and often the only corporate grouping, each containing a number of families whose members live, hunt, gather and worship together, and deal with common exigencies collectively. For such societies to achieve the structural consistency they need in order to operate and persist without structural conflicts, their family and band organizations must be mutually compatible; and also the relations between their bands. In such hunter-gathering societies as the Andamanese, bands sometimes engage in fratricidal war, unlike Pygmies of the Ituri forest, whose bands are exogamous and intermarry; while among the Kalahari Bushmen, individuals or families may move freely between bands as they feel necessary. As the Andamanese demonstrate, even when such non-corporate structures as the family or hunting groups articulate smoothly with the corporate organization, unless the bands that structure and regulate the society have equally harmonious relations, collective conflicts will recur to disrupt and perhaps destroy it. In short, besides the requisite levels of structural consistency within and between the corporate units that constitute its regulative framework, for a viable society, the various kinds of non-corporate units within it must simultaneously maintain sufficient degrees of consistency with one another and with its corporate organization to ensure its operational efficiency free of structural conflict. Unless the collectivities and non-corporate units of society are sufficiently congruent with one another and with its corporate organization as a structured complex of processes, the society can neither operate smoothly nor perpetuate itself. For this reason I have laid out extensively in various charts the differing kinds of processes, collectivities and social units we may expect to encounter in differing societies so that we may contemplate their distinctive forms and properties to determine which seem mutually compatible and which clearly would require alteration to avoid conflict with others.

In Chart H I have sketched a typological scale on which we may place societies in order of relative complexity. Despite its many dynamic aspects, the scale is not strictly evolutionary. The internal differentiation of these societies is indicated first by the variety of their social units, collectivities and interrelations; second by the number and variety of principles on which those units recruit their members. I expect that a society with ten or more diverse kinds of collectivities and social units and a corresponding range of inter-unit articulations will be substantially more differentiated and complex than one with only six or seven different kinds and correspondingly fewer types of relations between them.

In Chart H the hypothetically simplest society is illustrated in category A by the combination of family and band organization characteristic of surviving populations of hunter-gatherers. Considerably more complex and differentiated are those so-called tribal societies of category B based mainly on horticultural or pastoral economies that rely for order on multifunctional councils of elders and headmen, unilineal descent, with or without age organizations and men's associations, and local communities. Such tribal societies typically have weak stratifications, limited technological specialization, centralization, commerce or trade, tribally distinct religions, and no literacy. As societies become more differentiated and develop more complex divisions of labor, they develop centralized polities with elaborate monarchic institutions, palaces,

CHART H
SOCIETAL DIFFERENTIATION AND COMPLEXITY

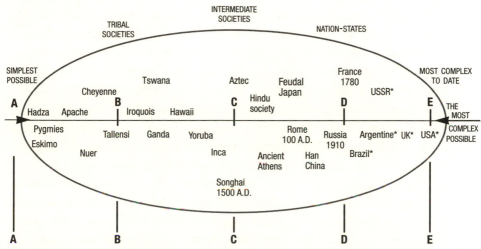

A	B	C	D	E
Foraging	Pastoral and/or agrarian	Complex predatory ecologies	Widespread literacy	Very complex ecology
Ethnic homogeneity	Ethnic homogeneity	Poor communications	Large-scale societies	Industrialized, capital intensive
Culturally uniform	Culturally uniform	Capital cities	More complex ecology	Multiple conurbations
Preliterate	Preliterate	Urban and rural sectors	Developing industry	Mass society
Very small scale	Kin based	Caste/estates/orders	Efficient communications	Mass communications
Low density	Large kin groups	Weakly centralized polities	Extensive markets	Mass movements
Family	Feud	Chiefship and councils	Strong D of L** by sex	Mass education
Bilateral kinship	Strong communities	Patrimonial administrations	Occupational specialization	General literacy
Band organization	Age organization	Authoritarian regimes	Wage labor	Organized research & science
Sharing	Gerontocracy	Armies. Empires.	Great gender disparity	Advanced technology
Weak D of L** by sex	Associations	Currencies. Guilds.	Increasing differentiation	Centralized administration
Near gender parity	Strong D of L** by sex	Markets.	Greater social mobility	World markets
Minimal leadership	Status ranking	Extensive trade	Universal cults	Extensive mobility
Little differentiation	Clientage	Slaves/serfs, clientage	Mixed stratification	Weak family, kinship, marriage
Egalitarian	Gift exchange and Debt	Ascriptive stratification	Universities, research	Non-hereditary stratification
	Consensual authority	Hereditary occupations	Centralized states	Polyethnic and multiracial
	Dispersed leadership	Great gender disparity	Central courts and judiciary	More complex plural societies
	Chief and/or councils	Strong D of L** by sex	Organized police and armies	Weak D of L** by sex
		Limited literacy, schools	Contractual bureaucracy	Functional D of L** dominant
		Polyethnicity	Imperialism, plural societies	Religious pluralism
		Alternative institutions		Ideological conflicts
		Polytheism/ Monotheism		

* 1990
** Division of Labor

capitals, extensive social stratifications of freemen, slaves, aristocrats, commoners and others, markets for internal and external trade, guilds and occupational groupings, limited literacy and some educational provisions. They may also display complex ecologies that combine cattle husbandry, agriculture, irrigation, craft production, mining, trade, slave raiding and predatory war with such elaborate polytheisms as Hinduism, the Olympian cults of Greece, Rome, and those of Mesopotamia, Peru, and Mexico before Pissaro and Cortez, or traditional Yoruba and Dahomey. Societies with such characteristics may be broadly classified as category C, intermediate, since they cluster in that part of the structural scale. More highly differentiated and of wider scale yet are those societies of category D, emergent nation-states with their central bureaucracies, armies, capital cities, monetized urban economies, extensive transport and communications systems, universities, schools, limited industry, literate ruling elites, impoverished and illiterate rural populations, poorly employed and ill-educated proletarians, and all the diverse strains and problems that beset aggregates whose composition and articulations are not sufficiently consistent to ensure their orderly and even development. France before the revolution of 1788-89, and Russia before 1917 illustrate the type.

The most advanced degrees of differentiation and complexity are illustrated on Chart H by contemporary society in Moscow or Shanghai and New York. The first two are substantially less highly differentiated and complex than the latter, given the prolonged centralization of political and economic resources and activities by the Communist Party and state, in contrast to the greater freedoms and opportunities for diverse political, economic and other activities and relations in polyethnic New York with its different racial, linguistic, religious and national collectivities. Since development continues to proceed in such great conurbations as Tokyo, Paris, New York, Mexico City and London, contemporary levels of complexity and differentiation in human societies increase annually and will certainly be surpassed in the near future as the differentiation of those world centers increases. The continuum is therefore open-ended at the complex pole, which hypothetically could coincide with a genuine world community and state under some form of global government in which all the diverse nationalities, religions, races and peoples of mankind would participate freely, democratically, and as fully as possible, if only they effectively controlled all levels of its bureaucracy.

However approximate these placements, this hypothetical scale demonstrates the utility of our structural framework for the comparative study of human societies by allowing us first to specify the principles that underlie and constitute their complexity and then to distinguish and compare their social structures from the simplest to the most elaborately differentiated range. It also shows how societies of similar levels of differentiation and complexity often present strikingly different arrays of corporate and non-corporate social units. For example, in precolonial days Northern Yoruba society had elaborate male associations, internally stratified secret societies with ritual functions and official directorates, age-set organization, localized unilineal descent groups with titled headmen, ritual chiefships and councils supported by elaborate hierarchies of slaves, eunuchs, clients and others, social stratification, an extensive market system for internal and external trade, temples and priesthoods, craft guilds, taxation, tribunals, and so on. To the north, by contrast, the Muslim Hausa had no comparable corporate associations except religious fraternities (*tariqa*), nor adult age organization, but numerous craft guilds, an elaborate system of long-distance caravan trade and local markets administered by office-holders, currency, a prestigious priesthood and clerical stratum, slavery, eunuchs, clients, tributary populations, taxation, courts, capitals, dynasties, councils, schools, nobilities, armies, literati and peasantries who had to support the rulers and state without any voice in its affairs. Yet despite such important differences in the composition of traditional Yoruba and Hausa societies, both fall in the intermediate range of this continuum, category C, unlike the Nuer, Gusii, Kipsigis, Ibo and Karimojong mentioned above, who fall into category B. They accordingly illustrate the approximate equivalence of certain alternative combinations of concrete structures as indices of differentiation.

In such comparisons the scale of a society corresponds to the number and diversity of the links through which its members may communicate freely with one another, directly or otherwise. Societies of the smallest scale depend on face to face relations between their members for communication and common action; while those of greater scale increasingly rely on indirect communications to coordinate their activities, and ultimately on mass communication. Such differences in the scale of societies clearly correspond with differences in their levels of internal differentiation and complexity, the latter being commensurate with the variety and number of collectivities and social units, corporate or other, that constitute them, their underlying principles, and the diversity of their internal and external articulation.

6. MODES OF INCORPORATION

To indicate the differing bases or principles on which social units of either kind, corporate or non-corporate, may and do recruit their members in different societies, in Chart I, I present a diagram of society as a cube in its environment and time, the dimension of change. Excluding time and the environment, with which, as the arrows indicate, the cube's relations are dialectic and reciprocal, the differing bases on which social units recruit their members are listed separately along the eleven remaining sides of the cube. Besides common locality or residence, these are property rights, gender, generation and age, racial or ethnic origin, common language, beliefs, kinship, descent and affinity, voluntary association, occupation and legal status.

By status here I mean legal or social status, summarized by such criteria as caste, race, ethnicity, religion, sex, or birth as serf, slave or free and enfranchised, which different societies use to classify and rank populations categorically as peon, serf, slave, free and freedman, noble and commoner, enfranchized and disenfranchized, conqueror and conquered, colonial and colonized. Another criterion that often furnishes the basis for such differing types of social units as formal and informal friendships, action-sets, cliques, clubs and fraternities, associations, factions, work-groups, sports teams, firms, sects, universities, political parties and much else, "voluntary" association denotes an equally elastic and variable condition. Otherwise the various recruitment criteria seem self-explanatory.

However, two or more diverse recruitment criteria are frequently combined by social units as membership conditions. For example, common language, locality, ethnicity and race are generally shared by members of most simple societies, who also often hold the same beliefs, homeland, and institutional culture. Likewise, membership in political

CHART I

SOCIETY AS A CUBE

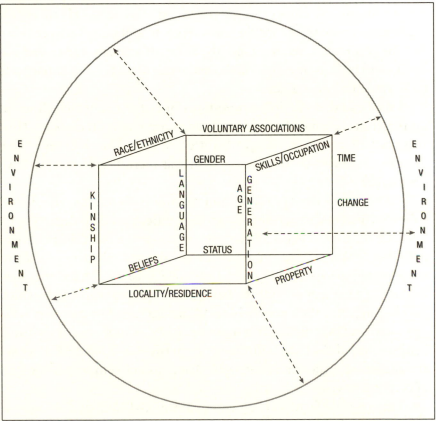

parties, sectarian and certain other organizations generally presumes shared beliefs and voluntary association. Together descent, affinity and kinship provide the bases for such diverse units as moieties, bands, lineages, ramages, kindreds and families of diverse types. By contrast with the homogeneous populations of unmonetized tribal societies, many complex modern societies contain collectivities of differing race, ethnicity, religious and other beliefs, language, occupation and forms of kinship and property. If social units recruit their members on several simultaneous criteria, such as language, religion and locality or ethnicity, or descent, locality and property rights, the requisites and entailments of those principles operationally defined and instituted must be sufficiently congruent with one another to provide the units based on them with firm but flexible foundations. The various *principles* or conditions on which social units recruit their members should always be mutually consistent and harmonious, whether those units are strongly or weakly institutional, non-institutional, corporate or other. At the level of corporate organization, among and within non-corporate units, and between those and the corporate level, to ensure the society's stability and to exclude disruptive conflicts, the structural consistency of all their essential parts is the prerequisite condition.

I shall call the principles, conditions or criteria on which all social units recruit their members and exclude non-members their *basis*. Thus corporations or other units with differing recruitment criteria have differing bases, while those with identical recruitment criteria have identical bases.

All four varieties of corporation discussed above, namely offices, colleges, corporate categories and groups, differ significantly in type or form. Of the four, colleges and corporate groups are most alike in form, but differ in that colleges are always minorities specially recruited from the corporate groups they regulate. Thus colleges cannot be defined solely by those criteria that provide the bases of the corporate groups to which they belong, since their members are always recruited by special criteria or procedures that distinguish them from others in their groups. Such institutional differentiae illustrate a particular mode of internal articulation in corporations aggregate that is also used to stratify the staff of corporations sole.

The formal features that distinguish commissions as quasi-corporations from these four corporations have already been noted. Besides their differing internal articulations, corporations differ in the ways in which they articulate with one another and with non-corporate units to furnish the structural framework of their societies. Since corporations are individually unique and identified externally as indivisible units, each has its own unique set of external relations with others of the same or differing form and base. Moreover, since appropriate external articulations are prerequisite for the efficient operation of corporations and non-corporate units alike, corporations of identical form and base should all have identical articulations with one another and with corporations of differing form or base, while corporations that differ in form or base should differ correspondingly in the kinds of external relations that they require to operate efficiently. We may therefore expect significant differences in the kinds of articulation requisite for corporations of differing form and base. We may also expect that when their external relations are inappropriate, the capacities of corporations to regulate their affairs are correspondingly affected.

As units that recruit and incorporate their members by special criteria and procedures, corporations are themselves incorporated in the societies they constitute in either of three distinct ways or *modes*. The three *modes of incorporation* are respectively the *universalistic, consociational* or *segmental,* and *differential.* Incorporation is *universalistic* when all individuals of similar sex and age are enrolled in some wider unit, which may be either a society or a corporation, directly, equally and on formally identical terms. When individuals derive their membership in a society or corporation indirectly from prior membership in one of its constituents, those units are therefore formally equivalent. I call this second mode of incorporation *segmental, equivalent* or *consociational,* since it constitutes the inclusive unit or society as a *consociation* of mutually exclusive *segments* of *equivalent* status and identical form. Accordingly, at any structural level, coordinate segments of a consociation should have the same articulations. Finally, when one corporate group or corporate section of a society enjoys superior rights and privileges, while others suffer corresponding disabilities, the inclusive unit is based on *differential incorporation,* and all its components are differentially incorporated. Such strata as slaves, serfs, helots, or disenfranchised, conquered and colonized populations illustrate alternative structures of differential incorporation. By contrast, societies subdivided vertically into a series of exogamous categorical clans illustrate segmental or consociational incorporation, since the members of these clans are all equally free to participate in the wider society. Societies with dual organizations incorporate their categories consociationally as intermarrying moieties. Comparative data demonstrate that corporate groups of equal autonomy that have the same base will only associate freely in a consociational mode. In a society characterized by differential incorporation, the dominant section will be constituted as an exclusive corporate group, its subordinates as corporate categories. Thus, while corporate units of differing form or base are incorporated differentially, others having identical base and form are equivalent and segmentally incorporated. In effect, these alternative modes of incorporation entail very different distributions of autonomy, resources and scope among the corporations they articulate, not all of which can freely administer their members' common affairs (Smith 1974:180-198).

Institutionally diverse populations may form a common society in various ways. Such variations may reflect differences in their history, in the number of their institutionally distinct components, in their spatial and ecological distributions, in their linguistic, racial, ethnic and religious characteristics, demographic structures and relative size, or in the relative degrees of their institutional differences, and the parts they play in the common society. We may best distinguish the regulative structures and processes of social organization from others that lack such significance by developing distinctions derived from Herbert Spencer (1969) and Meyer Fortes (1959). For Spencer, as we have seen, the institutional structure in all societies consisted of three subsystems, the *sustaining*, which is primarily economic and material; the *reproductive*, which consists primarily of family, kinship and marriage; and the *regulative*, which is represented by the prevailing forms of political and legal organization and the regulative aspects of religion. For Fortes, in all societies we can distinguish analytically two closely linked *domains*, the *domestic*, which he identified primarily with kinship and marriage in the simple societies that were his chief concern, and the *politico-jural*, through which these societies regulated other social relations, such as those of lineage and descent. Describing his distinction as analytic, Fortes showed that such institutions as kinship, religion and marriage had both domestic and politico-jural aspects, and participated simultaneously in both domains. Following those leads I redefined the domains distinguished by Fortes as *private* and *public* (Smith 1974:216-217), restricting the latter domain to those agencies and institutions through which societies and communities regulate such common affairs as defence and external relations, internal order, law, government, public activities, economic processes, education, exchange, and thereby determine the scope and autonomy of the private domain.

As we have seen, many of the organizations engaged in the public processes just listed, like those authorised to regulate them, are corporate in status and form, being established as unique, presumptively perpetual agencies to undertake or regulate the public's common affairs, including its economy, internal order and relations with other bodies. As the sphere

160

of common interests, affairs, activities and regulative institutions, the public domain plays an especially important part in structuring its society, since the jural and political status of people differs directly as an aspect of their differing relations with the public domain. This is most obvious in the familiar distinction made between "first" and "second-class" citizens of many contemporary societies, a difference that indicates the differential incorporation of their people. Since societal membership presupposes the members' incorporation, and since the modes of incorporation listed above differ essentially in the conditions by which they articulate units to the public domain of their societies, the three modes of societal incorporation entail corresponding differences in the articulation and participation of the units they incorporate in the public domain of the inclusive society, that is, in its central regulative processes and structures.

Differing forms and conditions of membership in a society correspond directly with these alternative modes of societal incorporation, which in turn denote differing relationships to its public domain. As stated above, there are only three modes of incorporation, namely, the universalistic, the equivalent and the differential. *Universalistic incorporation* consists in the immediate, direct and prescriptive incorporation of all individuals as members and formal equals on identical conditions in the public domain of a corporate unit or society. When individuals are incorporated in the public domain of an inclusive unit or society indirectly, by virtue of their prior membership in one or other of the units that constitute it, and those constituent units have the same form and equivalent rights as in Switzerland, the early American confederation, or in acephalous unilineal societies, the mode of incorporation can be described either as *equivalent, consociational* or *segmental*. By contrast, *universalistic incorporation* excludes intermediate structures as prerequisites for individual membership and participation. Finally, when one part of its population does not participate in the regulative processes and structures of the public domain which others control, such radically different membership status and conditions demonstrate their differing corporate statuses, and the society's *differential incorporation*.

Differential incorporation subordinates that section of the community which does not participate freely and fully in the public domain to those who do, under a regime of explicit political and legal inequality, whatever its ideological justification. By contrast, *universalistic incorporation* ensures the formal equality of individuals as citizens and members of society by prescribing their identical rights and duties in its public domain. *Equivalent* or *segmental* incorporation indirectly provides individuals of similar status who belong to different segments of a common society with equivalent rights and duties in its inclusive public domain. The three alternatives accordingly differ in their implications for social equality. While universalistic incorporation prescribes formal equality irrespective of wealth, race, religion, sex and other social conditions, the equivalent or segmental mode permits but neither prescribes nor excludes it, and the differential mode prescribes political and legal inequality between members of the sections it articulates. Thus the three modes of incorporation between them exhaust and define the alternative forms of societal membership, and corporate or personal equality.

To determine the precise conditions of societal membership in preliterate milieux, we have to examine with care the distributions of juridical and political rights among and between the members of all differing social categories and groups in the society. By so doing, we can normally identify the prevailing mode of incorporation for each of those constituent groups or categories. In societies with written laws and constitutions, such distributions of juridical and political status and rights are usually abstracted from the relevant legal texts. However, there are often great differences in the distribution of political and legal rights between the constitutional and legal prescriptions and prevailing practices. It is therefore never adequate to treat these constitutional and legal provisions as empirically valid without careful study of current conditions and relations. Such study will often reveal substantial discrepancies between the prescriptions of constitutional law and the actual conditions in which people live, as regards the distribution of political and juridical rights within society, and the condition of popular participation in the public domain. Wherever we find such discrepancies between juridical provisions and the prevailing conditions of daily life, that is, between the *de jure* and *de facto* conditions of societal incorporation and existence, then, as Weber (1947:137) taught, we should treat the *de facto* evidence as decisive. By that test, we can distinguish societies based on *de facto* differential incorporation from those which are *de facto* as well as *de jure* universalistic or consociational, and which differ correspondingly in their bases and implications.

7. PLURAL SOCIETIES

If corporate units provide the regulative structures of the public domain and order their processes and collective activities, the differential incorporation of collectivities in society will always entail significant differences in their institutions, and in the political and civic rights and status of their members. In such conditions, the differentially incorporated collectivities will also differ in their corresponding political, jural and ancillary institutions. Their differing civic statuses and rights entail those institutional differences, whether or not the differentially incorporated collectivities share identical institutions in their private domains. By their differential articulation to the public domain and resulting inequality, the society they constitute will therefore be institutionally plural and structurally hierarchic. In contrast, conditions of *de facto* universalistic incorporation prescribe the formally identical status, rights, privileges and duties of all their members in the public domain, irrespective of such differences as language, cult, kinship, family and marriage and other institutional patterns in the *private domains* of the units or collectivities incorporated, provided only that those differences do not affect the status and rights of their members in the societal *public domain*. Despite the *cultural pluralism* they manifest, if such cultural differences in their private domains do not involve corresponding differences between collectivities in the public domain, that sets the society apart from plural societies, hierarchic or other. That, for example, is the position among whites in the U.S.A. (Smith 1986). In short, institutional differences often prevail in the private domains of collectivities incorporated universalistically in a common society without corresponding jural or political differences between them. In contrast, if associated with differences in their political and jural status, such differences between or within collectivities of a common society identify them as social sections, and their societies as plural.

With or without institutional differences in their private domains, collectivities incorporated segmentally in a common society differ in their regulative institutions and *de jure* or *de facto* in their corporate status and public rights from those *hierarchic pluralities*. Such consociations constitute *segmental pluralities* of differing structure and properties from those based on differential incorporation. Examples include Malaysia, Cyprus before and after decolonization, Ulster, Yugoslavia, Sri Lanka and Lebanon, or, until recently, men and women in certain Swiss cantons, by virtue of the social pluralism of their segments. Frequently, however, as in Israel, South Africa, Mauritania and the former USSR, plural societies incorporate some collectivities differentially, others segmentally and yet others universalistically, thus using all three modes of incorporation to differentiate their corporate components, aligning them in complex structures that combine the principles of hierarchic and segmental disjunction with differences of regulative institutions to create more plural societies or *complex pluralities*.

To emphasize the significant difference between membership in corporations and non-corporate units, since corporations confer special status on their members, I shall reserve the terms *incorporate* and *incorporation* for enrolment in a corporate unit of any kind - group, category, college, office or society, - and describe enrolments in other social bodies as inclusion. Besides such social units as the family, work-group, peer-group, club or other informal association, individuals are often and simultaneously included in kindreds, networks, cliques and other quasi-groups. They may also be identified with such strata as status "groups" in Weber's terminology or "classes" in that of Marx, Lloyd Warner and others, age-grades, income "groups", regional populations, racial and sometimes ethnic divisions, or such loosely defined and bounded ideological divisions as radicals, moderates or progressives and conservatives, that lack both institutional and corporate status since the latter presumes the former.

Exclusion and inclusion denote opposite kinds of relation of individuals to social units or collectivities, and contrast with excorporation and incorporation. However, I reserve the term *excorporation* to denote societal exclusion, the opposite of societal incorporation. Perhaps the most general kind of excorporation is one country's exclusion of the citizens of others. Today that is easily done as nation-states are spatially distinct and most are mutually remote. In earlier centuries and differing conditions, various societies had to make special institutional arrangements to excorporate populations resident among them. Until recently that was how most Christian societies in Europe treated Jews, forcibly restricting them to practise certain occupations, to live in ghettoes under curfew, and, by various means, stigmatizing their identities and excorporating them from the community.

European states also excorporated the Gypsies who roamed across them, at different times deporting them. Most recently the Nazis tried to exterminate both Gypsies and Jews by starvation and poison gas. Among the Hausa of the Central Sudan during the 17th and 18th centuries, the situation of nomadic pastoral Fulani who grazed their herds in Hausa states was not dissimilar to that of Europe's Gypsies in benign states, since the sedentary Hausa regarded the nomadic Fulani as strangers who formed a separate society and treated them accordingly. In ancient Greece Athens and other city-states excorporated metics as resident aliens, while incorporating their slave populations differentially. By contrast, in the Ottoman empire, though excorporated as *millets* and excluded systematically from Muslim society, subordinate Christian communities administered themselves and rendered *jizia*, the Islamic tax on Jews and Christians. Contemporary Israel still excorporates Palestinians living in the Gaza strip and West Bank, and has done so for decades. In South Africa, while collectivities of non-whites are differentially incorporated under the institutions of *apartheid*, the Bantustans or "Bantu homelands", which white South Africans pretend are separate states, illustrate the familiar European program for excorporation of surplus subjugated indigenes by their settlement on reservations, whether they be Amerindians, Aborigines, Kanakas or other 'natives'. In China and the former USSR, 'national minorities' have likewise been confined on reservations, called autonomous or national republics.

The different institutional means and conditions by which dominant societies excorporate subject collectivities deserve detailed systematic study. When deemed expedient by their masters, entire communities have sometimes been deported, as happened in Spain after 1492 to Muslims and Jews, and recently to Asiatics in Kenya and Uganda. In other situations alien collectivities have been violently eliminated, as happened in Zanzibar and to the Armenians in Turkey. Such outcomes demonstrate dramatically the depth of the alienation from their hosts of those eliminated. So likewise do such wholesale peremptory relocations of population as the Kirghiz, the Kazakhs, Volga Germans, Tatars and others underwent, over great distances with minimal notice, and with great loss of life and property, in the former USSR at the hands of Joseph Stalin during World War II; or the Kurds of northern Iraq most recently, after decimation by aerial bombardments and poison gas. We should therefore study carefully the conditions and modes of societal excorporation in historic and contemporary societies, since in differing ways the situation of those excorporated is even more intolerable than that of such differentially incorporated populations as the colonized, peons, or slaves.

Such differentially incorporated populations as the patricians and plebs of early Rome, colonizers and colonized, slaveowners and slaves, enfranchised and unenfranchised, besides their radically different positions and rights in the societal public domain, differed also in their institutional culture, practices, beliefs and values, with the result that the inclusive society contained two or more institutionally distinct collectivities which were also differentially incorporated. Such were, *de jure* and *de facto*, colonial Jamaica, Swat Pathan society (Barth 1959), medieval Europe, India and other countries, and South Africa today. Institutionally distinct collectivities may also be segmentally incorporated as equals, as are the Terik and Tiriki of the Kavirondo Gulf in Uganda (LeVine and Sangree 1962), Switzerland, and until 1974, Lebanon. Since the decisive criterion of *differential incorporation* is the distribution of differential status and rights among groups or categories in the polity, law and other arenas of the public domain of their society, unless they share the same status and rights in that domain, men, women and children are differentially incorporated.

During the family's early years, when its children are young, their care is publicly recognised as the parents' responsibility, thus simultaneously sanctioning and balancing the inherently unequal relations of parents and children by parental obligations and responsibilities for which the lineage, clan, community or state ultimately holds them accountable. True that as infants children are utterly dependent and cannot act effectively to protect themselves. Hence besides such corporations as the lineage or state, various kinsfolk such as the mother's brother, father's sister and grandparents are authorized to intervene to protect the children whenever in their opinion the situation requires this. At that stage of its development, relations between family members of differing generation are so asymmetrical as to indicate their *differential incorporation*. So too

166

in most historical and contemporary societies are relations between husband and wife. In cultural theory at least, such asymmetries are institutionally balanced by corresponding inequalities in the distribution of responsibilities and duties between spouses and between parents and children, at least formally; and since the differentially incorporated statuses and roles together constitute a common institution, the family, whose members also share complementary relationships, their structured inequality is prescribed and sanctioned normatively by the institutional framework they all uphold, thus indicating their individual commitment to its order. Since both sexes participate in the same kinship and marital institutions as affines and parents of common children, the share a common institutional culture, and so form complementary halves of an institutionally homogeneous population.

By contrast, when institutionally distinct aggregates are also differentially incorporated in a common society, by virtue of their concordant inequalities and institutional differences, they differ so greatly from the more familiar model of the culturally homogeneous society in substance and form that they constitute the distinct category of *plural societies*. Most commonly, the institutionally distinct and differentially incorporated collectivities of plural societies differ also in their origins, ethnicity, language, culture, numbers and wealth, and sometimes in race or religion, each set of institutional differences progressively deepening and widening their social divisions which thus become correspondingly more difficult to bridge.

In segmentary lineages of the familiar African kind, by contrast, lineage groups of the same genealogical level and depth are culturally ascribed coordinate status, responsibilities and rights, as are their members of the same sex, generation and approximate age. In societies of hunters and gatherers whose largest residential units are local bands, those units also have equivalent status, rights and entitlements, as do the families that compose them, and, among the Hadza, adults of either sex. In such societies, as in those based on segmentary lineages, corporate groups of the same level and kind, with their memberships, are prescriptively equivalent. Such societies therefore incorporate their constitutive segments equally and consociationally, even though within the segments members may differ sharply in status, rights and duties. Thus while such structures often institute inequalities between men and women, and between the generations, in their consociations those groups, corporate and non-corporate, whether families, lineages or bands in different milieux, are all equivalent, having identical bases and form, and therefore formally identical status, rights and responsibilities.

We have distinguished such inclusive structures of status allocation from those found in nuclear families by contrasting the *equivalent* or *segmental* mode of their incorporation with the *differential*, which systematically prescribes inequalities between the social categories it differentiates. Among the Hadza (Woodburn 1982), whether married or not, men and women have identical rights and responsibilities to care for themselves. Ethnographers report comparable relations among some Pygmies, the Bushmen, and Philippine Negritos. In such situations adults should have the same rights and status irrespective of sex, and should therefore be equally free to engage in social relations, or to disassociate themselves without prescriptive bonds to any other unit. Such conditions, which hold equally for both sexes in private and public activities, are rather extreme and represent the most radically *universalistic incorporation* of adults in society known to us. In more differentiated societies, such as France, Italy, the former USSR or the USA, men and women may have formally identical status in activities and relations of the public domain, namely, the economy, government, universities or the bureaucracy, while remaining, at law and in fact, unequal in the private domain of family, religion, political and social life. The double standard of sexual behavior in most Western societies illustrates this pervasive discrepancy.

While many societies such as the Nuer, Tiv or Plateau Tonga which incorporate their corporate constituents as equals are institutionally homogeneous, since all members of those segments share the same institutions and culture, others, such as the Lebanon from 1945 to 1974, are not. In Lebanon, the constitutive segments of Maronite Christians, Jews, Sunni and Shia Muslims each had their own religion, social institutions, legal code, public domain and political authorities. In Cyprus at independence, Muslim Turks and Christian Greeks cooperated unequally to govern the state, each congregation having the right to administer its own affairs according to its religion and law. Thus while some societies based on segmental modes of incorporation are institutionally homogeneous, others like Cyprus and Lebanon are plural societies, but of a different kind from those incorporated differentially, since their institutionally diverse segments are formally status equals, despite their substantial differences in wealth, number and power. It was also the case until recently that in such consociations as Switzerland, whereas men and women had identical status in most cantons, in others they did not, women being denied the rights to vote or to seek electoral office. In the early U.S.A., despite the grand intentions and proclamations of civil rights at Independence and in the constitution, white women, Amerindians, hybrids and Blacks all had no vote or right to contest public office. Although white men and women shared common forms of culture, religion, family and marriage, and so had the same institutional culture, Amerindian tribesmen and Blacks, most of whom were slaves and born in Africa, differed sharply, with the result that each confederal state contained a plural society of Amerindian tribesmen and Black slaves ruled, like white women, by a population of dominant white males. Nonetheless, since all states as basic constituents of the confederation had the same status, rights, obligations and autonomy, that political society was incorporated segmentally as a consociation of equivalent units, in which a white male oligarchy shared identical status and rights in the national public domain, despite substantive differences among the plural societies in their respective member states.

In the early years of U.S. independence, only those white men whose states had together established the confederation had full rights as citizens, although white women were both subject to and protected by federal courts of law. Thus, until the state of Maine formally entered the USA, despite the common ethnic and cultural bonds its rulers shared with those of the other ex-colonies, the people of Maine had no status as U.S. citizens. During the next hundred years as New England abandoned slavery and reduced its Black and Indian populations, industrialized, and pressed to terminate slavery in the South, conflicts emerged that threatened federal unity and led to civil war. Thereafter the movement from confederation to a truly federal state in which citizens are incorporated directly and nationally, as individuals holding identical rights and obligations irrespective of their state, sex, religion, and formally of race, language and culture, has proceeded steadily despite reversals and prolonged arrest. Now, at least formally, American society is based on the mode of universalistic incorporation which if always valid *de facto*, should prescriptively enrol all native Americans in the national society directly and on identical terms.

Most contemporary states in their constitutions proclaim the universalistic incorporation of their citizens with full human and civil rights. However, in many and perhaps the majority of cases, the prevailing conditions of private and public life demonstrate otherwise. Commonly, despite the formal commitments of states to incorporate their citizens as equals and guarantee their political rights and security in their private and public life, the severe injustices and inequalities within their populations indicate *de facto* differential incorporation. This is equally characteristic of such former Marxist states as Poland, East Germany, the former USSR and Cuba, where the ruling party under Marxism in practice differentially incorporated its members, and the political or military autocracies of Africa and Latin America, where dictators and national armies now claim legal immunities and rewards for arranging the "disappearances" of citizens. Likewise in some consociations, the formally equivalent segments sometimes display such disparities of status, number, endowments, power and control of the state, that, as in Lebanon, Cyprus and Nigeria, groups that feel threatened may migrate or seek foreign help and take up arms to defend their interests and status. Angola, Mozambique, Zaire, Ethiopia, Uganda and Sudan have all experienced such developments, as have Kampuchea, Vietnam, Nicaragua, El Salvador, Chile and Malaysia. We should therefore give equal attention to the actual or *de facto* situations of citizens in such segmentally incorporated societies as Switzerland, India or the former USSR, and in such universalistic countries as France and the USA, to see whether the members of their differing collectivities and social categories do in fact enjoy equivalent or identical legal, political, economic and social rights as citizens of the nation-state. Differences between *de jure* conditions of incorporation and *de facto* realities of life in many countries are far too wide and general to be ignored. Wherever the two diverge, as Weber (1947:137) advised, we should study the bases, extent and implications of their divergence, and analyse the *de facto* conditions of collective life.

Societies that incorporate their members universalistically *de facto* as well as *de jure* differ from plural societies in ascribing equal rights and status as citizens to everyone in the public domain and in all processes regulated by the state, such as the economy, education, residence and housing, law, police, armed services, bureaucracy, the judiciary, legislature, and media. Even though the units and collectivities that constitute such societies differ in the institutions that regulate their private relations and activities, if their members are incorporated by public institutions that give everyone the same rights and opportunities, they differ radically from plural societies which distinguish sharply the *de facto* political, legal and other rights of such collectivities as slaves and freemen, lords and serfs, colonists and the colonized, Christians or Muslims, heathen, Marxists and others. Since many simple institutionally homogeneous societies like the Navaho, the Plateau Tonga, the Semang and Dayak, incorporate their members universalistically, we should distinguish them from those universalistic societies which are institutionally heterogeneous, such as Denmark and Portugal.

Besides universalistic societies, homogeneous or heterogeneous in their composition and institutional culture, we have also to deal with three kinds of plural society: *hierarchic pluralities* based on differential incorporation, *de jure* or *de facto*; *segmental pluralities* which consist of institutionally distinct collectivities incorporated equally or unequally as primary segments of an inclusive state; and finally, such *complex pluralities* as South Africa, the former USSR, India, Nigeria or Zaire, the segmental divisions of which are often more severe than the hierarchic disjunctions of differentially incorporated social sections. In short, besides institutionally homogeneous and heterogeneous societies that incorporate their people equally and directly under universalistic institutions, we have to distinguish structurally three kinds of plural societies, namely, the *hierarchic*, based on *de facto* or *de jure* differential incorporation, the *segmental* based on the coordinate status of institutionally diverse collectivities, and the *complex*, which as in India, South Africa and Indonesia, combines hierarchic and segmental incorporation in structures of greater complexity. As related above, segmental groups may also differentially incorporate their members, while differentially incorporated sections may contain institutionally dissimilar segments, as in South Africa.

8. STRUCTURE AND SUBSTANCE IN CORPORATIONS

The affairs that each corporation must administer centrally for its members are defined by its form and base, that is, by its structure as a group, college, category or office, and by the principles on which it recruits its members. The minimal body of common affairs that each corporation must regulate to assure its persistence without formal change is entailed by its constitution as a unit whose form includes its organization or lack of it, and by the principles on which it recruits and differentiates its members. In practice, however, the capacity of corporate units to regulate their distinctive sets of affairs reflects the prevailing conditions of their articulation with other corporations and collectivities in the society. For example, units that enrol members by criteria of descent or kinship will be directly concerned to regulate those kinship relations and interests presupposed or entailed by their recruitment criteria and procedures, as, for example, marriage, residence, inheritance, succession or descent in certain kinship systems. Corporations that enrol their members on local, occupational, economic, political or religious criteria, separately or together, will have different preoccupations and priorities, different issues, conditions, interests and activities they need to regulate. The extent to which corporate units can administer such essential affairs and pursue their interests autonomously and effectively within the wider society will depend upon and reflect their articulations, firstly, with other units of similar and differing type and base in the social environment and, secondly, with its non-corporate and non-institutional sectors.

While corporate categories, like categories of other kinds, are often based on a single criterion such as uterine descent or sex, corporate groups always require at least two, three or more criteria on which to recruit their members. Moreover, as we have seen, in order to recruit its members from others in the group, any college requires at least one criterion more than the corporate group of which it is part.

If a corporate category recruits members solely on one criterion or principle such as age, sex, religion or race, for its establishment it is only necessary to integrate the requisites and entailments of that principle with the requisites and entailments of its form as a corporate category in order to articulate its components with one another and with other collectivities and units in the society. For example, racially indifferent contexts should exclude corporate categories based on race, since racial categories can only articulate with one another as superior, coordinate or subordinate.

If, as the prerequisite of its institutionalization, a corporate group recruits its members by two criteria simultaneously, those principles, their requisites and implications, must be integrated coherently in order that the group they constitute may form a viable unit with uniform external and internal articulations. Within the limits set by its form, organization and societal context, the specific content and range of those external articulations will reflect the recruitment criteria that identify the unit's primary concerns. Thus the articulations of corporations with others of similar or differing base and form always reflect the general requisites and implications of their form, and the specific interests entailed by the principles on which those units individually recruit and organize their members. However, it is always first requisite that its recruitment criteria should be mutually consistent in order that together they may provide a sound *basis* for the unit's institutionalization. As a structural entailment, it immediately follows that those conditions will define the common affairs which the corporation must administer and uphold by procedures its members regard as valid. In the normal case, the central set of those common affairs are directly entailed by the principles on which the unit is based and the organization that determines its form.

We can call the affairs a corporation administers for its members and the wider society its *scope*. The population and area in which the corporation's rights to administer those affairs is recognized as valid is its *range*. The requisites for orderly regulation of a unit's corporate affairs include firstly, its comprehensive *organization*, which is usually its most important resource and which continuously needs regulation; secondly, appropriate levels and spheres of *autonomy*; thirdly, appropriate human, material and cultural *resources*; and fourthly, appropriate *external articulations* that define the *range* in which its authority is recognized as valid. Of these requisites, the organization is internal and structural, while autonomy and resources are internal requisites for its operation, and presuppose appropriate external articulations that define the range of its validity. Thus, those levels of autonomy and resource which are necessary for the unit's operation reflect the conditions of its external articulation. The latter are thus perhaps the most important external conditions that constrain the capacities of corporations to regulate their own affairs, internal and external. Of the critical conditions on which corporations depend for their efficacy, the conditions of their external articulations are therefore normally decisive for their formal and substantive continuity or change. Since corporations, being presumptively perpetual, recruit their members in ways that ensure their continuity across the generations, those that lack organizations may persist automatically as a consequence of recruitment by birth or some equally prescriptive condition, such as slavery, unless their articulations change dramatically. Others having comprehensive organization must use that to perpetuate themselves as units with their particular substance and form. We shall therefore not find many cases in which corporations with capacities for positive regulation independently initiate their dissolution; but we may find various situations in which the members of corporate categories act jointly to convert their units into corporate groups by instituting a common comprehensive organization with the procedures, authority and resources necessary to regulate their common exclusive affairs. Given also that corporations pursue their perpetuity as units of diverse form and base, to understand how and why they change, we must isolate those changes in the conditions of their external articulation that modify their resources, range, size or autonomy or their capacity to maintain their form and base. Alternatively, we should seek to identify *de facto* changes within the corporate unit that entail such changes.

The *capacity* of corporations to regulate their affairs efficiently is entailed as an internal operative condition by their form and base. Such capacities are impaired or reduced when the external articulations of a unit deviate from the limits set by its specific combination of entailments and requisites. If a corporation's external articulations are favorably modified, either its range, its scope, autonomy or resources will increase correspondingly, separately or together, along with its capacity to perform routine functions or to undertake new ones. This holds equally for all social units having that corporate form, however they may otherwise differ: chieftainships, churches, firms, armies, universities, guilds, lineages, age-sets, secret societies, or governments in tribal, Marxist or modern bourgeois societies. Conversely, if a corporation's external articulations are modified adversely, its range, autonomy, scope or resources should reflect that somehow, together with its capacity to regulate its usual affairs efficiently or undertake new ones. In direct consequence, the *estate*, or collective resources and interests of the corporation's members, will either expand or contract in security, range and scope as its external articulations alter, thereby extending or restricting their rights and obligations vis-à-vis one another and non-members. The implications of such modifications in a unit's membership conditions may be traced in detail by analyses of its members' role relations with one another and outsiders. To illustrate the analysis, let us consider the family.

As mentioned earlier, the family is both an institution and a group. Families vary greatly in structure and scope in different societies. As the nuclear family of two spouses and one or more children is a clearly structured group, familiar and widespread, though not universal, it will serve to illustrate the nature of articulation nicely. The internal articulations of a nuclear family consist in the relations between its essential components. Its essential components are the basic status pairs of wife-mother, husband-father, son-brother, daughter-sister, and the essential relations are those between husband and wife at one generation level, brother and sister at another, and between either parent and their children separately and jointly. Together those components and interrelations constitute the *internal articulation* of the family and summarise its essential structure nicely.

As a unit the nuclear family also has many diverse relations with other units in its environment, including the families and kindreds of the spouses, who may or may not live nearby, the local church, school, community associations, occupational and other economic groups, industrial associations and political parties, or their cultural equivalents. In addition, each member of the family has their own personal relations with friends, colleagues, rivals, enemies, neighbors and members of various social groups. The sum of those relations in which the family participates as a unit, jointly or otherwise, constitutes its *external articulations*. Together, its internal articulations define the family's internal structure as a set of roles, while the sum of external relations in which its members represent it, or the family participates as a unit, define the family's social position. Clearly, as a unit, the family's external relations must be consistent with the rules and relations that provide its internal structure in order that both sets of activities may proceed without dislocating one another, either by subverting the internal loyalties and roles that ensure its coherence, or by frustrating the operation of its external relations.

Unless consistent with its institutional code of reciprocal rights and duties, the external relations and activities of a unit's individual members often generate strain and conflict. If uncontrolled, they may either disrupt the group by obliging some members to leave, or destroy its original morale and solidarity by converting the relations of love and trust that they assume into antagonism, suspicion and fear by destroying the essential reciprocities on which its unity rests. For many Westerners the sexual infidelity of either spouse often leads to divorce and family dispersal. As children mature, fall in love and find their own future mates, their new bonds come to take precedence over old ties to their natal families, which they duly leave to set up their own homes and found families of their own. In many traditional societies with exogamous unilineal groups, on marriage all persons of one sex, most frequently women, leave their parental homes to join their husbands, whether their husbands live apart or with their fathers and agnatic kin, thus entailing different sets of external articulations for women in such families from those familiar in the West.

While the family is a transient, non-corporate unit, bands and lineages, as corporations, differ in their presumptive perpetuity, closure, uniqueness and determinate membership. If families, lineages and bands all have the organization they need to act as units, besides internal and external articulations, each will also have to manage its *scope*, that is, its distinct set of common affairs which includes its organization, the *resources* it normally requires to do so, the *range* or set of social units for whom its status and rights are valid, the *autonomy* its self regulation requires; and, in consequence, the *capacity* to improve its efficiency in conducting its affairs by doing so more swiftly, economically and efficaciously, or to undertake additional tasks without extra resources. If the unit cannot perform and manage its affairs or scope efficiently, due to lack of the resources, range and autonomy that presupposes, almost always that inability reflects its inappropriate external articulations, which must therefore be adjusted before it may do so. If a unit has all the resources, range and autonomy it needs to manage its affairs or scope, but still fails to do so, that inability reflects its inappropriate internal articulations, which must then be corrected before it can do so. The attributes listed, namely, scope, range, autonomy and resources, are requisites of all perfect corporations able to act as units; and of such non-corporate groups as the family, work team, clique or band of Indian braves on the warpath, all of which, being ephemeral, are clearly non-corporate. However, they are not the properties of quasi-groups, and so distinguish these two kinds of unit.

In short, non-corporate groups and perfect corporations have the same *structural* requisites, namely, coherent sets of internal and external articulations. They also have the same five kinds of *substantive* features, namely, the responsibility for managing their specific persons, interests and activities, i.e., their affairs, their scope; a population or territory in which their structures and institutional activities are regarded as valid, their range; the resources, material, technical, moral, symbolic and social that they control; the autonomy or freedom to undertake and manage the business that forms their scope; and the capacity to perform their normal duties more efficiently, or to undertake further activities without extra resources.

For non-corporate units of any kind, size or institutional level, as well as for corporations of all varieties, the internal and external articulations together identify a unit and constitute its particular structure. Though superficially it might seem that the structure of social units consists solely in their internal articulations as defined above, the precise composition and measure of their substantive contents depend directly on their external relations with other units in their social environment, as also often do their internal articulations. This is perhaps most evident in regard to corporate categories and certain collectivities, the former being prescriptively closed by some unambiguous criterion such as unilineal descent, race, religion, slavery, serfdom, sex, or votelessness, while perduring collectivities such as social classes, age-grades, income-"groups", or ideological conservatives, liberals and radicals, being ambiguous in their criteria and boundaries, all lack definite closure, membership status, determinate populations and distinct identities.

The lack of comprehensive organization that precludes corporate categories from acting as units to regulate or protect their members is entailed either by their status and external articulations with other social units, as, for example, is transparently true of such categories as slaves, serfs, helots, conquered, colonized, and heathen people, inferior "races", women, or the plebs of early Rome; or by the concepts that constitute the categories, such as uterine or patrilineal descent; or by the material, ecological or structural conditions that prevent their extensive internal articulation, as illustrated by women or Native Americans. In consequence, despite their determinate memberships, corporate categories, like collectivities, lack any specific scope or business, common tasks, affairs or interests to manage and regulate, as well as the autonomy, resources and range such action would require, and the capacity to act more efficiently, since as units they have none. Instead, they depend on the attitudes and activities of other units in their social environment for the range or area in which their structure is recognized to have validity, as shown by the historical failures of slave and serf revolts in very diverse milieux. Attempts to reconstitute such differentially incorporated categories as groups that manage their affairs effectively arise by revolt as direct reactions to the changes of their immediate situations evident in their deteriorating external articulations.

In like fashion the range within which particular role definitions and relations enjoy validity clearly influences their content and structure, since any innovations or departures from those norms in that range may and frequently do provoke negative reactions as deviations among others. Such negative sanctions are initially expressed in the behavior of those who interact directly with the offending role-incumbents; but whether negatively received or not, as departures from expected patterns, such innovations depend for their validity on the response and reaction of all interested in upholding the traditional patterns and resisting change. As an integrated complex of collective expectations and individual performances, institutional role-definitions therefore derive from and depend on their external articulations, that is, on popular endorsement and support. That is equally true whether roles are institutional, or anti-institutional as in terrorist groups. Such non-institutional roles as those of drop-outs, friends or lovers also owe their free contents and forms in Western societies to their external articulations which though lacking public sanction provide collective support for their privacy and freedom. When that support is missing, as in societies that regulate relations of friendship, arrange marriages, and punish extramarital love, individuals will normally lack the freedom and opportunity to create such relations.

When the Roman plebs in 439 BC re-constituted themselves as a corporate group, being by then perhaps more numerous than the patricians who ruled the city and relied on plebeian troops in their wars with Latium and Etruria, that extraordinary transformation was their collective response to increasing patrician demands for further troops, resources, labour, taxes and other services, coupled with their lack of legal and political rights, that is, the response to their external articulations as plebs. The immediate and future success of those developments alike depended on Rome's external articulations with its immediate environment. Under patrician leaders, Rome struggled first to dominate Italy, and then the Mediterranean, Northwestern Europe and Asia Minor, which made plebeian support for the Roman republic and its policies indispensable until Augustus established the empire centuries later.

Though the internal and external articulations of all social units, corporate or other, define their structure and delimit the scope, resources, validity, autonomy and capacity that each unit may have, it is necessary to distinguish the articulations of corporate units from others, since those articulations together constitute corporations, incorporate their members, demarcate societies, and provide their macrostructures. As we have seen, the different ways in which societies incorporate and articulate their corporations have profound implications for the non-corporate levels of their social structure.

Clearly the appropriate external relations of corporations presuppose a host of specific situational conditions, of which the levels and spheres of those units' autonomy are merely the most obvious direct entailments. When such corporate autonomies are drastically modified, as by conquest, colonization, or loss of the necessary public support, the mode, form and sometimes the basis of corporations may alter correspondingly. When ideological influences modify the interests, attitudes, loyalties and relations of the members of one corporation with one another, such developments normally reflect prior changes in its context, and entail shifts in its external articulations. Likewise, technological or economic innovations that impair or enhance a unit's capacity may change its external situation.

Given their effective organization, corporations are normally able to deploy collective sanctions to suppress internally generated innovations that threaten their order or viability. Being the chief traditional means of collective regulation within their respective spheres, such units are normally able to restrain their members and to deter or punish non-members for violating their appropriate articulations. Accordingly, the erosion or collapse of corporations as valid structures of collective regulation and frameworks of social order commonly reflects adverse developments in their immediate situations that involve articulations inconsistent with the levels of autonomy, resources and organization they need to maintain their form, scope and effectiveness. When the efficacy and significance of corporate units decline, consequent on such changed articulations, the roles, rights, obligations and relations of their members with one another and with outsiders are correspondingly modified, and the corporations may lose the ideological and normative foundations of their former validity in the eyes of members and others. The receptivity or resistance of diverse societies to change-inducing forces of all kinds, ideological and other, correlates closely with the ability of their corporate organizations to motivate, guide, regulate and satisfy the interests of their members in situations that vary in their degrees of exposure and modes of response to novel influences and conditions. Such phenomena as linguistic and cultural change, migration, the growth of towns and markets, the monetization · and marketization of command and traditional economies, cash-cropping, the spread of literacy and education, the emergence of new types of association, occupation, or cult, all illustrate the changing circumstances in which such corporations as chiefships, councils, tribal associations, communities and lineages lose their former capacity to regulate social action, the traditional situations with which they were once appropriately articulated having disappeared.

9. METHODS OF STUDY

The three most important aspects of all social units are their *form*, their *basis*, the principles on which they recruit their members, and their *mode*, that is, the set of conditions that regulate relations between their members, i.e., their internal articulations, and between their unit and others in the social environment, i.e., their external articulations.

As we have seen, social units are either statuses, roles, persons, dyads, categories or groups and quasi-groups, and either corporate or other. Units differ in the clarity and stability of their form and contents as aspects of their bases and variable institutionalization. Formal differences between such units as the status, role, person, office, dyad group, category and other kinds of aggregate, corporate or other, may be studied most clearly and fully by itemizing the requisites of those units and their entailments. This procedure applies equally to the diverse modes of the unit's incorporation, the universalistic, equivalent or segmental, and differential. Likewise, both the unit's basis, that is, the principles or criteria on which it recruits its members, and its internal and external articulations are best analysed to indicate their specific requisites and implications. The direct and immediate implication of any principle, condition or criterion is its entailment, just as the essential precondition of any phenomenon or concept is its prerequisite, or requisite, as I shall call it for simplicity. Moreover, as each principle or condition on which the unit recruits its members will have a distinct set of internal and external requisites and entailments, those principles should be itemized and analysed separately, to determine their requisites, entailments and interrelations. Those requisites presupposed by the unit conceptually, structurally and operationally are intrinsic and internal to it, while others, being extrinsic but no less essential, are external. Likewise the immediate implications or entailments of its internal requisites are intrinsic or internal to the unit, while those entailments are external that relate the unit to other units in its social context, conceptually, structurally or institutionally and operationally.

In principle, then, unlike collectivities, corporations and non-corporate groups of any kind, size, and institutional status should have the following seven attributes. Besides the *external and internal articulations* that together constitute and identify the unit, these are its *scope, range, resources, autonomy* and *capacity*, which together provide its substance or content. Corporate categories incapable of action due to their external and internal articulations accordingly have neither scope, autonomy nor capacity, and only such range or recognised validity and resources, material, moral or other, as their articulations and institutional status allow. Such units as roles, families, or corporate groups that act routinely, all have specific tasks, activities and interests to perform or pursue, which together form their scope. They should therefore have the autonomy, resources and range they need to do so, and the capacity to act more efficiently. Since both corporate units and non-corporate groups of any kind, institutional status or size should have these common attributes or properties, we may therefore use a single procedure to gather the data needed to construct a detailed inventory of the requisites and entailments of concrete structures or social units of all types and institutional levels in any society, irrespective of their size, complexity and pluralistic or other features. To collect the information necessary for such a descriptive analysis, we should proceed as follows:

1. List and classify all varieties of social units in the society by their:-
   a. differences of form as, e.g., status, role, person, dyad, group, quasi-group, category or other aggregate;
   b. differences of base (i.e., principles of membership recruitment);
   c. differing modes of incorporation, universalistic, segmental or differential, external or internal;

2. List and classify all kinds of collectivity in the society, specifying their characteristics and criteria.

3. Isolate and classify by form and base all corporations and quasi-corporations listed above; and specify the characteristic relations of each unit with other units of the same and differing base and type in the society.

4. For each distinct type of social unit, specify:-
   a. the principles on which it recruits its members - i.e., its base;
   b. its internal articulations, i.e., the principles on which it organizes its members and allocates statuses and roles among them;
   c. its external articulations with other units in the society;
   d. its scope or exclusive common affairs, if any.

5. Examine the principles on which each differing kind of unit recruits its members, to determine the minimal conditions necessary for their congruence and integration to establish the unit, institutionally or otherwise, given its specific formal properties.

6. Fill in the following categories of information for each type of unit. Then consider critically (a) their compatibilities or incompatibilities; (b) the adequacy and validity of your data.

   External articulations (its relations to other units) . . . . .a
   Internal articulations (its component parts & their relations)b
   Scope (the things it has to do and manage) c

Range (the demographic and territorial limits of its validity)d
Autonomy (internal, external) ....e
Resources (material, demographic, social, technical,
    moral/symbolic, situational) ....f
Capacities (manifest, latent) ....g

Determine how well the ethnographic data document these categories, and how best the categories may guide further research and analysis.

7. To analyse the basis of any social unit, first list as clearly as possible its recruitment principles or criteria, and then examine each of these in turn to identify their internal and external requisites, and their internal and external entailments. Then analyse those lists of requisites and entailments to identify and detail precisely any explicit or implicit contradictions and inconsistencies within or between them. Ideally such inconsistencies and contradictions should be excluded by the rules and procedures through which the unit recruits and articulates its members. Any discrepancies between the preceding analysis and empirical data should be examined further in selected situations and by case studies to identify their bases, nature and implications.

8. Having analysed the bases of all social units on these lines, we should then re-analyse each to specify and classify its differing requisites and entailments, conceptual, structural or operative.

    Let us assume that unit X has the form Y and the base Z, each having its specific requisites and entailments. Let us also assume that the base, Z, can be restated fully in detail as principles A-G. We may then distinguish and classify the requisites and entailments of each of those principles and of the unit's form as conceptual, structural, or operational, and as internal or external to it, as in Chart J on page 204.

9. We should then re-examine the logical relations of the intrinsic and extrinsic requisites and entailments of each kind of social unit: (a) first to determine their mutual consistency; (b) next to determine their several and joint consistency with the extrinsic requisites and entailments of other units of the same kind; (c) then to do likewise with the external articulations of all other kinds of social units. That analysis should identify in detail the mutual consistencies and inconsistencies of all kinds of unit and relations in the society,

and should therefore indicate the structural and operational implications of their relations.

10. To check and refine the analysis further, select a number of representative individuals of differing sex, age, social status, etc. from the population. List all the different kinds of social units to which each belongs and with which they interact recurrently; and enumerate their respective status/role sets in those contexts, and in such other relations as they maintain.

11. Then examine the various roles and social relations held by those individuals for their internal congruence and inconsistencies, analysing their respective requisites and entailments as sketched above. Next, list all the adjustments necessary to ensure or improve their reciprocal coherence, specifying the implications of those adjustments for the individuals, relations and social units involved.

    That done, to test and correct our hypotheses, and to further improve our understanding of the society, discuss the analyses of those role-combinations and conflicts with the principals concerned; and with their help reconstruct their social careers by mapping the sequential combinations of social statuses, unit memberships and relations of differing kind in which they have engaged.

12. Using these and any other detailed individual careers and profiles, we may then re-examine our conclusions and test the hypotheses derived from the preceding analysis of the requisites and entailments of various social units and relations, institutional and other, in the society; (a) to check, refine and as necessary, to modify or reject specific portions of the preceding formal analysis of unit relations and consistencies, replacing them with superior models; (b) to identify the likely sources, conditions, courses and directions of change for units of different kinds separately, and for the total ensemble or "social structure."

13. Finally, we should list the specific conditions or contexts in which we would expect those changes to occur to specific categories or groups of units, and then rank or group those conditions in orders of probability and structural importance, so that our analysis may be tested by future events and their outcomes, and thus be at least hypothetically predictive.

CHAPTER 4

STUDYING STRUCTURAL CHANGE

1. REQUISITES AND ENTAILMENTS

I would like to restate the commitment which I made at the start of these lectures to present a set of tools which can be used for descriptive, dynamic and comparative analyses of societies or parts of societies, historical or contemporary, free of the rather metaphysical ideas that have infected social theory as residues of its cultural inheritance from social philosophers and others. These ideas include the familiar shibboleths of causation, causality, and assumptions of causal determinism on the one hand, or their functional substitutes on the other, and the belief that the ultimate aim and test of sociological or any scientific study, whatever its nature and form, is to give a causal or functional explanation of the situation.

So far I have sketched a framework for the comparative study and descriptive analysis of societies. The scheme of social processes, collectivities and units, institutional, non-institutional or anti-institutional, and corporate or other, should comprehend all entities, including all kinds of membership units, that we may find in society, history or ethnography. It is thus at least theoretically possible that with the categories and criteria already discussed we should be able to identify and analyse all kinds of collectivities and social units, institutional or other, in any empirical situation. However, even if successful, such an exercise would at best only yield a static account of the social situation, and could only tell us about its process, collectivities, social units and their interrelations during the period of observation. Thus, even if the model of the structure of that society we derive from those data is correct, it could only yield a portrait as static as a snapshot. At best it might represent accurately the composition of the social field, that is, its component entities, including its membership units and their articulation, at a given point in time. Without further elaboration that model does not enable us to pull apart the items in that field to examine their interrelations, or catalog the conditions that underlie and support their individual and mutual adjustments, which, if changed, would destabilize them. To do so we must first develop various elements in our analytic framework, and then learn how to apply them. To that end I shall develop those concepts of requisites and entailments already familiar to you. I advocate this approach primarily because it avoids the unfortunate implications inseparable from concepts of causality and function. To avoid those familiar but essentially specious modes of "explanation", I shall therefore try to construct and substitute a logical frame of analysis for those substantive causal or functional "explanations" that have fascinated social theorists for so long.

An alternative to the approach pursued here is for us to study the analytic structures of societies, by developing analytic models of social processes according to criteria chosen to distinguish between economic, political, religious, reproductive and other kinds of activity. In that case we shall have to deal with a set of analytical sub-systems, hypothetically closed by the criteria we have used to distinguish and isolate processes belonging to each sub-system. In such a study the concept of system is central, the society itself being conceived as the most inclusive system. Insofar as collectivities and membership units participate in those analytic structures, we could apply such procedural analyses to entities of either class, following the leads of Talcott Parsons and Marion Levy. The structural-functionalists who developed and used that processual approach preferred to see society as sets of integrated and interdependent analytic systems, and rejected the present approach. This begins by classifying processes and collectivities, proceeds to social units, however small they may be, such as role and status, and moves from them through groupings and aggregates of intermediate size and different kinds to the macro-level of collectivities and units, and so to the totality, the society as the inclusive processual and concrete structure.

In the following models I have tried to develop Max Weber's concept of "necessary formal conditions" by identifying what appear to be the logically necessary preconditions for the existence and operation of a particular structure or pattern, such as "rational capital accounting", which is both an analytic construct, an empirical pattern, and a social institution. Though "rational capital accounting" is not a membership unit in Marion Levy's sense, Weber was able to specify several requisite conditions without which it could neither exist empirically in a pure form, nor be adequately conceived and understood. Even though empirically that pattern rarely ever existed with such purity of form, as Weber showed, an accurate concept of it is both useful and necessary, in order to analyse and compare systems of capitalism that differentially approximate the ideal of rational capital accounting by fulfilling or violating specific elements in its diverse array of preconditions. Following that example of Weber's, I shall first try to identify as requisites all components and conditions that are logically necessary in order that we may accurately conceive concrete social units of any kind, base or size, and then arrange those requisites in the correct order of their logical priority and succession.

To illustrate the technique, grasp the idea and apprehend it fully, let us think abstractly of a role. First of all one has to be able to formalize a conceptual model of that role that is appropriate and coherent, that is, a model that enables us to conceive the role as exactly or as closely as we can to its empirical reality. It is of course quite easy to conceive phenomena we can neither see nor institutionalize, as men have conceived for thousands of years the immortality of the soul, and Utopia, at least since Plato's day. Contemporary science fiction vigorously pursues such adventures. The converse holds equally, since, as history and ethnography show, societies often institutionalize many different kinds of social forms, structural and processual, without forethought, awareness, or understanding of those forms and their implications. However, as students of such forms, we shall proceed with care by conceptualizing analytically as clearly as we can the most exact models of their structure, following the procedures presented above. That done, to institutionalize the concept we will somehow have to anchor it structurally in some entity, and endow that unit with the various attributes and supporting sanctions it needs. For example, to establish a lineage, whatever its rule of descent, we must ensure that its requisites will be routinely observed, and that any breaches of them will be promptly corrected, offenders punished and nonconformity discouraged. Otherwise we shall not institute the intended lineage, but a self-defeating formula. Moreover, active social units have operational requirements without which they cannot routinely do what is expected of them by their members or others. One must therefore distinguish by their logical status and relations of priority three distinct categories of requisites and their entailments, the conceptual, structural, and operative, whether they are "functional" or "disfunctional", manifest or latent, and irrespective of their supposed causal origins. I refer here to the necessary conceptual conditions for the institutionalization and operation of a concrete structure or social unit, and to the entailments of those requisites for the structure and its performance. At another level, we should also distinguish between the internal requisites of the unit, or the principles that constitute it, and its external requisites, those requisites being internal which are intrinsic to the unit's conception, that is, those conditions and criteria without which we can neither adequately conceive the unit, nor institutionalize and operate it.

To illustrate, we cannot conceive human societies except as structures of status differentiation. If we look carefully in the zoo at a monkey house we can learn a lot about human societies. Monkeys have several discernible modes of differentiation, primarily sex, age and dominance. In baboon colonies, *Alpha* males behave aggressively more often and more noisily than *Betas*, the smaller baboons, and continue to do so as long as they can with impunity. To some degree, that kind of interaction is not unlike human society, except that humans misbehave more grossly than baboons, and do so in more complex ways. As a species we have far greater appetites and capacities for aggression and dominance than baboons or other primates. Equally important is the fact that apparently monkeys and baboons differentiate their mothers, siblings and offspring insufficiently to constitute families. With them anything goes, any kind of behavior that escapes punishment, sexual or otherwise. Yet, without assuming the minimal differentiation that prohibits such behavior, we can neither imagine nor institute the family nor develop a kinship system, and so would have no basis for further differentiation of status and role in society.

Sociobiologists have recently studied the sexual behavior and 'incestuous' mating patterns of monkeys, and they report several interesting patterns that variably approximate human norms. Yet there is always a clear, persistent set of differences between social relations among monkeys or great apes and those of humans. Those differences hang on the institutionalization of defined status. Status differentiations, and their accompanying roles, anchored in the primary relations of filiation and siblingship, and in the wider relations of kinship, are pivotal to the social order of human populations, and to the further development of more differentiated status structures and their role complements. So much is this so that we simply cannot conceive of any human society without assuming family structure and kinship with adequate degrees, levels and modes of status differentiation as its foundation. There are also, of course, many other structures that we cannot conceive without assuming other requisites. We shall therefore try in each case to formulate as clearly and precisely as we can the essential conditions we must assume, in order to conceive social units of diverse specific kinds; for without such concepts as bases, whether formulated in advance as structural blueprints or retrospectively by observation and analysis, those structures cannot be institutionalized. Neither, without first identifying these conceptual elements, can one adequately analyse them.

As regards relations within and between units, I spoke earlier of membership units and their relations as constituting the basic social structure; and also of collectivities, units, dyads, groups, quasi-groups, categories, and other kinds of aggregates. As indicated above, the two sets of relations which are structurally important for the model are those that articulate the elements of one unit to others within it, and those that articulate them individually and as a unit, whatever its base and form, to other units or their members in the social environment. If the unit is a corporation, together these two sets of articulations constitute its mode of incorporation, and are subsumed by that concept. To illustrate, as an ongoing corporate group, a university incorporates its members in particular categories, as undergraduates, graduates, faculty of diverse kinds, administrators, clerical and technical staff, alumni, regents or others. Normally each of those categories is also organised as a group. There may be a university senate or a students' union, but such structures vary from one university to another. Together these units and categories maintain very different relationships with one another, while the members of each category have distinct and complementary kinds of relationships among themselves. For example, students expect certain commonalities of treatment by outsiders and by one another. The sum of such differential patterns illustrates the university's mode of incorporation of its members. That is usually explicitly unequal, and involves the differential incorporation of different categories of personnel in the university, with their complementary privileges and expectations. Such intra-university relationships rarely prevail beyond its precincts, and then by accident as anomalies. So far as the wider society is concerned, university professors, administrators and other seniors have the same status and entitlements in the public domain, the law courts, the political process and voting booths, the market, church, synagogue, mosque or bureaucracy. Thus, the differential incorporation of its various categories of members within the university is quite consistent with their universalistic incorporation in the wider society, irrespective of their differing statuses within it. In much the same way the society incorporates families uniformly as units, despite the de facto differential incorporation of husbands, wives and children, all being partners in the same institution, which excludes pluralism.

Any university, whether of the top flight or not, is one of many similar units which all claim, as universities, more or less equal status and rights of treatment vis-à-vis the polity and society at large. As a category, the formal organization of the university world is segmental since, whatever their substantive rankings, they all have formal parity of status. Yet despite such formal equivalence, universities inevitably differ in their substantive resources, their endowments, size, histories, numbers of students and faculty, and achievements. Each university rightly treasures and strives to enrich its campus, history, contribution and organization. Formally, at a rather gross level, universities are more or less equal, like the lineages in a segmentary society, the cantons in Switzerland, or the member-states of the early U.S.A., each juridically autonomous within the proper sphere and scope of their relations and activities, the academic world. Vis-à-vis one another, universities therefore, internally and in relation to their societies, exhibit all three alternative modes of incorporation that may structure relations between individuals and groups within corporate units, whether an African lineage, an age-set, a church, a federal state or a society.

The same alternatives apply within and between units. We may find differential incorporation of men and women within such a segmental structure as the Swiss nation-state with its segmentally aligned cantons. Whereas in some cantons women can vote, in others they cannot, despite recent referenda. While women therefore are still differentially incorporated in certain cantons and cannot directly participate in the political process, in others not only do they vote, but they may stand for election to canton and state office. Such juridical differences between men and women do not, however, occur when they both enjoy identical status by their universalistic incorporation as members of a federal state in which the individual's jural and political rights flow directly from the conditions of their incorporation in the inclusive unit, rather than from their prior membership in any of its component states.

The complementary concepts of requisites and entailments or implications are the two main tools we shall use in order to develop dynamic analyses of social structures. First, let us briefly consider the relevance of such analyses to the descriptive framework outlined above. That framework has an inbuilt, heavy stress on change as a condition inherent in social structure. According to the framework, changes occur in society at three different levels. First of all, in its context the society interacts with other societies and with its material habitat. It is therefore involved in processes that are unlikely to be fully repetitive, being open to exogenous changes of various kinds. To illustrate, if a country suffers drought, that drought may not leave a permanent mark on its agriculture or economy, but if severe, it may at least modify the economy's operations and require unplanned adjustments. In small societies with frail economies, the effects of such natural disasters are especially harsh and may trigger riots, coups, migrations, and other unprecedented collective responses. In other cases, such as the spread of malaria in imperial Rome, or the decimation of aboriginal Mexico by European diseases and exploitation in the sixteenth century, societal disasters have social origins. As history relates, interactions between societies of many different kinds are also a very fertile source of change.

Secondly, our framework indicates the highly variable institutionalization of non-corporate structures in society. As we have seen, corporate units are also themselves sensitive to social movements, to ideological and economic changes and shifts in the composition or articulation of collectivities and non-corporate units which they have to coordinate and regulate. As illustrated above, such units as commissions, some of which may be anti-institutional, and corporate categories are also often pivotal in such sudden processes of structural change as those by which the Roman plebs created their council, the Shehu Usman dan Fodio his caliphate in 1804, or the Prophet Muhammad the *dar-al-Islam*, by his flight from Mecca to Medina.

Whether they are strongly institutionalised or not, social units may easily be destabilized and changed at any moment, if their institutional foundations are subverted or eroded. They may then even lose their institutional status and become obsolete. There is in fact nothing necessarily permanent about the institutional units in a social structure, except that illusion itself. To illustrate, forty years ago American sociologists proclaimed the status equivalence of husband and wife in American families, and generalized that equivalence to families in all societies without too much attention to anthropological data on the ethnography of family life. Their presumption was based on the prevailing male dominance of women in American society, which they regarded as equivalence, and assumed to be universal. Male dominance in the U.S.A. was then so complete that wives were identified with their husbands and ascribed status parity. Evidently many American women think otherwise, and they have objected latterly to such social subsumption under their husbands' *persona*. In consequence of feminist protest and criticism there is now increasing recognition of the differential statuses of husband and wife in American society. Such changes illustrate the lability of institutional structures, even those that seem most "natural" and secure.

Changes of this kind happen continuously. For example, until recently, Roman Catholics performed their liturgy in Latin, but after Vatican 22 they used the vernacular, whatever that was. Cognate changes also took place in the nature of the ritual, and in the church's orientation to the congregation, the clergy to the laity, to the world at large, and, for some, even to the Scriptures. These changes, both formal and substantive, were not effected solely to perpetuate ecclesiastical structures. We should recognise therefore that just as social movements may institutionalize themselves and provide the bases of new organizations, political, religious or other, so too, conversely, institutions that now appear consecrated and secure may for various reasons disappear and dissolve, to be replaced by others, because their basic preconditions are no longer valid, or are not routinely met. Changes of that kind and source are built into the structure of our analytic scheme, which recognizes the differential institutionalization and deinstitutionalization of structures and processes as inverse parts of the model.

There is a third and final source of change inherent in our static account of social structure. In that model all social units are structured by their internal and external articulations, internal articulations being the relationships between their components, while external articulations are the unit's relations to its material and social environments, including units of identical and dissimilar type. Being a concrete unit of very special type, any university is articulated to an environment that may include a few units of similar type and many others of different types, including its alumni, schools, city and state organizations, the public and the national academic community. As a unit, the university consists of its graduate and undergraduate students, faculty, technical and administrative staff, its premises, library and other resources, its senate, councils and faculties or subject groupings, etc., each internally and externally articulated in differing ways. Together those external and internal articulations define and constitute the unit's *structure* or *form*.

Those structures are not vacuous but full of content, namely, the powers, rights, resources and tasks of the organization, which are diverse and complex. Let us call the content or set of those properties its *substance*, and list them briefly in four or five categories to describe the unit fully in all necessary detail. First, there is its *scope*, namely, what the unit does or is expected to do, its affairs, business or aims. Next, there is its *range*, that is, the population and the area for which the unit and its institutional rules are valid. Of course, the population involved may be mobile, and both the population and the size of the area for which a unit is valid may change from time to time. Third, there are the unit's *resources*, which may be material, financial, technical, demographic, moral, ideological, social or situational. Fourth, there is its *autonomy*, that is, the degree to which the unit is free to discharge its essential tasks independently and regulate its business or affairs. For example, to achieve its objectives, a university has to select and organize its faculty to undertake the teaching, research and other activities expected of it. Together those four variables or categories describe the unit's *substance* or real content. Thus, despite Levi-Strauss' objection to the distinction, the unit has *structure* and *substance*, form and content. Together its structure and substance generate the unit's *capacity*, namely, its ability to do certain things, to fulfil its explicit goals. The unit may also have some *latent* capacity to undertake other tasks with no extra resources, and its latent capacity may be little or great. If these are conditions essential for all social units, corporate or other, they should also have their requisites and entailments which must be fulfilled in order that the unit can discharge its scope.

To handle its affairs and do what it needs to do efficiently, any social unit requires certain resources that will vary with its duties, basis, size and mode. It first of all presupposes a social *range* within which its existence and operations are recognized to be valid, so that it does not need to assert or defend its validity routinely against others within that range. It must also have the moral, symbolic, technical, material, fiscal, demographic and social *resources* it needs to perform its tasks; it should have sufficient *autonomy* to discharge its duties and manage its *scope* or exclusive common affairs, including its organization. Accordingly if either its *resources*, its *range* or its *autonomy* are significantly reduced, the unit's *capacity* to discharge its *scope* will be correspondingly impaired. This complex of variables that together describe the form and substance of social units demands detailed analysis of their requisites in order to identify the immediate implications or entailments of any change in its conditions of operation, including its articulation with others of the same or differing type.

2. STRUCTURAL AND SUBSTANTIVE CHANGE

To illustrate how we may use these ideas to analyse social change and isolate its structural dynamics, I shall cite my account of Daura, a small Hausa chiefdom in Northern Nigeria, whose political organization and history I studied in 1958. Having recorded its political history, to study the changes Daura had experienced as closely as possible, I first distinguished its three chief corporate structures, namely, the state, the government, of which the chief is the most senior member, and the chiefship. I then ordered the hundred and fifty years of history that I had recorded chronologically, and isolated sixty important "events" in that period as consecutive "moments of change." In treating these events as moments of change, I listed all incidents or processes which historically entailed some significant change in the condition of either of the three corporate structures under study, namely, the state, the government or the chiefship, subsequent to the immediately antecedent event in the series. Over a period of several months, as I recurrently reanalysed the changes those structures experienced during such political events as Daura's conquest by the Fulani and its surrender to Damagaram, in the order of their occurrence, I found that I could summarize their details most precisely by formulae based on the following notation (Smith 1978:463-490).

external articulations	**a**
internal articulations	**b**
scope	**c**
range	**d**
autonomy	**e**
resources	**f**
capacity	**g**

By using these letters to represent those variables, I could write formulae for each event to specify as precisely as the data permitted all changes that had occurred in either of the three structures by detailing the changes in each variable. To explain those formulae, let us look at some examples. Let us first write the formula to summarize changes in Unit X entailed by a specific event:

a b c/d ?f ?e g

As written, **a b** indicates that the first variable to change was **a**, namely, the external articulations of unit X, our reference point. After **a** had changed, X's internal articulations, **b**, the interrelations of its parts, changed next. Then followed changes in the scope of X, **c**, and its range, **d**. Both sets of changes occurred simultaneously, as the stroke that links the symbols indicates in our conventions. Thus, while the first two changes of unit X in this event are both structural and proceeded *seriatim*, the next pair of changes, involving its scope and range, affected the unit's substance and happened simultaneously. The question-sign before **f** in this formula means that I am not sure that the variable it precedes, the resources of unit X, also changed. It indicates my inability, perhaps due to lack of sufficiently clear criteria and concepts, or ignorance, due to lack of data, to say whether there was then any real change in the resources of X or not. Similarly, the following question sign indicates that I am also unsure whether, if the unit's resources did then change, its autonomy, **e**, also changed; but that if its resources and autonomy were both changed, then they changed *seriatim* in that order, and neither simultaneously, nor in any other sequence. In short, though we have to make conceptual distinctions between different aspects of structural change, these either occur sequentially, proceeding *seriatim*, or with such apparent simultaneity that superficially they seem concurrent, although analytically distinct.

Finally, the formula says that if all changes happened as recorded, that is, if X's autonomy, **e**, changed as well as its resources, **f**, then the unit's capacity, **g**, would also change. Thus, the formula makes four kinds of statements, namely, first, what specific units changed at a given event; next, it lists all aspects of those units that changed in the particular instance or situation; thirdly, it indicates our ignorance due to lack of data or inability to identify changes with confidence; and, fourthly, it lists the changes that occurred in the order of their occurrence, indicating whether they were simultaneous or *seriatim*.

We may also use this kind of formula to make a fifth kind of statement. If our data allow, as they often do, we may be able to say with certainty that as aspects of its change, the value of the unit's scope, autonomy, range or resources increased or decreased, extended or diminished. If its scope increased, that would mean that the unit's responsibilities had grown to take in other tasks and activities. Conversely, if its scope decreased, the unit's responsibilities had been reduced. Sometimes we can even say that as aspects of a given moment of change, the values of specific substantive variables, such as scope, resources, autonomy or range, increased in certain ways and reduced in others. We may record that by placing appropriate signs of plus (+) and minus (-) beside the variables involved, as, for instance, in the following formula:

$$\textbf{a b c-/d+ ?f- e- + ?g+}$$

As revised, this formula says that after the first two structural changes of its articulations, **a** and **b**, in that order, unit X's scope was reduced while its range increased simultaneously. If they changed in any way, its resources were reduced, while its autonomy reduced in some spheres but increased in others, as detailed in the data, but overall its loss probably exceeded the gains in significance. If affected at all, the unit's capacity probably increased after all the changes listed, the sequence in which that occurred or did not occur being as in the formula.

To illustrate some other patterns of empirical change in the variables of social units, let us translate another formula,

$$\textbf{b c d/e/f ?g}$$

The notation says that at this event the unit's internal articulations first changed, while its external articulation remained constant. Following that, the unit's scope was changed, but whether by gain or loss is not known. Next, there were simultaneous changes in its range, autonomy and resources, but whether these were positive or negative remains obscure. We also cannot tell whether or not the unit's capacity was changed by that event. With such conventions we may write these formulae as descriptive statements to summarize all modifications in the attributes of a social unit, including specific changes in its internal and external articulations, associated with any event. As we shall see, such formulae facilitate the application of requisite and entailment analysis to details of the units involved, and lay bare the structures of the processes of social change.

For an example from the history of Daura, let us consider the conquest itself. Until that event, c. 1804, Daura was a minor Hausa state under the suzerainty of Bornu in which the chief and senior officials shared an unchallenged authority over the territory and its people. As is normal in such regimes, there was continuous internal rivalry and competition within the establishment, but no direct challenge to the authority of the chiefship. In 1804, when the Shehu Usman dan Fodio established the caliphate of Islam in his struggles with Gobir, having appointed himself caliph, he immediately despatched selected flag-bearers, his commissioned representatives, to conquer and rule the various chiefdoms of Hausaland, and other areas of the adjacent *dar el-harb*, or land of the heathens. To Daura the Shehu sent his disciple, a local Fulani called Ishi'aku, a Muslim cleric and scholar who had studied with him.

On his return, Ishi'aku mobilized the local Fulani, attracted Fulani contingents from neighbouring Katsina, and overran Daura, expelling its Hausa chief and his court, who fled northeastwards. After recovering from shock, the Hausa chief, Abdu, reassembled those who had fled north with him and went to Bornu to seek assistance from his suzerain there. His appeal failed, as Bornu was then confronting another Fulani invasion. So the disappointed chief and his officials eventually returned towards Daura, and over the next ten years assembled sufficient support to reassert his claim to the northeastern part of the former state. That, briefly, is the story of the conquest of Daura, which we can treat as one event.

What constituted that event? Analytically, first there was an abrupt and significant change in the external articulations of Daura chiefdom. In consequence there were also significant changes in its internal articulations, by which I mean that the chiefship and the government were evicted from the territory and its people and forced to flee. A recent parallel from European history provides a helpful illustration. When the Nazis overran Holland in 1940, Queen Wilhelmina and the Dutch cabinet fled to Britain, and there proclaimed the continuing independence and integrity of the Dutch state, even though it was no longer based in Holland, as they did not live there and the Dutch population was then under Nazi rule. The USA and several countries besides Britain nonetheless took cognizance of that claim, and did what they could to assist the Dutch government in exile, as they had done to the French government in exile and others. Thus, although states normally incorporate and regulate their homeland territories and populations, if having lost both, they are still recognized as valid by several other states, that is, if they retain an appropriate range, they continue to exist and assert their rights as corporate structures. That was the case of Daura after 1804, as well as Holland in World War II. Even though he no longer controlled the territory and population of Daura, the Hausa Sarkin Daura accordingly continued to be recognized even by his enemies as the legitimate leader of an independent polity in exile.

With the conquest and associated changes in the status and content of Daura's external and internal articulations came a simultaneous and considerable reduction in the range and scope of the Hausa state. All prior responsibilities for the administration of local communities within the territory had been lost to the conquering Fulani. In consequence there were material losses of territory and population as well as range. Thereafter only Hausa and others loyal to the evicted Sarkin Daura, and other rulers who recognized his legitimacy, recognized the validity of the Hausa chiefship and government. There were thus material reductions in the state's resources and autonomy. Autonomy to regulate the internal affairs of the pre-jihadic chiefdom and to control and use its resources had been appropriated by the Fulani conquerors. Whereas the first two structural changes happened *seriatim*, those substantive reductions seem to have happened simultaneously, and should therefore be so represented. Together they represented a significant reduction in the state's capacity, that dependent variable being largely determined by the set of resources, range, autonomy, and scope, all together. To summarize the changes at this event formulaically, its conquest affected the Hausa state of Daura as follows:

a b d-/c-/f-e- g-

What is particularly interesting in the Daura study, and in another study (Smith 1997) of the much larger state of Kano over a period of 600 years, which contains fewer "moments" of structural change than Daura had in 150, is that of one hundred "moments of change" in both studies there is not a single case in which the substance of a unit changed in any way without some prior change or changes of its structure, that is, in its internal or external articulations. That is an extraordinary finding, and exactly the reverse of Herbert Spencer's belief that all changes of structure presupposed changes of function, which may overlap loosely some variables that denote the substance or content of social units. Theoretically, it is possible that a unit's internal organization or external articulations may change without correlative changes in its substantive properties. To date, despite detailed analysis of all cases, I have not found any changes in those substantive properties occurring without some preceding change in either or both sets of articulations that together constitute and identify the unit.

Another interesting result of those studies is the finding that while changes in the internal or external articulations of a unit always proceed *seriatim* and never simultaneously, changes in its substantive properties may proceed simultaneously or *seriatim*. Analytically we can distinguish between simultaneous changes of a unit's scope and resources, and sequential changes first of its resources and then of its scope, or first of its scope and then its resources.

I think it is therefore useful to ask whether this kind of analysis is fruitful; and if it is, whether it may enable us to say what conditions are requisite for stability in the scope, resources, range and autonomy of a social unit, and what are the logically unavoidable implications or entailments of specific changes in the unit's requisites for those variables. If, in the course of some imaginary experiments, we look at relevant empirical data to see whether our expectations are falsified, to what degree, in what ways and with what effect, the results may either mean that we shall have to abandon this approach, or that we need only go back to the drawing board and rethink our model, then try like engineers to fill in its gaps, or refine its particulars. In essence that is the kind of approach I believe we can use, both to examine and to determine the reciprocal articulations of social units of the same and different kinds within the inclusive structure of society, and to study all changes in the properties of those units linked with changes in other conditions.

To show how we may use such formulae to abstract the structures involved in processes of change so precisely that we can test our analyses for their adequacy and validity, I shall briefly review two or three examples of abrupt corporate change referred to at different points above to summarize their details in formulae. These events are first, the creation of the *concilium plebis* and election of the ten plebeian Tribunes at Rome in 439 BC, when the plebs transformed themselves from a category incapable of joint action into a corporate group so formidable that the patrician rulers of Rome had to accept that group as an ongoing feature of the Roman state throughout the republican era. Second, we shall examine the Shehu Usman dan Fodio's creation and assumption of the caliphal office at Degel in Kwonni in 1804 AD, thereby converting his charismatic commission into an office, and the community of his followers, the *jema'a*, into a corporate group, and their lands the *dar al-Islam*. Finally, as an example of the reverse process, we shall consider France's abolition of the kingship and state of Dahomey following its conquest and occupation of that West African territory on the eve of this century.

As we saw, the assembly of plebs on the Aventine that established their ruling college, the *concilium plebis*, and elected ten tribunes, was preceded by increasing demands and pressures on them by the ruling patricians who commanded the Roman armies in frequent campaigns against Latium and Etruria, and who steadfastly refused to accord plebeians the same legal rights and securities they themselves enjoyed under the patrician Law of Twelve Tables, then unknown to the plebs. Thus the basic pre-conditions of the assembly on the Aventine in 439 BC were the deteriorating external articulations of plebs as resident aliens and the patricians who ruled Rome. Until then the plebs had lacked any comprehensive organization, and therefore could not act collectively against the patricians, while the latter, having the senate and its hierarchy of officials as their executive college and agents, were constituted as the group that monopolized state power and resources. When their common situation was sufficiently grave for most plebs to assemble on the Aventine to consider and take collective action, by so doing they radically transformed their preceding internal articulations and initiated the process through which they converted their corporate category into a corporate group. This unprecedented plebeian gathering on the Aventine was thus preceded and provoked by the progressive deterioration of plebeian relations with the patricians. Those changes in the external and internal articulations of the plebs proceeded sequentially, and should therefore be written a b, following the notation and conventions adopted above.

After assembling for collective discussion of what action they should take, the plebs created their council of tribunes as a concrete structure, charged to supervise and protect their welfare and interests, and responsible ultimately to them at periodic elections. To legitimate such action in their own eyes, they swore a collective oath to uphold the council and invest its members with the autonomy and right to do whatever they deemed necessary or appropriate to uphold plebeian interests or to enforce their decisions. Since the wide responsibilities of the new *concilium plebis* could not be discharged without such autonomy and legitimacy, those powers were promptly vested in it by the plebs. Moreover, since the plebs appointed the council and its members to supervise and protect their interests against patrician demands and pressures, the demographic and territorial range within which the tribunes were authorized to act cannot be separated from the definition of their responsibilities. Thus the scope, autonomy and range of the new council were established simultaneously at its creation, obliging us to record those details as **c/e/d**. Besides the autonomy and legitimacy requisite to fulfil the scope which was invested in them, and the power to veto senatorial decrees independently or together, other resources which became available to the council and its members accrued subsequently and situationally. Initially such resources were material, financial, moral and symbolic, but when the Law of Twelve Tables was finally written down and made known to plebs, they also became legal. Since those resources, represented by f, accrued piecemeal after the council's creation, that should be recorded by appropriate placement and spacing. Likewise, the council's capacity to perform the tasks initially assigned to it more efficiently or to undertake new ones, presupposes its prior existence and operation. Hence, to record in detail the sequence by which those structural and substantive changes occurred on the creation of the *concilium plebis*, we should write the following formula:

$$\text{a b c/e/d f g}$$

That formula also describes the sequence of structural and substantive changes through which the plebs created and filled the tribunate on that occasion. It does so because, although they differed substantively in their resources and capacities, the *concilium* and its components, the ten tribunes, were formally identical.

By contrast, the transformation of the plebs from a corporate category into a corporate group began when the plebs took the essential first step of assembling to consult together on how to protect themselves, thereby at least temporarily constituting themselves as a provisional group for that purpose. They then assumed the collective *autonomy* to decide jointly what to do, and chose to remain together at Rome rather than to disperse or withdraw, thereby identifying the *range* in which they would act. They then identified the kinds of action their security required, that is, the protection of all plebeian interests as the *scope* of their common affairs, for which they needed adequate *autonomy*. They then set about creating the appropriate organisation to protect their interests and welfare, and so endowed themselves simultaneously with the *concilium plebis* and with the tribunate as deliberative and executive *resources* that together provided the comprehensive organization needed to reconstitute them as a corporate group.

Those substantive changes clearly unfolded *seriatim*, however swift the process of their occurrence, and should therefore be recorded thus. The *capacity* of the new corporate group to protect its members and interests efficiently, or to undertake further tasks, only became evident later. Thus, to record the sequence of changes by which the plebs transformed themselves from a corporate category into a corporate group on the Aventine in 439 BC, we should write the following formula:

$$a\ b\ e\ d\ c\ f\ g$$

When the Shehu Usman dan Fodio realised that the conflict with his former student Nafata, the Hausa chief of Gobir, could not be settled peacefully, and that he had to organize his followers for effective defence, he considered how best to do so, and, according to an eye-witness account, having fled from Gobir to Degel in Kwonni, called all who had followed him to assemble at a set time and place. The community (*jema'a*) having assembled, the Shehu prayed, announced his intention to establish a caliphate, and assumed the caliphal office, thus undertaking to act as the Prophet's deputy and Commander of the Faithful, *Amir el Mu'minin*, in this region of the Central Sudan. The Shehu felt driven to create his caliphate by the deteriorating external relations between himself and his Muslim community on the one hand, and the chief and people of Gobir on the other. Those deteriorating external articulations of the *jema'a* entailed immediate changes in the internal articulations of the Shehu and his Muslim followers. Together those developments led him to establish an authoritative central office which would fulfil the requirements and prescriptions of Islamic religion and law by creating a caliphate which, as he stated explicitly on that occasion, assumed full responsibility for the welfare and protection of all Muslims. The Shehu thus first created the caliphate as an autonomous office, and then announced its scope and range. The caliphate claimed authority that extended throughout Kwonni, Gobir and surrounding regions up to its border with the nearest legitimate caliphate. Together those measures were sufficient to proclaim the caliphate; but to be established it needed a caliph and, being its creator undoubtedly the fittest person for that office in the region, the Shehu formally assumed the office himself. By so doing he clearly conferred his great personal authority, large body of followers, moral, symbolic, material and other resources on the central office of the caliphate. But as at Rome in 439 B.C., only the future could reveal the true capacity of the new unit. Thus to record as exactly as we can the structure of the process by which this dramatic change took place, we should write as follows:

$$a\ b\ e\ c/d\ f\ g$$

The same formula describes the process by which the Shehu converted his *jema'a*, or unorganized body of followers, into the *dar el-Islam*, the corporate group over which he presided as caliph, and from which he recruited his lieutenants and officials.

Our final example is France's abolition of the Dahomean state following its military defeat. Clearly, this sequence presupposed drastic changes in the external articulations of Dahomey, following which its historic internal articulations were eliminated by abolition of its central chiefship and government, the state's autonomy, scope, resources and range were simultaneously abrogated, and its capacity abolished, at least formally. Thus, to record the structure of the process involved in the French abolition of the Dahomean chiefship and state, we should write as follows:

$$a\ b\ e/c/f/d\ g$$

That formula also summarises in detail the changes by which the chiefship was abolished.

Together these examples illustrate how we may use the criteria and categories summarized to analyse the requisite elements and properties of corporations, and provide detailed accounts of the successive steps by which their structures and substance changed, even in moments of apparently simultaneous transformation. Such analyses demonstrate the usefulness of these criteria and categories for the analysis of continuity and change in the structures and content of concrete units, corporate and other. Further analysis of the prerequisite conditions in which such changes take place, and of the implications of those changes, should further expose the principles and requisites that underlie the structures involved.

3. THE ANALYSIS OF ROLE CHANGE

To develop a systematic framework for the analysis of social units in terms of their requisites and entailments, let us begin with an elemental unit often regarded as indivisible, the role. We can distinguish as *requisites* of a role, all those conditions that must obtain in order that the role may be routinely and adequately discharged by all or most of those who hold it in a given society at any given time. We can also distinguish as *entailments* those conditions that derive directly from the definition and modal performances of the role in its social context. Thus the role definition and performance link its requisites and entailments. The role can have no existence either conceptually or institutionally apart from them nor they from it. In short, we have here an indivisible empirical unit, which can only be segmented by logical criteria for analytical purposes. The role's distinctive requisites and entailments apply equally in contexts of its continuity or change.

Before proceeding, it is useful to distinguish the internal and external conditions and implications of the role under study, whatever its specific nature, content and context. Some requisites and entailments are internal, or *intrinsic*, features of the role, while others are external, or *extrinsic*. By an internal requisite I mean any concept, feature or condition which forms part of the role as an intrinsic component, such that we cannot conceive the role fully without invoking this requisite. By an external requisite I mean any concept, feature or condition which forms an extrinsic precondition of the role as a social unit.

Internal and external entailments are likewise distinguished by their reference to the role. Those entailments are internal that attach directly to the role and form essential parts of it as immediate implications of other features within the role. Those entailments are external which relate the

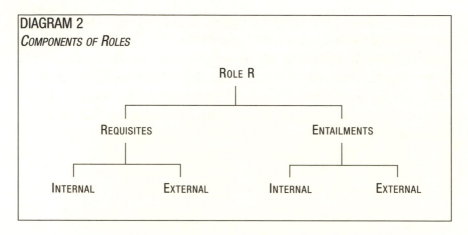

DIAGRAM 2
COMPONENTS OF ROLES

ROLE R

REQUISITES   ENTAILMENTS

INTERNAL   EXTERNAL   INTERNAL   EXTERNAL

role to units other than itself in its social and material context.

To explore these distinctions, examine your roles as graduates or undergraduates of a department, college and university; or your roles as spouses, kin or members of any dyadic social unit. You may learn a good deal of sociology that way.

The requisites and entailments of Role R are illustrated in Diagram 2. Those features of the role that its conceptualization presupposes, whether prerequisite or entailed by its other intrinsic features, are intrinsic requisites and entailments of the role under study, while all other requisites and entailments are external or extrinsic.

We should also classify requisites and entailments according to their bases and their nature. Some are conceptual in kind, others structural, and the remainder operational or operative. All requisites and entailments discussed below are logically essential and inseparable features of roles and other institutional social units. They are therefore distinguished by logical criteria, and identified by logical analysis of the necessary and invariant conditions of roles as social units. However, while some requisites and entailments are purely conceptual and ideational, others relate to the institutional or non-institutional status of the units as structures in their societies, and yet others to their conditions of effective operation.

A conceptual or logical requisite is any concept that is assumed or presupposed by another. If B assumes A, we should distinguish A as a logical requisite from all other types of requisites that B assumes. The converse holds equally. If the concept A directly and always entails B, then

B is a conceptual or logical entailment of A. Thus conceptual requisites and entailments are essential components aligned by conceptual or logically invariant relations that exclude empirical contingency.

We may distinguish a second category of requisites and entailments which admits several degrees of contingency as structural, to indicate that they denote specific features or conditions of a social unit which are either requisite for or entailed by the principles that constitute it, or some specific component of it. Elements of contingency in this category reflect the theoretical and practical probabilities that alternative structural arrangements or features that provide substitute entailments or requisites are possible, which neither assume nor produce any other changes in the structures of the unit or its social context. For example, while the contents of these categories enable us to analyse institutional units, including categories, they apply also to such non-institutional forms as collectivities, provided only that we take their ideal or distinctive attributes into account, along with their diverse requisites and entailments, internal and external. In comparative work, we can expect to find different structures as requisites or entailments of similar social forms, such as the family, in differing societies. The illusion of their perfect equivalence reflects the general tendency of sociologists and social anthropologists to identify social structures by inexplicit functional criteria. To discriminate structural requisites and entailments precisely, to minimise erroneous claims of structural equivalence, comparatively or with reference to any single society, we should always define structural units by structural criteria. For present purposes social units are identified by their membership. Their structural requisites and entailments accordingly reflect the substantive preconditions and implications of the principles on which these members are recruited and the units based, as well as their form and institutional status. Such conceptions of structure and structural relations include all elements of contingency in the specification of structural requisites and entailments necessary to accommodate units of differing form, base and institutional status.

Still wider levels of contingency characterize the category of operational requisites and entailments, given the conditions to which those concepts refer, and the generality of their functional equivalence. A unit's operational requisites are the preconditions of its efficient operation to fulfil its structural requisites and entailments. By a precondition or requisite, I mean here any activity, resource, situational factor or capacity that is assumed by or necessary for the structure of a chosen unit.

Given institutionalization of the unit under study, namely, role X in society Y, the operative requisites of X are all those substantive conditions which are necessary in order that the role may operate or be performed as expected with routine efficiency. The operational entailments of X thus approximate but do not correspond to that usage which defines function as observable effects. In this scheme, however, all operational entailments are direct and immediate logical implications of the structures that entail them, in contrast with other effects of the operations of those structures. Thus my operational category is not exactly homologous with the familiar anthropological conception of function.

The operational level of the analytic scheme exhibits the widest degrees of contingency of its three levels. We should therefore exercise the utmost care and rigor if we seek to specify the variable and casual empirical data that correspond exactly to the substantive conditions of the categories in this scheme.

I have tried to do so in Chart J, which simultaneously strives for the greatest possible generality and abstraction, in order that it may be used to analyse institutional and non-institutional units of any type. The unit's conceptual, structural and operative levels have already been distinguished, as also its requisites and entailments, both internal and external. In Chart J, Unit X represents a social unit of any kind and size, from the role to a society. Almost all such units are distinguished by names, whether those are class terms or individually specific. A social unit's most prominent and important attributes are the size or number of its membership; its form, as a group, category, quasi-group or other aggregate; and its nature, as corporate or non-corporate, and institutional or other. Generally, the name of the class to which a unit belongs, such as nation, role, party, village or sect, allusively indicates most or all of those attributes, while that which identifies it precisely, such as the French nation, the doctor's role, the Kpagwak lineage among Kagoro, the U.S. Democratic Party, Giwa village, or the Plymouth Brethren sect, subsumes the features that distinguish it from all others of that class, type and status. Most of these distinctive features derive from the unit's base, that is, the principle or principles that serve to constitute it as it is by stipulating criteria for the recruitment of members, together with their prerequisites

CHART J
ASPECTS OF UNIT X

ASPECTS	UNIT X			
	REQUISITES		ENTAILMENTS	
	Intrinsic	Extrinsic	Intrinsic	Extrinsic
Conceptual	1	2	3	4
Structural	5	6	7	8
Operative	9	10	11	12

and requisites and their entailments. For Kpagwak lineage, such recruitment criteria include agnatic descent from Kpagwak men and, for men, residence within the group. Among the Ashanti of Ghana, lineage filiation is traced through women, and lineage units are further differentiated from one another by post-marital residence patterns which change as persons age, marry, and their unions mature. In much the same way the prescribed training, examinations, internships and other prerequisites distinguish those entitled to pursue general practice in Western societies as physicians from other kinds of doctors and medical personnel, or lawyers, policemen, politicians, clergy, and other occupational specialists. As used here, the term Unit X designates all information necessary to identify the particular social unit under study and to specify its constitution. Summarized algebraically, Unit X = (SxFxIs) x B, where S=membership, F=form, Is= institutional status; and B (base) = Pa-N plus their Requisites and Entailments, Pa-N being the set of principles that together regulate its recruitment and so constitute the unit's base.

Based on Chart J, Chart K provides a framework for discriminating analysis of the requisites and entailments of any institutional or non-institutional role. Having expounded its details, I shall apply these to two examples of social change in colonial West Africa, and then show how the

CHART K
ASPECTS OF ROLES

ASPECTS	ROLE R			
	REQUISITES		ENTAILMENTS	
	Internal	External	Internal	External
Conceptual	**1** (a) Status (b) Expected performance	**2** (a) Complementary statuses (b) Complementary roles	**3** (a) Status anchorage (b) Role definition	**4** Congruent relations with complementary statuses
Structural	**5** (a) Status differentiation (b) Recruitment criteria and procedures (c) Institution-alization	**6** Congruence with other roles attached to the same status	**7** (a) Transferability (b) Disposal of dyadic sanctions	**8** (a) Restraints imposed by other roles in the same set (b) Exposure to dyadic sanctions (c) Exposure to collective sanctions
Operative	**9** (a) Certain social capacities, e.g., age, sex, health, linguistic & cultural skills, knowledge, authority, power, etc. (b) Resources, material & social	**10** (a) Specific situations features, e.g., place, time, etc. (b) Access to complementary roles	**11** Routine performance	**12** Reciprocation, i.e., reactive responses by others

same scheme may be used to analyse corporations and corporate change.

To expound Chart K, I must first clarify the meanings of particular terms placed in its various boxes, and indicate why each occupies its respective place. To facilitate reference, the twelve boxes of the chart are numbered from left to right; but for convenience before discussing Role R's internal and external entailments, I shall proceed from its internal to external requisites to the internal and external entailments; and will then discuss their conceptual, structural and operative aspects in turn.

Firstly, then, status is an intrinsic, that is, an internal requisite of any institutional role, since every role presupposes some specific status to which it is attached. Moreover, the role consists of certain generally expected types of performance or action by those who hold that status.

Those expectations are therefore intrinsic features of the role, though not the only ones. Since such expected performances presuppose the status they manifest, the latter is their prerequisite, as indicated by their places in box 1 of Chart K.

When writers identify a status as a particular combination of rights, privileges, duties and liabilities, the role consists in the exercise and fulfilment of these capacities (Linton 1936:113-114). However, many others treat roles as patterned forms of action without attention to status (Parsons 1952; Parsons & Shils 1951). As we have seen, neither alternative is valid or necessary. To distinguish status and role while recognizing their relations, it is merely necessary to identify statuses as differentiated positions within related sets of similar units. If those positions are institutional, their relations will express the institutional entailments of the principles and criteria that differentiate and articulate them. If the positions are not institutional, so likewise their role requisites and entailments. As illustrated below, such relations, if institutional, are generally consistent with differing distributions of right, obligation and reciprocal performances between pairs of statuses within the wider set. The structural and operative relations of mother's brother (MB) and sister's son (ZS) may be modified by events that abrogate some of their institutional features, such as their respective obligations and rights. However, such modification of the rights and duties of MB and ZS vis-à-vis one another neither alters the nature and definition of those statuses, nor their genealogical places and relations within the system of kinship statuses of which both are part.

The first structural requisite of any institutional role is thus a set of differentiated statuses, to one of which that role can be attached. As concrete membership units, each of those differentiated statuses will be filled in accordance with specific recruitment criteria, which may, for example, indicate the sex, age, descent, experience or skills of those competent to hold it. Such recruitment criteria presuppose prior differentiations of the statuses to which they refer. Finally, to enjoy validity and regulate the allocation of statuses and their associated roles, such recruitment criteria must either be institutionalized or structurally reserved for individuals to choose and apply. These conditions ensure that all features of roles which express those criteria prescriptively and directly will be institutionalized as operative requisites. The order in which these internal structural requisites are listed in box 5 of Chart K accordingly indicates the relations of logical priority that hold between them.

The operative internal requisites of a role are of two kinds. First are those attributes and capacities predicated at the structural level by the recruitment criteria and institutional status of the role as intrinsic and requisite for its incumbency and operation, for example, maturity, sex, age, physical condition, ethnic identity, descent, linguistic and cultural skills, religion, etc. Specialist competence, authority and, in certain cases, power, may all be intrinsic operational necessities and features of a role. Roles are distinguished from one another primarily by their combination of such specific capacities and operative criteria on one hand, and by the criteria that govern their allocation to statuses and individuals on the other.

A second set of operative requisites intrinsic to any role consists in the material or social conditions and resources required for its adequate performance, such, for example, as equipment, cattle, capital, trade goods, an entourage, family or school, etc., depending on its context and scope.

Given the variable institutionalization and mutability of roles, we cannot conceive any role, institutional or other, that either exists independently in isolation from some specific status or from other roles which are themselves anchored in specific statuses. Sociologists who seek to analyse social processes in terms of roles without relation to specific statuses, find the postulate of their institutionalization their essential condition, even though, as we have seen, many roles lack institutional status and are neither normative nor collectively sanctioned, but optional and variable. One solution which some prefer, though it seems analytically obscure, is to substitute vague indeterminate value complexes as an institutionalizing mechanism for roles, in place of the status structure. An alternative approach emphasizes the instrumental, situationally variable character of interpersonal transactions which may and do generate change in social relations and behavior, while leaving obscure the roles that are simultaneously the agents and subjects of change. Operationally neither of those solutions is entirely defensible. If the role assumes some specific status, that status is itself defined by its differentiation from and articulation with other statuses in the set or matrix to which it belongs. In consequence, any role, institutional or not, has as external conceptual requisites a set of complementary statuses with their complementary roles to which the unit relates symmetrically or asymmetrically. Such complementary statuses and roles, although extrinsic, are requisite for adequate conceptualization of the role as a differentiated set of expected performances. They are thus appropriately classified as its external conceptual requisites.

Since every status is aligned with several others in related social situations, and since each role relates its status to some specific complementary status or status set, each status will have a set of attached roles that mediate its relations with incumbents of its status complements in all situations that involve their interaction. Though all express the status that they enact, any role is simply one of a set attached to a common status and not, as Linton assumed, its full expression. Roles in a common set are analytically and operationally distinct from one another. All accordingly share the common requisite of mutual congruence, since unless they are mutually consistent, structurally and operationally, they cannot be coherently integrated, and will obstruct, controvert, dislocate or exclude one another. The requisite congruence of any role, R, with others in the set, RST, is clearly extrinsic to R in so far as roles S and T are distinct from role R. Such congruence of R with S and T as expressions of the same status is thus a primary external structural requisite for their simultaneous institutionalization in a common set.

At the operational level, the major external requisites of any institutional role are those situational factors which are necessary for its operation and which are commonly taken for granted by the society in which the role occurs. Such situational factors include those spatial and temporal arrangements without which the role cannot be routinely performed. For example, some universities explicitly stipulate that undergraduates must pursue courses in residence for three consecutive years before qualifying for the bachelor's degree. Other stipulations may regulate the residence of graduate students. However, in many simpler organisations and societies, the situational requirements of ordinary role performances remain unperceived or unformulated. Thus, a tribal chief may be expected to maintain order and to subsist his destitute subjects, among much else; but the material and social conditions under which he is expected or able to do these things are often left undefined, particularly in a stable traditional society. Some of these conditions may be situational. Given the resources at the chief's disposal, their performance may assume certain dispersions of demand by space and time. If simultaneously required to deploy his resources to maintain order and relieve the destitute, the chief might fail to do either satisfactorily.

Since any role requires its complements on conceptual and structural grounds, the accessibility of those role complements is an external requisite for the successful operation of each role. To emphasise this, in box 10 of Chart K I have set the condition of accessibility apart from other situational requisites of role operation, even though such accessibility is often contingent on those situational factors, since it should be separated from other requisites of role performance.

We may now consider the internal and external entailments of roles. The first conceptual internal entailment is that the role should be attached to a specific status; the second, which follows immediately, is that it should have some clear shape or definition. Both are direct entailments and immediate corollaries of the internal logical requisites in box 1 of Chart J. Role transferability is likewise an internal structural entailment of the internal structural requisite that role incumbents must be recruited on specific and appropriate criteria. That condition entails role transferability. Indeed such recruitment criteria may allocate the same role to many members of a community at once. Thus, most villages contain several husbands, wives, householders, sons and daughters.

A second internal structural feature of roles which is entailed by their definition and allocation, whether institutional or not, consists in the implicit deployment of positive and negative sanctions within the role for exercise by its incumbent in dyadic relations with the incumbents of other roles. Such dyadically distributed sanctions owe their content, form and effect to the prevailing definitions of the specific roles whose complementarity and interdependence are thus regulated. They are normally also the only sanctions available to role principals in non-institutional dyads. Most institutional roles also involve collective sanctions in certain situations. Such collective sanctions are distinguished from those interpersonal sanctions intrinsic to dyadic relations by their specifically collective nature, authority, procedures and forms. Police, magistrates, chiefs, priests and other public persons may be charged with such collective capacities by virtue of their public offices. In so far as specific roles are instituted with such capacities for such ends, the sanctions they apply illustrate the operative entailment of their institutionalization, namely, their adequate routine enactment.

The last intrinsic entailment of any role, which is obviously operational, is its routine performance. This is logically entailed by all preceding internal and external requisites and is clearly intrinsic to and inseparable from the role. By routine performance here, I mean whatever actions illustrate the institutional definition of the role, that is, its normal enactment.

The final column of the chart lists the external entailments of role R. Normal role enactments are one component in the socially expected or culturally prescribed alignment of complementary statuses. That such interaction should be guided by reciprocal roles which are intrinsically congruent with one another and relate their complementary statuses, is directly entailed by the conceptual requisites of either role. In short, box 4 is entailed by box 2 in Chart K.

A role is subject also to various constraints imposed by the necessities of its congruence with others in the role-set of which it is part. Such role-sets being external conceptual requisites of roles, the restraints they impose on the roles they integrate are extrinsic structural entailments of those roles. So too are the liabilities of those roles to dyadic sanctions deployed in the course of interaction by incumbents of reciprocal or complementary roles; and so finally, but only if the role is institutional, is its incumbent liable to positive or negative collective sanctions for exemplary or inadequate performance. Those sanctions to which role incumbents are exposed are clearly external structural entailments of the particular role that each performs, institutional or other. The normal purpose of such sanctions is to reenforce prevailing definitions of the role. When role definitions are normally and adequately fulfilled, diffuse approval is a common positive sanction.

The external operative entailment of role enactment is reciprocation, that is, the appropriate response of incumbents in the complementary roles. For continuity and smooth operations, such interaction assumes the complementarity of reciprocal roles, their congruence within their respective sets, their routinely adequate performances, and the host of unspecified situational factors such performances assume. Those include the mutual accessibility of interacting incumbents, each of whom possesses the requisite resources and social capacities for the normal enactment of his role. Thus, as box 12 of Chart K is directly entailed by boxes 9, 10 and 11, discordances between the requisites of boxes 9 and 10 and empirical conditions may well entail corresponding deviations from the normal pattern of role performance and response.

I cannot claim that all the aspects or conditions of institutional roles distinguished above are placed in appropriate categories in the boxes of Chart K. I may have made some logical errors in distinguishing or ordering them, although I do not think so. However, I do claim (1) that the twelve categories in those boxes are necessary and sufficient to distinguish all analytically important aspects or features of any social, institutional or other role; (2) that they are also necessary and sufficient to indicate the connections and relations of these elements within that role, and of the role as an operational unit with its social matrix; (3) that together they allow us to analyse systematically all changes in the content and structure of roles to see whether there is any constant structure in the processes by which roles change; and (4) that the same analytic categories may be economically applied to study continuities and changes of social units of greater complexity and span than roles, to see whether such changes they experienced proceed in any constant order.

4. EXAMPLES OF ROLE CHANGE

Following a brief digression, to illustrate and test this analytic scheme, I shall apply it to two unrelated examples of social change in West African societies. However, before proceeding, let us assume that traditional definitions of role R have been subverted by ideological currents which formerly had no place or little weight within its society. If those ideological elements originated outside the society, they are exogenous. Hence, if they induce any changes in the definition or performance of role R and in those social relations that involve it, such changes originate exogenously. Conversely, if the disturbing ideological current arose within the society, as, for example, by some prophet's proclamation of a new message, or some new interpretation of old ideas and values, it is endogenous, and any changes associated with it are endogenous in origin. We shall therefore classify changes as of *endogenous* or *exogenous* origin by reference to the source of stimuli that induced them. Once it is clear that such stimuli have destabilized an antecedent pattern and induced a process of change, we shall not regress further to determine their genesis, since we are engaged neither in historical study, nor in 'causal' analyses. However, it is first necessary that we should clearly identify the set of factors that initiated the sequence of change, in order that we may then study the sequence and its manifestations in detail. The analytic scheme enables us to identify such initial stimuli or conditions by tracing the process of change backwards from the unit's final to its original state, through the logical chain of requisites and entailments that together describe the process, and its result.

Some may wish to describe this analysis as essentially 'causal'. However, since it operates at a strictly logical level and seeks to specify logically necessary relations of presupposition and entailment between changing categories, rather than demonstrable substantive relations of cause and effect between empirical entities or events, I do not accept that view. Moreover, instead of observed or recorded empirical sequences, given sufficiently detailed descriptions of any social units and their structural matrices, we can devise various imaginary experiments merely by assuming that different stimuli or conditions have destabilized or discontinued some particular feature of the unit or its context by modifying one or other of their components. From such predicates we can then use the chart to determine the logical entailments of each of those different changes, and so unravel the structure of the sequence by which they took place.

That said, I should note that exogenous stimuli rarely appear singly. Normally we will have to deal with a variety of social changes that proceed simultaneously at different rates and often in different directions, induced in various levels and sectors of a society by the operation of diverse stimuli, internal or external, that fluctuate in their intensities, immediacy and relations. To discriminate the specific effects of each of those external stimuli, we must first identify and distinguish them, then isolate the particular units or social relations that underwent change, examining each in turn as illustrated above, in order to determine the sufficient and necessary conditions that account for the alterations we have observed. By such procedures of logical analysis, we can identify and distinguish those specific exogenous stimuli that are analytically necessary and sufficient to account for the sequence of changes under study in those social units and/or relations. We should then be able to specify particular relations between specific external elements and clearly defined changes in various units and sectors of the structure in change, including its social and ecological situation, to the exclusion of other features, each of which in turn may likewise be related to developments in other parts of the society. This procedure merely assumes that all the units involved and the changes under study can be reduced conceptually to their essential elements and conditions and their logically necessary relations of presumption and implications, in order that they may be investigated separately and exhaustively. We may then use requisite and entailment analysis to unravel the logical structure of the processes by which those changes developed in each of the social units or sectors under study. Such analyses should represent advances on the selective accounts of social change, abstracted from history or field studies and structured by "explanations" derived from the dichotomous assumptions and typologies of Western thought, or from the causal and functional theories of classical social evolution.

Endogenous conditions or stimuli that modify social roles and relations frequently emerge as reactions to remoter conditions, and often develop together rather than singly, even when they may ultimately derive from a single source, such as the teachings of a prophet or some technical innovation. To analyse the impact of such stimuli on a given role or social relation, it is both necessary and sufficient to identify the structural feature that was first modified as the initial point of impact, in order that we may trace ensuing developments within the unit and its social environment. To analyse the formal and substantive modifications of the structure affected, we do not need to pursue the initial endogenous stimulus further back to some ultimate source, or to the conditions that generated it. Instead, having isolated the endogenous stimuli that initiated those changes, we need only determine whether or not they express recent changes. If they do not, we should then identify those conditions in the antecedent situation that protected the unit against their influence, and then investigate their current status and recent development. Otherwise, first by assembling the necessary empirical data, then by conceptualizing the structures and processes involved appropriately in terms of their basic principles, requisites and entailments, and finally by analysing their relations for consistency, we should locate the social unit or complex of units in which progressively earlier adjustments enhanced or reduced their internal and mutual consistencies, and modified or preserved their articulations with others in the social context. By such regressive analyses, we should be able to disconfirm various 'causal hypotheses', and progressively to narrow the search for the original event or sign of change, to some specific condition or unit in a defined structural context, whose composition and articulations we may then analyse logically, using the methods of requisite/entailment analysis. For that analysis we must first convert empirical units into conceptual structures of varying form, based on their principles of recruitment, then specify their substantive requisites, resources and entailments, and convert the changes under study into a series ordered chronologically and structurally by details of their composition and articulation. By such means we should be able to trace back the process of change to its original matrix, and reconstruct the sequence of its development logically without invoking causal or functional relations. In short, for this analysis we may treat all forces that operate to change a unit, other than those demonstrably generated within it, as external, although some of these may arise within and others beyond the society of which that unit is part; and, of course, we may also define the milieu or society as a unit. We can then distinguish those changes which are generated entirely within the unit affected, from others which reflect its response to forces that operate on it from the social environment or beyond.

To illustrate the analytic procedure, let us assume that the initial modifications in two roles under study were ideological in source, character and impact. To institutionalize modifications in those roles, such ideological influences would have had to be strong and general, and not mere idiosyncratic deviations which are readily suppressed by the normal mechanisms and collective sanctions that validate institutional roles. For purely operational purposes, we may therefore assume that some ideological developments were the source of changes in the roles under study, which were expressed as changes in the antecedent definition of the institutionalized role. Our two examples are these: in traditional Ashanti society, the mother's brother (MB) was entitled to sell or pledge his sister's son (ZS) into slavery, but under colonial rule he lost this right. In Tiv society, as brothers and fathers, men were traditionally free to exchange their "sisters" for brides, but under colonial rule they lost those rights. If provisionally we ignore the colonial situation, and treat those changes as

219

ideologically based redefinitions of these two roles, we can trace all changes that ensued in detail through Chart K.

First, given the ideological shifts we have assumed, the internal conceptual requisites of the affected roles changed to include corresponding alterations in their expected performances, at the same time that the traditional relations of both roles with their status-complements altered to suit. In the Ashanti case that would involve the MB and ZS (sister's son) directly, and the sister's husband (ZH), the father of ZS, proximately. In the Tiv case, it would involve the reference man's sister (Z), wife (W), wife's brother (WB) and other agnates in his *ingol*, the Tiv woman-holding patrilineal unit discussed below.

If status positions are socially identified by collections of particular rights and duties, such abrogations of the rights formerly exercised by the Ashanti MB and by Tiv men obviously represent direct modifications of these statuses. However, the fact that such modifications do not alter the nature of the positions involved, nor their requisites or entailed relations, indicates the inadvisability of conceiving statuses in such essentially mutable, jural terms. As mentioned earlier, MB and ZS occupy the same positions in the kinship grid vis-à-vis one another and other consanguines before and after the abrogation of MB's right against ZS. The positions of men and their sisters in Tiv society are in these respects identical. We should therefore distinguish each status conceptually as one position among others from the particular complex of rights, duties, privileges and liabilities by which it is identified and distinguished from other statuses in its society. On those grounds item **a** in box **1** of Chart K is unchanged by the modifications in boxes **1b**, **3b** and **2b**.

However, the roles of both senior men in these Ashanti and Tiv examples are affected by the elimination of certain traditional features of their roles, namely, the authority of MB over ZS in Ashanti, and of men over their kinswomen as "sisters" in Tiv. By definition the initial change, which we assumed was ideological, modified the internal conceptual entailments of both roles, that is, item **3b** in Chart K. Of the two external conceptual requisites of these roles, only **2b** is affected; and their external structural requisite was unaffected by this measure. In both cases the abrogation of these traditional powers also modified the sanctions intrinsic to the senior roles (**7b**), and thus improved the status of the Ashanti ZS and Tiv "sisters" reciprocally (**8b**), while exposing the Ashanti

MB and Tiv B to the risk of collective sanctions for violations, thus altering the traditional content of **8c** and institutionalizing the change (**5c**).

Moreover, since both these senior roles then lost significant social capacities and resources, both categories of their internal operative requisites were appreciably altered, namely, **9a** and **9b**, but *seriatim*. How such cancellation of a traditional sanction or capacity affected performance of other features of senior and junior roles in either pair, if that is the only relevant factor, would depend largely on the resources and capacities that remained with the senior role. However, in Ashanti these changes in the traditional relations of MB/ZS involved compensatory redefinitions of the roles and relations of ZH and his son ZS, since the latter was no longer subject to MB's discipline by removal from ZH on that account. Thus, reduction in the authority of MB over ZS significantly strengthened the tie between ZH and ZS, improving simultaneously the relation which MB enjoyed with his own begotten son. Clearly, such linked revisions of roles and relations may either generate new orientations and alignments, or extend and strengthen older ones in the relations of F and S, as happened in Ashanti. These derivative changes in the relations of fathers and sons were associated with the progressive weakening of the traditional relation of MB/ZS as guardian and heir as regards discipline, residence, ritual and jural responsibilities. However, in the Ashanti case, the changes were also affected by other influences, among which monetization, cocoa farming and derivative changes of land tenure are important. They are clearly not logical entailments of the abrogation of MB's right to sell or pledge ZS into slavery, and cannot be regarded as such.

However, since this initial change indirectly alters the relation of ZS and his father, we should examine the relation of MB and ZH to determine how that was changed. We shall find that the major change in that relation consequent on the redefinition of MB's role vis-à-vis ZS was the reduction of sanctions at MB's disposal against ZH, at the same time that ZH gained a new resource, namely, a right of appeal to the colonial authority, which he could use against MB should the latter use the abrogated right. In that event ZH could appeal to the colonial administration, the chief or the courts, to enforce the new rule, and restrain or punish MB. Thus, the initial change in the relation of MB and ZS had wide ramifications, and imposed new responsibilities on those who exercised collective authority, whether as lineage heads of MB and ZH, or as chief and councillors obliged to uphold the new rule.

We should also note that although MB lost his former right to pledge or sell ZS, the boy's father, the ZH, received no such right. Thus, while the paternal relation of ZH and ZS was enhanced and secured *in rem* by the abolition of MB's former right, that change did not increase the father's rights over the boy *in personam*.

To determine precisely how the loss of MB's initial right to pawn his ZS affected the boy, we need firstly to retrace its implications for the boy's relations with his MB and his F. For both analyses, we should adopt the boy's role as frame of reference and object of study; and in either case we shall have to deal directly with changes entailed by modifications in some precise feature of the role in relation to others in its set. For example, MB is simultaneously aligned with Z, with ZS, and with ZH in a set of congruent roles. The Ashanti MB is also aligned to his lineage head, and less directly to the lineages of his W and ZH, and to their common or respective chiefs and councils. Such role-clusters illustrate how an apparently single instance of simple role change may ramify to a complex integrated role set. For example, freed of the jural control previously exercised over him by MB, ZS was not placed under his father's *potestas*. He could therefore elect to leave the vicinity to find independence in some distant town such as Accra, to join the army, go abroad, or engage independently in social relations which formerly required his MB's assent. According to the ethnographic accounts, many young men chose to follow these various alternatives. The autonomy that ZS enjoyed thus increased vis-à-vis his MB and other kin.

The Tiv case illustrates similar extensive ramifications consequent on the apparently simple modification of a single role. Traditionally the Tiv, organized in exogamous patrilineages, married by "sister" exchange, that is, by transferring one woman for another as wives between men of different lineage. Tiv men of the same lineage grouped themselves in corporate units known as *ingol,* to pool and trade their kinswomen in marriages. Each *ingol* operated as a woman-holding unit for a group of adult kinsmen, who would deposit and "lend" one another their junior kinswomen or "sisters" for marriage exchanges, to be repaid later with other women by the debtor. Thus, abrogation of the traditional rights of Tiv men to exchange their "sisters" for brides modified relations between the following status incumbents in order of immediacy, and materially redefined the role relations of B/Z, F/D, H/W, H/WB, and *ingol* members. Elimination of exchange marriages deprived Tiv *ingols* of their original purposes, resources and validity, threatening their dissolution. How the *ingol* institution adapted to this abrupt change, I do not know. It faced three alternatives: dissolution; persistence, by undertaking new ways of transferring women as brides, for example, by co-operative provision of bridewealth or bride service; or persistence in some form by undertaking other activities and resources, the two last alternatives not being mutually exclusive.

In the Tiv case, the initial change in the relations of H and W was formerly mediated by that between H and WB. Traditionally when two men, A and B, had exchanged "sisters" as wives, if either woman broke her marriage, the other woman was returned. However, if B's wife, A's sister, had borne 3 children, while B's sister, A's wife, had borne less, A might either claim compensation for the extra children his sister had borne, or he could elect to retain B's sister until she had borne him that many. Under such arrangements, a woman's relation with her husband was always open to disruption by her absent brother and his wife. With the proscription of exchange marriage by the colonial authorities, women were relieved of those risks, and so could develop their own marriage policies. Short-term fertility scores ceased to be decisive measures of the relative value or equivalence of women as wives.

To examine these changes in Tiv society, having first analysed the changed relations of men as "brothers" and husbands, we should do likewise to women's roles as "sisters" and wives. We could then continue to examine the relations of men to their ZH and WB, and conclude by studying their roles in *ingols*. Such sequential analyses demonstrate clearly the connections between roles integrated as sets by attachment to the same statuses.

The preceding classification of role requisites and entailments should enable us to unravel their sequence and determine precisely how and in what order such implications ramify to alter related roles in dyads, or relations linked in sets and chains. One point valid for both the Tiv and Ashanti examples should be noted. For the purpose of exposition, I have treated both sets of change as initiated by ideological stimuli. However, in both cases the initial changes were historically decreed by the British colonial authorities who abrogated the traditional right of Ashanti MBs to pledge their ZS as pawns, and who also prohibited exchange marriage among the Tiv. Do such empirical corrections materially alter the preceding analyses? Only by removing the point of impact initially postulated for the exogenously generated ideological change from box **3b** to those situational factors which were operative external requisites for routine performance of the traditional roles, that is, to box **10a** of Chart K.

British rule drastically modified the precolonial situations and institutions of both Ashanti and Tiv. Those modifications included abrogation of the traditional rights of the Ashanti MB to pledge or pawn ZS. They also included abolition of the traditional rights of Tiv men to transfer their "sisters" in marriage directly or through *ingols*. The immediate effect of those measures, **8c,** was to reduce the social capacities and resources of the MB in Ashanti and the B in Tiv, thus redefining their roles vis-à-vis ZS in Ashanti and junior kinswomen among Tiv. In short, by identifying these administrative proscriptions of specific Ashanti and Tiv institutions as the critical bases of change, we can correct and amplify the preceding analyses of the serial changes in the components of these two roles. First, in Ashanti the role and relation of MB to ZS changed in the following order:

a) (8c) $\rightarrow$ **10a** $\rightarrow$ **3b**$\rightarrow$**2b** $\rightarrow$ **7b** $\rightarrow$ **8b** $\rightarrow$ **5c** $\rightarrow$ **1b** $\rightarrow$ **4** $\rightarrow$ **9a/9b** $\rightarrow$ **11** $\rightarrow$ **12**

Items **1a, 2a, 3a, 5a, 5b, 6, 7a, 8a** and **10b** of the original role remain unchanged. However, as noted above, as aspects of the change, along with **9a, 9b, 7b, 8b, 8c, 11** and **12**, items **1b, 2b, 3b** and **4** altered to express the changed relations of MB to ZH.

In the Tiv case changes in the relations between men and their "sisters" unfolded in an identical sequence:-

b) (8c) $\rightarrow$ **10a** $\rightarrow$ **3b** $\rightarrow$ **2b** $\rightarrow$ **7b** $\rightarrow$ **8b** $\rightarrow$ **5c** $\rightarrow$ **1b** $\rightarrow$ **4** $\rightarrow$ **9a/9b** $\rightarrow$ **11** $\rightarrow$ **12**.

For the Tiv also items **1a, 2a, 3a, 5a** and **b, 6, 7a, 8a** and **10b** of B's initial role and relation with Z remain unaffected, while item **4, 9a** and

9b altered to express the changed relationships of men to their wives, their wives' brothers, and to other members of their *ingol.*

Is such exact parallelism of the formulae accidental, or is it invariant because logically necessary?

If I have erred in listing the precise order in which these role components changed, or in distinguishing these components and situating them in the various boxes of the chart, my errors should affect both series of changes equally, and therefore cannot affect their formal identity. Whether such sequential uniformities illustrate an invariant sequence by which roles, the essential components of social relations, change in all instances and contexts, or only in all contexts of the kind these examples represent, we cannot pause to examine; but it is obvious that structural changes associated with technological, economic or other kinds of development should lend themselves as fully to this type of analysis as those induced by political or ideological factors. It is equally clear that the differential impacts of change-generating stimuli will be shown by the differing number, scope, range, resource and autonomy of the roles, relations and social units such processes affect. Such differences in the number and nature of the social units affected indicate corresponding differences in the structural significance of those processes.

5. CHANGES IN CORPORATIONS

We shall now try to use this general approach to study changes in structures broader than roles and dyads. This is less difficult than we might expect. Since, as elements of social relations roles are essential constituents of all larger structures, beginning with the dyad, to analyse their constituent roles we always have to reduce the internal articulations of such wider structures to sets of dyads.

To recapitulate briefly, besides dyadic relations which are variably institutional, societies include groupings and categories of differing type, base, scale and institutional status. For example, boys and girls form categories in all societies; but, although present in all, such categories are institutionalized as formal age-grades or age-sets in relatively few societies. Aggregates that have ill-defined boundaries and no membership status are inchoate collectivities rather than corporate categories or groups. Nuclear families also may be found everywhere as transitory intermediate groups; but in some societies they are embedded in perduring joint families, and thus acquire enhanced complication and significance.

Besides such institutional structures, societies also contain non-institutional collectivities, groupings and relations, and display non-institutional action of different kinds that sociologists study as *collective behavior* by variably large sections of the population in various situations.

Though roles and dyadic relations are central components and foci of microsocietal processes and microsociology, such elements, being ubiquitous, are also critical for the organization and operation of macrostructures. Those larger perduring units furnish the frameworks within which dyadic relations of differing type and range proceed, each having distinctive properties. These larger units may prove intrinsically simpler to analyse than roles. As we have seen, all societies include some units institutionalized as perpetual concrete structures, along with many others that are temporary, conditional or transient. Units of the first, presumptively perpetual, kind should be distinguished as *corporations* from all other social units such as dyads which are transient. The various kinds of corporations are all distinguished from quasi-corporations and non-corporate units by the following four features: (1) their presumption of perpetuity; (2) their unique social identities; (3) their distinctive rules of recruitment and closure; and (4) their determinate memberships. To develop and adapt the analytic framework of Chart K for the study of corporate change, we need to look more closely at the requisites and implications of corporate organization, as is done in Chart L.

It is obvious that we cannot conceive any concrete social unit or membership structure as perpetual without first apprehending its identity. Having done that, if we assume the unit's perpetuity, we create the problem of ensuring its persistence, given human mortality. Thus, specific rules and procedures by which the unit can recruit its members generation after generation are directly entailed by the presumption of its perpetuity. Such criteria and rules of recruitment are further conditioned by the unit's postulated uniqueness, which entails a distinct and determinate membership; for only if the rules and procedures by which a unit recruits its members are sufficiently precise to exclude ambiguities of individual identification will it display the requisite uniqueness. Thus in Chart L, while the criteria of uniqueness (**1a**) and presumed perpetuity (**1b**) are

CHART L

ASPECTS OF CORPORATIONS

ASPECTS	CORPORATION Y			
	REQUISITES		ENTAILMENTS	
	Internal	External	Internal	External
Conceptual	1 (a) Uniqueness (b) Perpetuity	2 Complementary Units	3 (a) Recruitment criteria (b) Membership	4 Similarity and differences of complementary units
Structural	5 (a) Status differentiation (b) Institution-alization (c) Comprehensive organization	6 Appropriate external articulations	7 (a) Common affairs = scope (b) Regulatory procedures (c) Internal articulations	8 (a) Range (b) Exposure to sanctions by other units
Operative	9 (a) Autonomy (b) Resources	10 (a) Specific situational conditions (b) Access to complementary units	11 (a) Capacity to regulate its internal affairs (b) Routinized performance	12 (a) Capacities re. external affairs (b) Expectations by others (c) Reciprocation by others

internal conceptual requisites of corporations, criteria of precise recruitment (**3a**) and determinate membership (**3b**) are internal conceptual entailments. By that I mean that we literally cannot conceive corporations correctly without first assuming those two requisites, which entail recruitment criteria and determinate membership as their immediate logical implications.

Those four formal features are inseparably linked and exclude contingencies. Assuming or implying one another, they form an irreducible set of conditions that distinguish corporations as a class from all other classes of social unit. Nonetheless, those four criteria do not exclude the possibility that corporations may differ among themselves in form as well as basis. Indeed, one type of corporation, namely, the *corporate category*, a unique, externally indivisible, and presumptively perpetual social unit containing a plurality of members recruited under precise criteria that exclude non-members, is almost completely defined by those four criteria. Clans, moieties, castes, slaves, bondsmen, peons, helots or serfs, ethnic or racial categories, some types of age sets, and all acephalous societies illustrate varieties of this type. Formally, corporate categories are fully described by the four criteria that separate corporations as a genus from other social forms; but to persist and retain those qualities, all corporate categories must be institutionalized as units of distinct status whose validity is supported by appropriate external articulations and endorsed by their societies. At this point, as we found to be the case with roles (page 206), alternative conditions may be institutionalized, thus introducing corresponding structural contingencies. In Chart L, following boxes **1a, 1b, 3a, 3b, 2** and **4**, those structural conditions are listed as **5a, 5b, 6, 8a and 8b**. Of those, **6** as an external requisite follows **5a** and **5b**, which also entail **8a** and **8b** externally.

Like other corporations, corporate categories are concrete social units with determinate memberships. As intrinsic structural requisites, they assume their own status differentiation as units and that of their members, as well as their institutionalization. The lack of comprehensive organization which renders them incapable of acting as units to manage or undertake any matter for their members is another structural requisite of corporate categories. Hence, given their operational incapacities, it follows that the articulation of these categories with other social units is presupposed by the criteria on which they recruit their members and exclude non-members. Such collective articulations specify for members the implications of their membership, with one another and with members of other units of the same and different type in that society. For example, if clansmen recruited by unilineal descent are forbidden to marry one another as an entailment of their common descent, they must marry members of other clans. If slaves are forbidden to marry one another or free persons, they must mate without marriage, if at all. Finally, the institutional status of corporate categories, and the distinct statuses of their members, entail their recognition and acceptance as valid by the societies of which they are part, while exposing them to sanctions by other units. Those external structural entailments listed as **8a** and **8b** in Chart L complete the requisites and entailments of corporate categories. Lacking the necessary organization, **5c**, they also lack the properties listed in boxes **7, 9, 10, 11** and **12**.

Chart L classifies the essential elements of all three kinds of corporation that act as units, the college, group and office, in the same twelve categories as those we have used to analyse roles, namely, conceptual, structural and operative requisites and entailments, though in view of the differences between corporations and roles, the contents of these categories also differ. The charts help us to appreciate fully the critical differences between corporate categories on the one hand, and colleges, offices and corporate groups on the other. Since appropriate external articulations are structurally requisite in order that corporations may enjoy the resources and autonomy they need to regulate their respective affairs, such articulations are listed in box **6** as external structural requisites. The corporation's affairs, its scope (**7a**), must be regulated by appropriate procedures (**7b**), which include besides relations among their members, the relations between their members and other non-members. These external relations will vary in their particulars for corporations of differing type and base in correspondence with the unit's form and recruitment criteria that differentiate it from other colleges, corporate groups and offices.

It might be argued that the autonomy and resources that such corporations require for their routine operation are directly entailed by their appropriate external articulations, and should therefore be placed in box **8** of Chart L. That the autonomy and resources these units enjoy will vary with their external articulation is clear and established; but those relations do not always satisfy the structural requisites for the unit's efficacious operation; and the criteria that define the latter derive rather from the conditions of the unit's organization, the affairs it administers, and the procedures it employs, than from its prevailing external articulations. Alternative definitions of those criteria being theoretically possible, it follows that their institutionalization involves some structural contingency and greater contingency at the level of operational requisites and entailments. For these reasons among others, I regard adequate autonomy (**9a**) and resources (**9b**) as intrinsic operational requisites of these corporations rather than external structural entailments that derive directly from their prevailing external articulations. Moreover, given those articulations, the corporation's capacity to regulate its internal affairs by positive action (**11a**) is an internal operative entailment of the relation between its resources and autonomy on the one hand, and the affairs it has to regulate on the other, which also demonstrates contingency.

As already mentioned, governmental bodies endowed with appropriate authority sometimes create unique commissions by approved procedures to undertake special tasks. Presidential or parliamentary commissions of enquiry illustrate the type. Such commissions differ from others in their uniqueness, their self-liquidating character, the authority they enjoy to create their own patterns of procedure, and their normal constitution as a committee of several members. We should thus distinguish those commissions of the parliamentary or presidential type which are characteristic of modern complex societies from the self-authenticating charismatic commissions that figure prominently in many different kinds of society, simple, intermediate and advanced.

I shall not include here the charts that classify these three types of commission by their essential elements and implications. Those charts illustrate the differences in their nature, operation and articulation, and demonstrate the advantages of analysing units of such differing type and base comparatively in terms of their internal and external requisites and entailments. They also show that the two varieties of individual commission, the self-authenticating charismatic form, and that included in some ranked perduring series, approximate more closely the role structure set out in Chart K than that of corporations illustrated in Chart L. In contrast, a chart constructed to analyse government-appointed commissions of the parliamentary or presidential type would correspond more closely in its requisites and entailments to one that describes corporations with positive regulatory powers.

Thus of all these kinds of unit, only corporate categories lack positive regulatory capacities; yet even they, being defined and sanctioned negatively by precise conditions that regulate the conduct of their members with one another and with outsiders, are significant as agencies of collective regulation.

The preceding analysis of role structures has shown that we could express their modifications either as changes in the capacities of antecedent arrangements to regulate the action of role incumbents in conformity with prevailing norms, or as changes in the scope or type of affairs that such roles regulate. Thus the Ashanti MB and adult male Tiv lost capacities to place their ZS in slavery, or their Z in marriage respectively. We have also seen that unless individual divergences of role performance from institutional expectations are routinely restrained by dyadic or collective sanctions, the prevailing definition of a role is likely to keep on changing until either some other definition is institutionalized, or the role segments or disappears as an institutional unit. In short, inadequate or inappropriate regulation of conduct in changing circumstances is a normal condition of changes in roles. Appropriate regulation of conduct is therefore equally critical for role stability or change; and since the four varieties of corporation and three types of quasi-corporation just reviewed, together subsume all forms of collective regulatory agents in all societies, they have a central place in all studies of macro-social change.

An important external requisite of all corporations at the conceptual level is the existence of complementary units, **2**. Every corporation is one of a set of such units. Even the society as a corporate unit is simply one of a set of societies that share the same formal status and properties. As an external entailment, that condition involves complementary relations between similar corporate units. That external entailment therefore will demonstrate the corporation's similarity or difference of form, basis, mode, location and content with its complementary units, **4**. If a corporation fulfils these conceptual requisites but lacks comprehensive organization, it must either exist as a corporate category in the wider society; or form a society incapable of co-ordinated activity as a unit, because it lacks the requisite organization. For corporations to be capable of routine effective action as units, the conditions listed in box **5**, namely **5a, 5b and 5c**, must be institutionalized. Especially critical is the latter, namely, the institutionalization of its organization (**5c**), since that establishes the unit normatively with the sanctions necessary to ensure its continuity, and provides the set of relations and procedures through which the unit can mobilize its members for common action.

Such institutionalization assumes that the unit has appropriate external articulations, **6**, since if those are inappropriate, the conditions its operation requires may not be met. Moreover, if its organization is a necessary condition for a unit, that organization becomes the central structure it has to manage and strengthen, and its maintenance or renewal becomes a primary interest for the unit in order that it may perpetuate itself, **7a**. This really requires the unit to have appropriate regulatory procedures and internal arrangements to ensure the continuity of its organization, **7b**. Those procedures and arrangements are therefore internal entailments of the unit's comprehensive organization. An external entailment of the organization's institutionalization is the societal range in which the unit's organization and authority enjoy validity, that is, the territorial range of the population which regards the normal unit and its normal activities as legitimate; **8a**. Another external structural entailment of its institutionalization as an organized unit is the corporation's exposure to sanctions by other units for actions of its members and representatives; **8b**. In different societies and cultures this may lead to blood feud, or to the suspension of marriage arrangements or trade.

The operative requisites of corporate activities are adequate autonomy and resources for the corporation to manage its affairs, to satisfy its needs, and to perpetuate itself; **9a, 9b**. As external requisites, any corporation also exists in various specific conditions which become contingent needs, **10a**. For example, if a cattle herding lineage loses its cattle, as happened to Fulani pastoralists in rinderpest epidemics during the 19th century, it must either scatter and dissolve, replace the lost herds, or struggle to survive by undertaking some equivalent activity such as herding camels, horses, goats or sheep. That was also the plight of Tuareg camel herders of the West African sahel who suffered severely during the prolonged droughts of the 1970s, and lost their stock. Such cases show that, like other social units, corporations assume specific situational conditions for their efficient routine operation, the specifics and operative contingencies varying with the unit's nature and the culture in which it is set. Access to complementary bodies of similar and differing kinds is also necessary for the operation of any unit, as, for instance, when exogamous villages or lineages have to marry members of other units of similar basis and type, **10b**.

Two operative entailments, listed in box **11a** and **b**, are the corporation's ability to regulate its internal affairs and routinely to satisfy its requirements and fulfil its obligations by its normal procedures. Finally, given adequate autonomy, resources, a suitable situation, and access to complementary units, the external entailments of a corporation are its ability to manage its external affairs and relations as expected by other units which will react reciprocally to it; **12a, 12b, 12c**.

While stressing once more the preliminary and tentative character of this approach, it seems particularly useful as a tool to break down social units into their essential components, so that we may see exactly how they are constituted and how their components articulate with one another. To do so we must determine the logical order and status of their conceptual, structural or operative requisites and entailments, so that we may then employ that instrument to analyse instances of corporate change in order to lay bare the structure of the sequence through which it developed in differing contexts and corporations.

6. EXAMPLES OF CORPORATE CHANGE

To illustrate these techniques, let us consider what happens when structural change occurs, whether it develops endogenously within a society or exogenously. As a first example, let us briefly review the rise of Shaka and the Zulu chiefdom. As far as we know from their early history, the ethnic core of the future Zulu nation was a set of small localized exogamous patrilineages and clans, which were all formally equal and coordinate in status and power, spoke the same language, and shared a common culture. Shaka, who succeeded lineally to the head of his lineage, was a military innovator, who changed the fighting equipment and organization of his forces, and consequently had enormous success in battle. The growth of his power and of the Zulu people were meteoric and parallel. To begin his conquests, Shaka first of all mobilized his own clansmen and ethnic group, the Zulu, against non-Zulu outsiders, and then forcibly incorporated the manpower of the defeated tribal forces into a series of age-regiments he created and kept ready for war in barracks as a standing army under his control. In consequence, as he defeated and overran nearby populations, his armies expanded by the forced recruitment of those defeated like a snowball, until they were too unwieldy for a single commander. They then either split and moved away under independent commanders, or were subdivided among several whom he selected for their loyalty and talents. In this continuing process of rapid conquest and expansion, Shaka's lineage soon ceased to be equals of other Zulu lineages as they were initially, and became a much larger dominant unit of a quite new kind. In what was hitherto an egalitarian structure of corporate lineages and clans, a powerful royal dynasty began to develop, even though Shaka had no sons. That, briefly, is an example of endogenously generated change which proceeded through the successful use of military force and political innovations to develop the Zulu kingdom and empire. During that process many thousands lost their lives in battle, Zulus and others.

If we look at Chart L on corporations, and consider these developments, we shall find that the uniqueness and perpetuity, the recruitment criteria and the membership of the lineage corporations involved remained the same. However, even at the conceptual level the initial complementarity of those units ceased to hold, and changed in box **4** as a direct external entailment of the emergence of the royal lineage, which by establishing new articulations, **6**, became a new kind of unit that claimed superior status to all the lineages and clans that were formerly its peers, **4**. There was corresponding modification of the original status structure, since new modes of status differentiation emerged with the rise of this royal lineage and the incorporation of conquered non-Zulu in new age-regiments, **5a**. Those status differences became manifest through the changed external articulations of Shaka's lineage with other Zulu clans as well as the large conquered population, **6**, and its institutionalization as the dynasty, **5b**. Otherwise the lineage organization remained unchanged, **5c**.

These changes entailed simultaneous changes in the scope or exclusive common affairs of the ruling Zulu clan, **7a**, which now had more matters to look after, including the new standing army of age-regiments, each commanded by an appointed *induna* or general, responsible to Shaka. To administer these tasks and resources entailed new regulatory procedures and internal articulations, **7b**, **7c** and greatly changed the demographic and territorial range of Shaka's authority, **8a**. Simultaneous increases in the autonomy claimed by the Zulu chief, and reductions in the autonomy and resources of other Zulu clans subjected to his overriding jurisdiction, were internal operative requisites of the new royal power, **9a**, **9b**. The situational conditions that were externally requisite for the continued exercise and growth of Zulu power now included peaceful relations with whites in Natal and adjacent Transvaal, as well as other native peoples, **10a**. In consequence of its enhanced resources and autonomy, the Zulu chiefship and royal clan were able to regulate their own internal and external affairs routinely and efficiently, **11a**, **12a**, thus generating appropriate expectations and responses by other units, **12b, 12c.**

This sequence of changes may be written thus:

$$(6) \to 4 \to 5a \to 5b \to 7a \to 7b \to 7c \to 8a \to 9a/9b \to 10a \to 11a \to 11b \to 12a \to 12b/12c$$

In Chart L, which classifies the essential elements of corporation Y by their status relations as internal or external requisites and entailments, the four conceptual requisites which are sufficient to constitute corporate categories and to distinguish corporations from all other types of social unit, are listed in boxes **1** and **3**, while the organization and its implications that enable some corporations to act as units and distinguish them from categories, are listed in boxes **5c, 6, 7** and **9** to **12**. Of the elements of corporation Y itemized in Chart L, status differentiation and institutionalization are intrinsic structural requisites of all types of corporation, noted in **5a** and **5b**. All corporations share those internal requisites, and need appropriate articulations with other social units for their members. Excluding status differentiation, institutionalization, appropriate external articulation, societal range and exposure to sanctions by other units, **5a, 5b, 6, 8a, 8b**, corporate categories lack **5c** and all other items listed in boxes **7, 9, 10, 11** and **12** of Chart L. Since they have no comprehensive organization, such units cannot have any common exclusive affairs, common procedures to regulate such affairs, corporate autonomy or resources, and therefore have no positive capacity for regulatory action.

It is possible that I have placed some of the features that constitute corporations and corporate categories as requisites and entailments inappropriately in Chart L, though I do not think so. Though it might be argued that the lack of comprehensive organization is an operative requisite of corporate categories, it seems to me that the presence or absence of such organization is structurally requisite to differentiate units with positive capacities from those without. That these are structural rather than conceptual features of a unit is shown by the fact that they may be present or absent in units of the same general kind, namely, corporations aggregate. However, while such uncertainties indicate the subtlety of the criteria and procedures required to analyse these units, they also illustrate the utility and adaptability of the framework originally devised to analyse the composition and structure of roles and the details of their continuity or change, and its applicability to social units of broader span and greater variety. Chart L also reveals that the collective requisites and properties of these larger social units may prove less difficult to study than those of roles.

To test the results of such analyses, we should cross-check their conclusions by reanalysing the data using other concepts and methods. To that end we may use the requisites and entailments presented above to re-analyse the same events already analysed to determine changes in the set of seven variables. This should show whether there is any material difference between results yielded by studying the changes in those attributes and articulations, and that derived by reanalysis of the data in terms of the requisites and entailments of those corporations.

To that end I shall re-analyse the corporate transformations already discussed in Rome, Gobir and Dahomey, to determine their effects on the structures involved, such as offices, categories and groups. Since those events all involved corporations of some kind, I shall first re-analyse their processes with the help of Chart L to test and hopefully refine the preceding analyses, by determining the precise nature and order of those changes, beginning with the creation of the *concilium plebis* by the plebs in 439 BC.

As that event created new structures and changed some that already existed, while leaving others unchanged, before seeking to detail its sequence I should first list in their order of logical priority those elements or aspects of the antecedent structures and situation that remained unchanged, those that changed but persisted, and those created *de novo* by the event. However, for brevity, I shall omit those steps and concentrate on the event itself. As indicated earlier, that sequence began with changes in the external articulations, **6**, of the Roman plebs, which led to the specific situation of their assembly on the Aventine, **10a**. That provisionally redefined their status, **5a**, by providing them for the first time with an opportunity for comprehensive organization, **5c**, which they promptly institutionalized, **5b**, by deciding to establish their council. Thus, following the distribution of categories in Chart L, to record those developments, we should write:

$$(6) \to 10a \to 5a/5c \to 5b$$

Being already a unique, presumptively perpetual and closed category of the Roman populace, even at that stage the plebs were recruited by specific criteria and had a determinate membership, **3a, 3b**. Before their assembly on the Aventine that day, they were distinguished from the ruling patricians in various ways, including their legal and political status as non-citizens, being non-Roman by origin. Following the decision to establish their own comprehensive organization, **5c**, the plebs identified its scope, regulatory procedures and internal articulations, **7a/b/c**, as well as its range, **8a**; and, being exposed to various pressures and sanctions from the patricians, **8b**, to improve their situation, endowed their central college and offices with the autonomy, **9a**, and resources, **9b**, it needed to override senatorial decrees and officers and ensure peremptory access to the Senate when desired, **10b**.

Accordingly, the assembly of plebs endowed those newly created units, the council and their tribunate, with authority to regulate their internal and external affairs, **11a, 12a**, thus ensuring their efficient routine operation, **11b**, and appropriate expectations and responses from the patricians and senate, **12b and 12c**. To record the sequence by which this development occurred using the categories and sub-categories of Chart L, we should therefore write as follows:

$$(6) \to 10a \to 5a/c \to 5b \to 7a/b/c \to 8a \to 8b \to 9a/b \to 10b \to$$
$$11a/12a \to 11b \to 12b/c$$

If we compare that formula with its equivalent on page 202, the first briefer set of seven categories, **a b c/e/d f g**, we shall notice various divergences that are due mainly to differences in the number, structure and content of the categorical schema on which both formulae are based. As necessary, such comparisons should compare and examine critically the correspondences and divergences of the two sets of formulae designed to describe the same event or process, in order to test and refine both analyses and the categorical frameworks that underlie them. Interested readers may undertake this comparative analysis themselves, in order to determine the mutual consistency of the two frameworks, and to see whether the combined analyses shed more light on the changes to which the unit is subject than either does separately. Especially also we should try to develop both analyses further to yield greater detail, understanding and demonstrability.

To detail the structural changes involved in Shehu Usman's assumption of the caliphal office on proclaiming the caliphate in 1804, we should recognise that both events responded to the changing situation of the Shehu and his people, marked by their deteriorating relations and increasing conflict with the chief and state of Gobir, **6**, which provoked the specific situation of the assembly at Degel, **10a**. Until then the Shehu had exercised a unique charismatic commission which, being personal, was not perpetual. By proclaiming the caliphal office, he established a unique and presumptively perpetual corporation, **1a/b**, and by assuming it, he identified its essential recruitment criterion and first holder, **3a/b**. Since that event took place in the context of conflict between the Shehu and his followers and the chief and people of the Hausa state of Gobir, the latter already existed as a complementary unit whose difference from and opposition to the Islamic caliphate matched that between the caliphal office and the Hausa chiefship, **2/4**. In thus proclaiming and assuming the caliphal office, the Shehu transformed his original commission into an office, a quite new and different status, **5a**, having an institutional organization, **5b** and **5c**. To ensure its efficacy, he then assumed and defined the scope, range and autonomy of his office, which claimed authority over all Muslims throughout the Central Sudan, **7a, 8a, 9a**. Thereby he undertook to establish appropriate regulatory procedures, **7b**, to secure the necessary resources, **9b**, and to regulate the unit's internal and external affairs, **11a, 12a**. We may therefore summarize the development of this sequence as follows:

$$(6) \rightarrow 10a \rightarrow 1a/b \rightarrow 3a/b \rightarrow 2/4 \rightarrow 5a \rightarrow 5b/c \rightarrow 7a/8a/9a \rightarrow 7b \rightarrow 9b \rightarrow 11a/12a$$

Using the notation set out above to describe these changes in the seven attributes of a social unit, on page 204 we found that the Shehu established his caliphate, and simultaneously converted his *jema'a* (following) into a corporate group, by processes having the structure of **a b e c/d f g**. We should surely ask what, if anything, do the differences in these two sets of formulae signify. Are both correct, or equally incorrect? Or do the formulae supplement each other where they do not directly overlap?

Clearly, the formula set out on page 204 differs greatly from that based on the 12 boxes and 23 distinct conditions of Chart L. For example, although restricted to 7 variables, the first briefer formula includes one item, capacity, which Chart L does not. Moreover, as indicated on pages 195 to 197, the category of internal articulations, **b**, subsumes the principles on which social units recruit their members, and also denotes their organization, or lack of it. By contrast, Chart L includes the following categories, which refer solely to the constitution of corporations - **1a, 1b, 3a, 3b, 5a, 5b**. While these are sufficient to describe corporate categories, offices, colleges and corporate groups also require **5c** (comprehensive organization) and **7c**, to which the term internal articulations, category b, in the shorter formula, corresponds. To record in detail the internal articulations of any corporation, Chart L also requires the information listed as **7b** (regulatory procedures), **11a** and **12a** (capacities to regulate internal and external affairs), though not in that order. In the short formula, category **a** (external relations) corresponds in Chart L to **6** (appropriate external relations), **2** (complementary units), **4** (of similar and differing form), and **10b** (access to complementary units) whose reciprocation (**12c**) is guided by their expectations (**12b**). Thus item **a** in the short formula corresponds to **6, 2, 4, 10b, 12b, 12c** in Chart L whereas item **b** in the short formula corresponds to **5c, 7c, 7b, 11a, 12a** in Chart L, boxes **1** to **4** and **5a** being assumed for all social units, and **5b** for corporations which are always institutionalized. Together these comparisons denote the chief differences between the set of 7 variables and those listed in the twelve boxes of Chart L.

Further analysis of the two attempts we have made to describe the creation of the *concilium plebis* that transformed the plebs into a corporate group, and the Shehu's assumption of caliphal office which transformed his *jema'a* into a corporate community, will show that the correspondences between these different sets of formulae greatly outweigh their apparent differences. The latter are reducible in almost all cases to differences in the level of detail provided by the divergent frameworks of both analytic schemes, that in Chart L being specific to corporations, whereas the set of 7 variables is equally applicable to all classes and kinds of social unit, whether institutionalized or not. However, I cannot be sure that I have made no error of substance in listing these formulae until they have been used by others to analyse different sets of data, and their results have been repeatedly checked. I therefore invite those of you who have followed the argument thus far, and who may think there is something more to this approach than I have seen or presented, to experiment with it as a tool to use and develop it as freely and fully as you can. That is the spirit in which I have written.

Moving now to the last of the three substantive transformations summarized on page 204, the French abolished the Dahomey chieftaincy and state when they had established appropriate relations, **6**, by the defeat that created the specific situation of conquest. Abolition of the unit *qua* unit erased all features listed in the earlier boxes **1** to **5** and **7c**, namely, Dahomey's uniqueness, perpetuity, recruitment criteria, membership, similarity or differences of complementary units, status differentiation, institutionalization and comprehensive organization. It also entailed the cancellation of **7a, 7b, 8a, 8b, 9a, 9b, 10a, 10b, 11a, 11b, 12a, 12b, 12c** simultaneously. Since the abolition of the Dahomean chiefship and state involved the simultaneous elimination of the unit's scope, regulatory procedures, range, autonomy, resources, capacity to regulate its internal and external affairs, routinized performances, expectations and reciprocation by others, the summarizing formula,

$$(6) \rightarrow 10a \rightarrow 1a/1b/2/3a/3b/4/5a/5b/5c/7c \rightarrow$$
$$7a/7b/8a/8b/9a/9b/10b/11a/11b/12a/12b/12c$$

corresponds closely to that entered above on page 204 for the same event, namely, **a b e/c/f/d g.**

From these tests we may therefore conclude that these processes of social change have a similar structure, whether analysed in one way or the other, by the short formula or the 12 boxes of Chart L, neither of which involve causal or functional explanations. If the order of those processes is as invariant as it seems, allowing for contingencies at their structural and operational levels, those changes could not have proceeded otherwise, since each successive step or stage in the process presupposed the changes that preceded it, even though those changes do not directly entail them. This explains the astonishing invariance of political changes in Zaria from which in 1960 I abstracted three laws of political change. No change initiated in any other order, even by autocrats, ever achieved institutional status. Years later I was able to test these laws against historical data from Daura, and found that they held. The mystery dissolves when we realise that concepts ordered by logical priority are aligned as a hierarchy of prerequisites; hence their empirical expressions should invariably reproduce this logical order, as has been shown in all my studies of political change among the Hausa to date (Smith 1960a; 1978; 1997).

The corollary of this fundamental principle is that structural change can only be institutionalized when it follows that order, and thus that all other attempts to produce structural change are self-defeating and futile, in much the same way that all attempts to start the engine of a motor car are futile until the ignition is switched on. This means that unless properly designed to replicate the relations of logical priority among their components, programs of social development and structural change are doomed to failure, since even changes in their substantive attributes presuppose prior structural changes in their articulations (Smith 1978:384-388). The present analysis therefore reveals the basis of those regularities I found in the study of political change among the Hausa. Moreover, besides summarizing these historical processes, it reveals why, in the given instances, nothing else was possible. Thereby it assures us that on this foundation we can tentatively predict the outcomes of programs of change, which may then be falsified or confirmed by subsequent events. Alternatively, if our predictions are accepted, we may then propose modifications to those programs to ensure success in achieving their goals.

Whether either the shorter or longer analysis is more useful in helping us to understand the processual structure of social change remains to be seen. One may hope that the proof of the pudding lies in the eating. For the method of this study commits its results to the tests of replicability and verifiability by the independent enquiries of colleagues.

REFERENCES

Aberle, D.F., A.K. Cohen, A.K.Davis, M.J. Levy, Jr. and F.X.Sutton.
    1950 "The Functional Prerequisites of Society." Ethics 60:100-111.

Banton, Michael.
    1965 Roles: An Introduction to the Study of Social Relations. London: Tavistock Publications.

Barth, Frederik.
    1959 Political Leadership among the Swat Pathans. London: Athlone Press of the University of London.

Barton, R.F.
    1919 *Ifugao Law.* Berkeley: University of California Press.

Bertalanffy, Ludwig von.
    1973 *General System Theory: Foundations, Development, Application.* New York: G. Braziller.

Bohannan, Paul.
    1965 "The Differing Realms of the Law." *American Anthropologist* 67:33-42.

Burton, Michael L, Lilyan A. Brudner and Douglas R. White.
    1977 "A Model of the Sexual Division of Labor." *American Ethnologist* 4:227-251.

Cohn, Norman R.C
    1957 *The Pursuit of the Millennium.* London: Secker and Warburg.

D'Andrade, Roy.
    1976 "A Propositional Analysis of U.S. American Beliefs about Illness." Pp. 155-180 in *Meanings in Anthropology,* edited by D. and H. Selby Basso. Albuquerque: University of New Mexico Press.

Durkheim, Emile.
    1947 *The Rules of Sociological Method.* Glencoe, Ill.: Free Press.
    1951 *Suicide: A Study in Sociology.* Glencoe, Ill.: Free Press.

Epstein, A.L.
    1958 *Politics in an Urban African Community.* Manchester: Manchester University Press.

Firth, Raymond.
    1951 *Elements of Social Organization.* London: Watts.

Fortes, Meyer.
  1959 "Descent, Filiation and Affinity: A Rejoinder to Dr. Leach." *Man* LIX:193-197, 206-212.

Furnivall, J.S.
  1948 *Colonial Policy and Practice: A Comparative Study of Burma and Netherlands India.* Cambridge: Cambridge University Press.

Goodenough, Ward H.
  1965 "Rethinking 'Status' and 'Role': Toward a General Model of the Cultural Organization of Social Relationships." Pp. 1-24 in *The Relevance of Models for Social Anthropology.* London and New York: Tavistock Publications and Frederick A. Praeger, Publishers.

Goody, Esther N.
  1982 "From Craft to Industry: The Ethnography of Proto-Industrial Cloth Production." in *Cambridge papers in social anthropology.* Cambridge and New York: Cambridge University Press.

Halbwachs, Maurice.
  1980 *The Collective Memory.* New York: Harper and Row.

Levi-Strauss.
  1953 "Social Structure." Pp. 524-553 in *Anthropology Today,* edited by A.L. Kroeber. Chicago: University of Chicago Press.
  1963 *Structural Anthropology.* New York and London: Basic Books.

LeVine, Robert A. and Walter H. Sangree.
  1962 "The Diffusion of Age-Group Organization in East Africa: A Controlled Comparison." *Africa* 32:97-110.

Levy, Jr., Marion J.
  1952 *The Structure of Society.* Princeton, New Jersey: Princeton University Press.

Linton, Ralph.
  1936 *The Study of Man.* New York: Appleton Century.

Maine, Henry S.
  1861 *Ancient Law.* London: J. Murray.

Malinowski, Bronislaw.
  1944 *A Scientific Theory of Culture and Other Essays.* Chapel Hill, North Carolina: The University of North Carolina Press.

Marx, Karl and Friedrich Engels.
  1948 *The Communist Manifesto*. New York: International Publishers
         Company.

Mayer, A.C.
  1966 "The Significance of Quasi-Groups in the Study of Complex
         Societies." Pp. 97-122 in *The Social Anthropology of Complex
         Societies*, edited by M. Banton. London: Tavistock Publications.

Merton, Robert K.
  1949 *Social Theory and Social Structure*. Glencoe, Illinois.

Nadel, S.F.
  1957 *The Theory of Social Structure*. London: Cohen and West.

Parsons, Talcott.
  1952 *The Social System*. London: Tavistock Publications.

Parsons, Talcott and Edward A. Shils.
  1951 *Toward a General Theory of Action*. Cambridge: Harvard University
         Press.

Radcliffe-Brown, A.R.
  1930-31 "The Social Organisation of Australian Tribes." *Oceania* 1:34-
            63, 206-246, 322-341, 426-456.
  1952 *Structure and Function in Primitive Society*. London: Cohen and
         West.

Rivers, W.H.R.
  1924 *Social Organization*. London: Kegan Paul.

Rudé, George F.E.
  1964 *The Crowd in History: A Study of Popular Disturbances in France
         and England*. New York: Wiley.

Smith, M.G.
  1960a *Government in Zazzau* 1800-1950. London: Oxford University
          Press.
  1960b "Social and Cultural Pluralism." Pp. 763-785 in *Social and
          Cultural Pluralism in the Caribbean*, edited by Vera Rubin. New
          York: New York Academy of Sciences.
  1962 *Kinship and Community in Carriacou*. New Haven and London:
         Yale University Press.

1974 *Corporations and Society: The Social Anthropology of Collective Action*. London: George Duckworth.

1978 *The Affairs of Daura*. Berkeley, Los Angeles and London: University of California Press.

1984 "The Nature and Variety of Plural Units." Pp. 146-186 in *The Prospects for Plural Societies*, edited by David Maybury-Lewis. Washington, D.C.: American Ethnological Society.

1986 "Pluralism, Race and Ethnicity in Selected African Countries." Pp. 187-225 in *Theories of Race and Ethnic Relations*, edited by John Rex and David Mason. Cambridge: Cambridge University Press.

1991 "Pluralism and Social Stratification." Pp. 3-35 in *Social and Occupational Stratification in Contemporary Trinidad and Tobago*, edited by Selwyn Ryan. St. Augustine, Trinidad: Institute of Social and Economic Research, University of the West Indies.

1997 *Government in Kano 1350-1950*. Boulder, Colorado: Westview Press.

Southall, A.

1956 *Alur Society: A Study of Processes of Domination*. Cambridge: University Press.

Spencer, Herbert.

1969 *The Principles of Sociology*. London: Macmillan.

Sykes, J.B.

1976 *The Concise Oxford Dictionary of Current English*. Oxford: Clarendon Press.

Weber, Max.

1947 *The Theory of Social and Economic Organization*. London: William Hodge.

1978 *Economy and Society*. Berkeley: University of California Press.

Wolf, Eric R.

1969 *Peasant Wars of the Twentieth Century*. New York: Harper and Row.

Woodburn, James.

1982 "Egalitarian Societies." *Man* 17.